LEARNING COMMUNITIES IN EDUCATION

The independence of participants in the learning process, inclusivity and diversity in education and the roles of teachers in different settings have been increasingly debated in recent years. The result has been an international movement towards learning communities, led by both researchers and practitioners of education.

Learning Communities in Education explores the theory and practice of learning communities from an international perspective. Covering primary/elementary, secondary and tertiary levels in a variety of educational contexts, leading researchers discuss:

* theoretical issues and debate
* processes and strategies for creating learning communities
* learning communities in action.

The current experience of the learning community is examined with reference to case studies from England, Ireland, Canada, the USA and Australia.

With comprehensive coverage of this much-debated topic and a careful balance between theoretical analysis and case-study material, *Learning Communities in Education* will be a valuable addition to the literature in this field.

John Retallick, **Barry Cocklin** and **Kennece Coombe** are all Senior Lecturers in Education at Charles Sturt University, New South Wales, Australia.

ROUTLEDGE RESEARCH IN EDUCATION

1 LEARNING COMMUNITIES IN EDUCATION
Issues, strategies and contexts
Edited by John Retallick, Barry Cocklin and Kennece Coombe

LEARNING COMMUNITIES IN EDUCATION

Issues, strategies and contexts

Edited by John Retallick,
Barry Cocklin and Kennece Coombe

London and New York

First published 1999
by Routledge
11 New Fetter Lane, London EC4P 4EE

Simultaneously published in the USA and Canada
by Routledge
29 West 35th Street, New York, NY 10001

Typeset in Garamond by Routledge
Printed and bound in Great Britain by Biddles Ltd,
Guildford and King's Lynn

British Library Cataloguing in Publication Data
A catalogue record for this book is available from the British Library

Library of Congress Cataloguing in Publication Data
Learning communities in education/edited by John Retallick,
Barry Cocklin, and Kennece Coombe.
Includes bibliographical references and index.
1. Education – Aims and objectives. 2. Educational
sociology. 3. School environment. 4. Educational change.
I. Retallick, John. II. Cocklin, Barry. III. Coombe, Kennece.
LB14.7.L43   1999
98–36953
370.11–dc21
CIP

ISBN 0–415–19760–0

CONTENTS

CONTENTS

CONTRIBUTORS

Richard Butt is Professor of Education at the University of Lethbridge, Canada. He is interested in professional development from teachers' perspectives and their participation in the facilitation of classroom and school-based change through emancipatory forms of professional learning, development and research.

Barry Cocklin is Senior Lecturer in Education at Charles Sturt University, Australia. His research interests include adult students at secondary school, rural women principals, outcomes-based education, teachers' workplace learning, critical theory and pedagogy, learning communities and creative teachers.

Kennece Coombe is Senior Lecturer in Education at Charles Sturt University, Australia. She has taught in early childhood, primary and secondary and university settings in Australia and New Zealand. Her teaching, research and writing interests include early childhood education, sociology of education, education administration, gender issues and feminist research, and teacher professionalism and ethics.

Neil Davidson is Professor of Curriculum and Instruction at the University of Maryland. A teacher and adviser throughout the Professional Development Doctoral Program, he served as coordinator after 1992. He publishes extensively on cooperative learning and leads numerous faculty development workshops.

Susan Groundwater-Smith is Adjunct Professor of Education at the Centre for Applied Education, Griffith University, Australia. She is an independent researcher and professional development consultant. Her most recent book, written with Robyn Cusworth and Rosie Dobbins, is *Teaching: Challenges and Dilemmas*, published by Harcourt Brace, Sydney, 1997.

Shirley Grundy is Associate Professor of Education at Murdoch University, Western Australia, and currently on secondment as District Director with the Department of Education. She has written extensively in areas relating to curriculum policy and theory, action research and teacher professionalism.

Jim Henkelman-Bahn is Associate Professor Emeritus at the University of Maryland. Until his retirement in 1992, he coordinated the Professional Development Doctoral Program in the College of Education. He is currently an international consultant in human resource development.

Garry Hoban is Lecturer in Science Education at the University of Wollongong, Australia. He completed his Ph.D. at the University of British Columbia, Canada, in 1996. His research interests focus on establishing frameworks to support long-term professional development programmes for high school and elementary school teachers.

Neville Johnson is Senior Lecturer in the Faculty of Education, University of Melbourne, Australia. He has worked as a researcher and consultant throughout Australia, the USA, the UK and Canada. His current research includes investigation of learning teams in school settings and long-term studies of schools as learning communities.

John Retallick is Senior Lecturer in Education at Charles Sturt University, Australia. For more than twenty years he has been involved in pre-service and in-service teacher education, and for five years he was Director of the Centre for Professional Development in Education at Charles Sturt University. His current research interests are teacher workplace learning and professional development.

Thomas Sergiovanni is Lillian Radford Professor of Education and Administration at Trinity University in San Antonio, Texas. He is also a senior fellow at the Center for Educational Leadership and founding director of the Trinity Principals' Center. His previous books include *Moral Leadership*, *Building Community in Schools* and *Leadership for the Schoolhouse*.

Paul Shaw is responsible for the Peel Universities Partnership in Ontario, Canada. This brings together the diverse interests and resources of a number of partners to focus on supporting schools and teachers in dealing with change. He is a member of the International Centre for Educational Change, OISE/University of Toronto.

CONTRIBUTORS

Ciaran Sugrue is Lecturer in Education at St Patrick's College, Dublin City University. His major fields of interest are qualitative research, educational change, leadership and school renewal, as well as the life history of teachers. His most recent book, *Complexities of Teaching*, was published in 1997 by Falmer Press.

Pamela Wells is a freelance education consultant and director of collaborations. She has conducted consultancies in Australia, the USA and Canada. She is a part-time lecturer for Southern Cross University, Australia, and presents summer school courses for Boise State University, USA.

Peter Woods is Professor of Education at the Open University, England, where for several years he was Director of the Centre for Sociology and Social Research. Recently, he has been researching creative teaching and learning in primary schools.

INTRODUCTION

The idea of 'learning community' is now featured prominently in many educational contexts. In schools, colleges and universities it is a focus for discussion about the increasingly interdependent nature of all stakeholders in the educational process, and it is supported by research on how teaching and learning are best facilitated. It is an international movement which appreciates inclusivity and diversity while valuing the role of teachers in different settings. This book explores and analyses the terrain of learning communities from a range of perspectives and issues, advocates processes and strategies for reconstructing organisations into communities, and presents a number of case study examples from Australia, England, Ireland, Canada and the USA.

The idea for the book grew out of a small research project funded by the School of Education at Charles Sturt University, Wagga Wagga, Australia. The three editors formed the research team and we sought to explore what we perceived to be an emerging discourse in a number of places around the notion of the learning community. In different ways we set about trying to understand what it was about and how the ideas were beginning to impact on schools and other educational settings. Through our explorations we became aware of the learning community movement in a number of other countries, and we were most grateful for the many positive responses from international colleagues when we flagged the idea of the book.

In searching for a statement that would encapsulate the spirit of this book we were fortunate to come across a teacher's story written by Darlene Witte-Townsend when she was a doctoral student at the University of Alberta in a course taught by Richard Butt. It is not a happy story but it is true. Unfortunately it represents the life of the vast majority of teachers in schools where learning community ideas do not prevail. If ever there was justification for reconstructing schools into learning communities it is to be found in Darlene's story.

1

ONE TEACHER'S STORY

I like my classroom. It is a huge sunny space, and there is lots of room for my handful of students. I have made this place as comfortable as I can, mostly by using colour. There is a pile of pillows in pastel shades, with bulletin boards, desks, tabletops, and balloons hanging from the ceiling in the same soft colours. I am enjoying the feeling of the place I am in when the bell rings and within seconds Ossie, Chris, Don, Dale and the rest of the class come in. They progress down the hallway in short bursts of sound and movement. I meet them at the door, and they walk in and settle themselves on the oval rug. Between themselves they sort out which of them gets to hold the two classroom teddy bears, and they begin the morning in the usual way, that is by spending a few minutes either reading a book or writing in their journals.

I begin the morning by sitting in the corner with them, writing. I am writing an adventure story that stars the kids in my classroom, and they are quite eager for each new day's instalment...the one girl in the class, Beverly, is, of course, the princess in the story. The boys all ride milk-white or coal-black steeds, and fight dragons and wild bears in order to save her from an evil queen. Their eyes glow when I read the story to them, Sir Ossie the Powerful, Sir Chris the Magnificent, Princess Beverly the Wise, and so on. They each have a part and they listen for the mention of their own names with the same eagerness each day. Today's episode is 'Rescue at the Stone Bridge', which involves a confrontation between Sir Dale and the Red Fairy. I feel a sense of achievement as I write because the children are all either reading or writing too, and there is an air of happiness about them. It is going to be a good morning. They are looking forward to the story that they know is coming out of the end of my pen, and nobody has as yet chosen to break the calm.

Twenty minutes later the calm is still holding and with a flourish I put my pen down and announce that it is 'story time'! The children watch me closely, fascinated with this process of seeing and hearing a story come alive in their presence. I begin to read aloud. But suddenly there is a knock at the door. Olivia, the school secretary is standing in the doorway looking at me expectantly, and I realise that it is time for my one-on-one, that is my evaluation meeting, with the principal. How could I have forgotten! Olivia has come to take my class to the library, and Mr. Jones will be here soon. The children go ahead with her, and I go to my desk to make a few notes in my plan book before he comes in.

As I wait I feel hopeful that he will see that progress is being made even though it is still slow, but I hear someone shouting. Sounds like Ollie. I go to see. Yes it is. On the way down to the library through one of the classroom doors he spotted a kid who had been 'on his case' before school, and he has decided that the time has come to settle the score. He has marched into the classroom (Mr. Smith's) and without warning has started to punch. Deciding that Olivia and Mr. Smith are capable of sorting out the confusion, I return to my desk, but I feel so empty. It seems that no sooner do I manage to get these kids focused on something good than an interruption arises. How will they ever learn to sustain a meaningful activity if they are constantly interrupted? It seems that there is little awareness of the kind of privacy that teacher and students require if they are to really accomplish very much.

A glimpse of my working reality must include a description of the children with whom I work, and the way in which I know them. I have a very special class. There are usually between seven and fourteen children, and they come to me for language arts and math only. They are in my class because they cannot cope academically or behaviourally in the other classrooms in the school. Some children stay only a few weeks, as I am to prepare them to return to the 'normal' classroom as quickly as possible, and some are with me for the whole term.

There is Ossie. Ossie explodes with anger at least three times every day in the way I have described above, and during these episodes he will damage anyone or anything near him. He has scars all over his face from his mother's fingernails. He does not listen to adults' words. Words do not reach him unless they are spoken very, very gently. He watches my eyes. If my eyes love him and are gentle he can relax and listen, but if I react in any other way to his outbursts his violence just escalates. Usually he shelters behind anger and keeps it close by him on a hair-trigger. Anything can set it off, a look, a word, an accidental bump from one of the other children.

With some positive social/emotional growth happening, it becomes easier to focus on academic learning. I feel that it is so important for these kids to start experiencing personal involvement, or ownership, of this part of their school experience. One day Chris comes up with the idea of having a spelling test. We haven't had one of those before, and I'm not sure where he has run across the idea. Maybe he has seen an episode of 'Little House on the Prairie', but his face is alight with the idea of having a spelling test, and the other children catch his enthusiasm. So we agree. We choose a set of words and decide to work on them all week and then have a test on Friday. Tests and spelling lists are something that just don't happen in my classroom, so the idea is a bit of a thrill...something new, something different. I tell the children that the words they contribute should be important to them for some special reason. Ollie's choice is 'Black Stallion'. There is a sense of ownership, a sense of fun, and of excitement. I am especially pleased that Chris has thrown off his normal apathy.

This day is also the day of my 'one-on-one' with Mr. Jones, the one mentioned above. He comes into my classroom after the children have gone to the library with Olivia, and looks around. He notices the list of spelling words and the printed announcement that the test will be on Friday. He sits down and informs me that he expects me to run a whole language programme in this classroom, and that 'there is no such thing as a spelling list or spelling test in whole language. Never.' He also says that he is disappointed that I have not done more to 'individualise' my programme. That means that everyone must be doing something different all the time and that no, several kids couldn't be interested in the same thing at once. Working together is not 'individualising' and therefore not acceptable. What can I say to him? I say nothing. I do not know the words to say what I want to say. He says he knows what whole language is, although I had never yet been able to get anybody to explain it to me. He has been to at least two workshops on whole language, and is therefore more informed than I.

How can I explain my gut feeling that these kids need to learn in a social context before they will be able to learn on their own. It's only a feeling I have, an intuition, a sense of direction. What can I say? What do I know? Only that my whole life has been a project of being immersed in words and sounds of words and the magic of knowing myself through language, becoming human through the community of language, sharing the project of being alive through language, and that there is something about the socialness of living, about humanness itself, that IS the wholeness in whole language, a drumbeat that must be heard if you are to march in the rhythm of the dance of knowing a symbol as it hides itself in meaning and then reflects our own souls back into our own eyes again and suddenly you know more about being alive than you did before. He has not asked me why but he has made an assumption, and seems to assume that I have no reason for what I do in the classroom, that I would only have the most superficial of reasons for having a spelling list on chart paper standing in my classroom. I feel that I have been disembowelled. His words bear down on me and roar in my ears like a freight train. I cannot breathe. I feel that I need freedom, the freedom of trust and acceptance, or I will die. I am so unhappy. I feel trapped.

I cannot tell Mr. Jones any of these things. For some reason my words are frozen inside me as usual. I feel sad, I feel angry, I feel that once again I have not been heard, but I really don't know what to do about it. I point out that the words on the list were selected by the children, but I am unable to say that there is a special relationship between those words and these children and I can't argue with the fact that the words are in a list, and the plan was to have a test on Friday. I can't seem to find the words to tell him that the list was only intended as a place to hold them because they were important for other reasons.

But I know that he has not heard me. I cannot make him hear me. He may have even decided not to hear me before he came.

So I agree that there will be no more lists. In the morning I tell the children we cannot do what we were going to do and they are disappointed, and I am angry. I am quietly, desperately angry with a system that seems to leave me voiceless. I prove my competence every single day that I work in this classroom, but there always seems to be one more challenge to prove my competence, and he walks in here seeming to have assumed I am not a professional with reasons for everything I do. He doesn't give me a chance to tell him that these kids are accomplishing things socially and academically that they have never accomplished before and I am angry with myself because I cannot speak out in my own defence. I am frustrated with my own lack of knowledge, and my lack of being able to give an informed answer to his criticism. I don't know what whole language is, and I just haven't had the time or opportunity to find out. It's not because I don't care.

You may think I am an unforgivable milquetoast for giving in to the principal this way. Aside from my own difficulty with speaking up, let me share a little more about my 'working reality' with this man. During the two years that I worked with him, I saw four teachers give up their careers because they could not stand the pressure that he exerts. The only male member of the staff gets into yelling matches with him quite regularly, and I see other teachers cry every day, quietly in their classrooms, alone. I sometimes cry too, but I am determined that he will never see me do it. I will not let him know he upsets me. My instinct tells me that if he ever smells blood he will not stop ragging me until he has me down – how does a man like this get away with it? (Does this explain something of my resolve to discipline myself with calm at all times while I am in the school, and thus also the reason for the little centring routine I go through every single day before I enter that environment?)

Shortly after the day the spelling test dies our school is due for a review by the language arts consultant from the School Board. A woman I have never met before comes to visit my classroom. She tours the room, and at the end of her visit she announces that the Michael Knight book she sees on one of the student's desks is 'totally inappropriate for this age group', but otherwise she can't see anything wrong. Again, I am unable to justify to her why it is there - I explain, but my words feel limp to me as they come out of my mouth and I know she is unconvinced.

Once again I am confronted with this assumption that I don't think about what I do, that there is no reasoning behind my actions and what disturbs me most is that I'm not even asked if I have a reason. The judgement is made without asking, and I feel anything I say is going to be heard as an excuse, not a reason. Again I feel miserable. Where is the encouragement I need to give me energy to keep myself on the cutting edge for these kids? It doesn't come from their parents, or from my principal, or the consultant. They only seem to want to find something wrong, but the things they find wrong are so silly that they really seem to undermine their own validity...but again I feel that my lack of concrete, research-based information has contributed to my inability to speak up confidently.

This story points to some things that are fundamentally wrong with schools as they are presently constituted. Not all schools, but enough to be a major concern for those of us who seek a more caring and liberating environment in which learning can flourish for all students and teachers. Whilst this book is not meant as a panacea for all the ills and problems of contemporary schooling, it does put forward an alternative set of ideas to those that are generated in the story above. We hope that the reader will find them both challenging and helpful.

Part I

LEARNING COMMUNITIES
Issues and debate

1

THE STORY OF COMMUNITY

Thomas Sergiovanni

Stories tell us about events, what these events mean and how these events affect our lives. Different stories lead to different values, beliefs and decisions about what is real and what is possible. What is the story of community? How does this story differ from other stories about schools? What narratives does the story of community encompass? What stories compete with community for the attention of policy makers and administrators in education?

The story of community includes unique ways of thinking about connections, human nature and societal institutions. In schools that are traditionally organised, for example, connections are understood using the narrative of social contracts; human nature is understood using the constrained narrative; and schools themselves are understood using the narrative of formal organisations. In schools that are striving to become learning communities connections are understood using the narrative of social covenants; human nature is understood using the unconstrained narrative; and schools themselves are understood using the narrative of social organisations.

SOCIAL CONTRACTS

The major story line in the narrative of social contracts involves a deal within which each of the parties to the contract gives up something to the other party in order to get something else back that is valued. In this narrative, teachers, like workers in other sectors of our economy, hand over to their employers time, muscle and brain in order to obtain money, health benefits, psychological fulfilment and security. Similarly, children endure the rituals of schooling in order to get the gold stars and praise they covet from teachers; the attention they want from parents; and the grades they need to be admitted to college. A social contract is maintained as long as each of the parties gets what it wants. When teachers, for example, no longer receive the contracted amount of money, health benefits, fulfilment

9

and security, they are less willing to hand over to the school time, muscle and brains. And when students no longer get the gold stars, attention and grades they want, they are less willing to endure the rituals of schooling. This narrative is about calculations involving trades that offer incentives in exchange for compliance. Self-interest is presumed to be paramount and let's make a deal is the order of the day.

The narrative of social contracts guides the practice of the principal of the Locke Elementary School. He promised the student body that if 2,000 books were read during the month of October, on Halloween night he would dress up like a witch and kiss a pig on the roof of the school building. This goal was achieved and, to the apparent delight of the students, the deed was done. The Locke principal believes that contracts are important motivational devices and that unless students get something tangible for their efforts they will not be motivated. You can't expect a manager to manage well, a worker to be diligent or a football player to play hard unless there is something in it for them. So, he asks, how can we expect teachers to teach well, students to learn well and schools to reform themselves without incentives? How can we expect them to display proper behaviours without providing exhaustive lists of rules and regulations or outcome requirements that are linked to clear consequences for non-compliance?

SOCIAL COVENANTS

The major story line in the narrative of social covenants is much less conditional. In this narrative, connections are covenantal and thus are more moral than calculated. Marriages, extended families, civic associations, faith communities, caring groups and friendship networks are examples of affiliations characterised by covenantal relationships. Connections among people are created when they are together connected to shared ideas and values. Once achieved, this bonding together of people and this binding of people to ideas forms a fabric of reciprocal roles, duties and obligations that are internalised by members of the group. This is a fabric that cannot be torn apart when one or another party no longer likes the deal. This is a fabric that perseveres even when the fun is gone, when needs are not being met or when self-interests must be sacrificed.

The narrative of social covenants guides the practice of the principal of the Rousseau Elementary School. She encourages teachers and students together to develop a description of how everyone in the school should lead their lives together. Connected to a larger vision of school purposes, critical values and pedagogical beliefs, this 'covenant' provides the basis for an ongoing discussion about how teachers, administrators, parents and students can meet their commitments to each other and to the school. Students at Rousseau, for example, expect teachers to work hard, to be caring, and to teach well. Since relationships are reciprocal, teachers expect students to respond similarly. Students are given considerable latitude in deciding important things at Rousseau. They help decide how learning goals will be achieved and help make decisions about how they will spend their time. But decisions must be responsible ones that embody and advance the school's covenant. Both teachers and students work hard to make reading fun and useful while also increasing mastery. Rousseau's students are avid readers as a result.

The Rousseau principal believes that when given the opportunity to make important decisions about school goals, purposes, values and other important school matters, teachers and students will respond by being morally obliged to embody these decisions in their actions. Further, the bonding of school members together and their binding to shared ideas and ideals provides a normative environment that encourages moral responsiveness. Social contracts, she reasons, have important roles to play in the real world. But so do social covenants. The school is the place, she argues, to learn about social covenants, to practise developing them, and to use them in a practical way to govern affairs.

In comparing the two narratives, Sacks (1997) argues that a social contract is maintained by the promise of gain or the threat of external force. A social covenant is maintained by loyalty, fidelity, kinship, sense of identity, obligation, duty, responsibility, and reciprocity. A social contract, he points out, 'gives rise to the instrumentalities of the state' both corporate and political. 'A covenant gives rise to quite different institutions – families, communities, traditional and voluntary associations. It is the basis of civil society' (Sacks 1997: 16). Social contracts are at the core of what connects people in *Gesellschaft* enterprises and social covenants are at the core of what connects people in *Gemeinschaft* enterprises (Tonnies 1957). The former are rules-based and the latter are norms-based (Sergiovanni 1994a).

THE NATURE OF HUMAN NATURE

Related to the social contract and social covenant narratives are two narratives about the nature of human capacity and will – constrained and unconstrained (Herzberg 1966; Sowell 1987; Etzioni 1988). The constrained narrative is aligned with the selfish side of human nature rooted in the satisfaction of physical needs and psychological egoism. The unconstrained narrative is aligned to the altruistic side of human nature rooted in moral conceptions of goodness. The altruistic side includes our capacity to practise such virtues as moral bearing, self-sacrifice and cooperation aimed at the enhancement of the common good. The selfish side includes our propensity to put self-interest first, to compete to win, and to strive to accumulate advantages such as wealth and power aimed at enhancing our individual pleasure and position.

The major story line in the constrained narrative emphasises controlling the impulses of self-interest thought by Hobbes (1950) and others to dominate human nature. According to this narrative, people are inclined to be self-centred, competitive, devious, addicted to gratification and even unscrupulous as they seek to maximise their own gains with little regard for the common good. Thus, the constrained story avers, principals, teachers and students must be 'constrained' if they are to overcome these brutish impulses and instincts. Without constraints they will not be inclined to do the right thing. Society therefore must use rewards and punishments to provide the necessary constraints that will channel human behaviour in the right direction – be it paying taxes, communing with God, providing leadership, preparing lessons, being collegial, or studying and behaving at school.

The major story line in the unconstrained narrative emphasises the capacity of people to embody such virtues as altruism, moral bearing, and cooperation aimed at enhancing the common good, even if doing so occasionally requires sacrificing one's self-interest. Instead of viewing people as being cost-benefit machines who make individual choices rationally in an effort to win, the unconstrained narrative includes the emotive, normative and altruistic side of people. Motivation, in this story, is a result of the complex interaction not only between our emotions, values and beliefs, but between these and our ties to others (Etzioni 1988). Connections, in the unconstrained narrative, are normatively derived and have moral overtones (Sergiovanni 1992).

Policy-makers who subscribe to the unconstrained narrative believe that principals and teachers can be trusted to act morally, and therefore should be provided with the freedom to optimise their moral propensity to do what is right. Principals and teachers, for example, have both the capacity and the need to sacrifice their self-interest for causes they believe in and for conceptions of the common good that they value. As professionals, they willingly accept responsibility for their own practice and they commit themselves to the learning needs of their students above other concerns. A similar tale is told for students.

Within the constrained narrative, by contrast, it is believed that principals and teachers will act selfishly if given the chance. Their primary concern is to maximise their self-interest. Thus constraints in the form of incentives and penalties must be provided to force them to do the right thing. Principals and teachers may have the capacity to do the right thing, this narrative concedes, but this capacity will only be motivated if constraints are provided. A similar tale is told for students.

Though some may view the two narratives as being mutually exclusive, in most people they coexist in reasonable balance. The selfish side of human nature described by Hobbes (1950) provides the constrained narrative with its plot – a plot that can help us when navigating through many aspects of our lives. Similarly, the altruistic side of human nature provides the unconstrained narrative with its plot – a plot that can help us when navigating other aspects of our lives. The selfish side, for example, dominates when we are buying a used car, negotiating a pay rise, shopping for jeans, or playing the stock market. The altruistic side dominates in our family relationships, in our spiritual lives and in our interactions with friends and neighbours.

The principal of the Rousseau school recognises this duality. Further, she believes that the school is a setting for evoking the altruistic side of human nature. Thus, she is strongly influenced by the unconstrained narrative. The principal of the Locke school, by contrast, either does not recognise this duality or feels that the school is not a compatible setting for evoking the altruistic side of human nature. Thus, he is strongly influenced by the constrained narrative.

FORMAL AND SOCIAL ORGANISATIONS

Cutting across the narratives about connections and human nature are two narratives about societies' institutions – formal organisation and social organisation (Sergiovanni 1994b). Formal organisations are the institutions of political and economic society. Most of us were born in formal organisations and now work in them. We use formal organisations to obtain health care, to invest in and protect our economic future, to provide protection from fire, war and other calamities, to obtain needed government services, and otherwise to enhance our material well-being. Formal organisations include IBM, the Xerox Corporation, Qantas Airlines, Harrods Department store, McDonald's Restaurant, the New York Yankees, the Royal Marines, Bell Research Laboratory, and hundreds of other valued enterprises. Social organisations, on the other hand, are the institutions of civil society. They include the families we love, friendship networks we enjoy, volunteer associations we value, faith communities we belong to, and other family, neighbourhood and community groups where moral connections characterised by intimacy, caring, shared commitments and reciprocal responsibilities are the norm.

Differentiating among organisational types has a long history. Peter Blau and W. Richard Scott made an important distinction between social organisations and formal organisations in their seminal work *Formal Organisations: A Comparative Approach* (1962). They pointed out that 'We would not call a family an organisation, nor would we so designate a friendship clique, or a community, or an economic market or the political institutions of our society' (1962: 2). To Blau and Scott what differentiates formal organisations from social enterprises is how human conduct becomes

13

socially organised. By this they mean the regularities and behaviour of people in the enterprise that are due to the social condition in which they find themselves rather than to their physiological or psychological characteristics as individuals.

Similarly, Philip Selznick (1957) provided an 'institutional' theory of leadership and organisation as a more viable explanation for how some of society's entities work than 'organisational' theory. He suggested that institutions evolve naturally as a result of social needs. They become infused with values which enable them to become more responsive and adaptive than organisations. To Selznick,

> Organisations are technical instruments, designed as means to defi-
> nite goals. They are judged on engineering premises: They are ex-
> pendable. Institutions, whether conceived as groups or practices,
> may be partly engineered, but they also have a 'natural' dimension.
> They are products of interaction and adaptation: They become the
> receptacles of group idealism: They are less readily expendable.
>
> (1957: 21–2)

Selznick noted that organisations are made up of standard building blocks that lend themselves to manipulation by administrators who are interchangeable across all organisations, and whose leadership involves the use of generic theories, concepts and skills. Adopting this generic approach, according to Selznick, commonly results in a lapse of integrity and a loss of character that leads to undifferentiated organisations and mediocre performance. Institutions, he points out, are more successful than organisations because they maintain integrity and character by being unique in their purposes, structures and ways of doing things. For institutions, elements such as situations, contexts, purposes, and traditions count.

Schools that are more like 'institutions' than 'organisations' develop distinctive ways of making decisions, distinctive commitments to their purposes, distinctive ways of operating, and distinctive internal connections as well as connections to the people whom they serve (see, for example, Sergiovanni 1994a).

> In this way the organisation as a technical instrument takes on val-
> ues. As a vehicle of group integrity, it becomes in some degree an
> end in itself. This process of being infused with value is part of
> what we mean by institutionalisation…The building of integrity is
> part of what we have called the 'institutional embodiment of pur-
> pose' and its protection is a major function of leadership.
>
> (Selznick 1957: 138–9)

Community is an example of what it means to be an institution. In a community, theories of leadership and culture are not transferred from generic sources but are constructed in the light of that community's unique purposes, traditions and responsibilities.

As a further example, Oakeshott (1975) distinguishes between two kinds of associations in our society: enterprise and civil. Enterprise associations are instrumental in the sense that they have formal goals and they require a layer of management whose job it is to decide the choice of needs and to establish the structures needed to achieve the goals. Civil associations, by contrast, are substantive in the sense that they do not have formal goals. They are, instead, places within which members go about their self-determined pursuits guided by norms, standards, covenants and other artefacts of culture that inform the decisions that they make (see, for example, Elkin 1993). In enterprise associations, people are connected to their work by organisational hierarchies, rules, systems of supervision and incentives. In civil associations, member 'citizens' are connected to their work by covenants and norms.

A THEORY OF COMMUNITY FOR SCHOOLS

Communities are much more like social organisations than formal organisations; institutions than organisations; and civil associations than enterprise associations. In the story of the school as a learning community, connections are governed more by social covenants than by social contracts; the altruistic side of human nature embodied in the unconstrained view is emphasised more than the constrained view's self-interest side; and schools function as social organisations that are distinct from formal organisations.

Communities are organised around relationships and ideas. They create social structures that bond people together in a oneness and that bind them to a set of shared values and ideas. Communities are defined by their centres of values, sentiments and beliefs (Shils 1961) that provide the needed conditions for creating a sense of 'we' from the 'I' of each individual (see, for example, Tonnies 1957; Bellah *et al.* 1985; Etzioni 1988).

In schools that are striving to become learning communities connections are based on commitments not trades (Sergiovanni 1996: 12). Teachers are expected to do a good job not so that they can get rewards from administrators, but because it is important to do so. Discipline policies are norm-based, not just rule-based as in ordinary schools. Instead of relying primarily on trading rewards and punishments for the right behaviour, learning communities seek to connect members to what is right and wrong, to obligations and commitments, and to moral agreements. When these moral connections are in place, students and teachers are compelled to action by obligations to embody shared commitments and values. In schools that are

15

struggling to become learning communities, members live their lives with others who have similar intentions. In ordinary schools, relationships are constructed by others and become codified into a system of hierarchies, roles and role expectations.

Both ordinary schools and learning communities must deal with issues of control. Since learning communities rely more on norms, purposes, values, professional socialisation, collegiality and natural interdependence than on external control measures, control mechanisms are institutionalised as part of the school's culture. When the ties of community become a part of the culture of a school they become substitutes for formal systems of supervision, evaluation and staff development. In time, they gradually become substitutes for leadership itself. As community strengthens, more and more of the action for individuals and groups is compelled from within and less and less of the action is required from the outside. Parents, teachers and students alike become increasingly self-managing partners tied together by reciprocal webs of moral obligation.

The strengthening of community ties redefines how empowerment and collegiality are understood. In ordinary schools, empowerment is focused on shared decision-making, site-based management and similar schemes. Within learning communities, the focus of empowerment begins to change. Rights, discretion and freedom become connected to commitments, obligations and duties that people feel toward each other and toward the school. Collegiality in ordinary schools is often equated with congeniality (Barth 1990) and often results from administrative arrangements, such as variations of team-teaching, and from the team-building skills of principals who encourage people to work together (Hargreaves 1989). In learning communities, collegiality is something that comes from within. Community members are connected to each other because of felt interdependencies, mutual obligations, and other emotional and normative ties. Further, the focus and substance of collegiality is less interpersonal and more the work of teaching and learning itself (Little 1992).

Schools that are striving to become learning communities are also communities in a larger sense (McLaughlin and Talbert 1993). Becoming a learner-centred community can be thought of as an end result variable. Leadership and culture can be thought of as initiating variables. Both are linked by mediating variables that are composed of *enabling* forms of community. As leadership is provided and as school cultures are changed, the mediating variables go to work enabling the learning community to emerge and strengthen. Sergiovanni (1994a) shows that schools become productive learning communities as they become:

- *reflective communities* – within which students (and teachers too) develop insight into their own strengths and weaknesses as learners, and use this information to call upon different strategies for learning

- *developmental communities* – within which it is acknowledged that students (and teachers too) develop at different rates, and at any given time are more ready to learn some things than others
- *diverse communities* – within which different talents and interests of students (and teachers too) are not only recognised, but acknowledged by decisions that are made about curriculum, teaching and assessment
- *conversational communities* – within which high priority is given to creating an active discourse that involves the exchange of values and ideas among students, among teachers, and between students and teachers as they learn together
- *caring communities* – within which students (and teachers too) learn not only to be kind to each other and to respect each other, but to help each other to grow as learners and as persons
- *responsible communities* – within which students (and teachers too) come to view themselves as part of a social web of meanings and responsibilities which they feel a moral obligation to embody in their present behaviour as students, and future behaviour as citizens.

As the enabling forms of community emerge, the school is able to respond better to the needs of teachers, students, parents and principals to be connected to themselves, to each other, to their work and to their responsibilities.

BUILDING BLOCKS FOR THE LEARNING COMMUNITY

The enabling forms of community and the learning community itself will not prosper without principals and others striving to create within the school a:

- community of relationships
- community of place
- community of mind
- community of memory
- community of practice.

As a school develops a community of relationships, connections among people are close and informal; individual circumstances count; acceptance is unconditional; relationships are cooperative; concerns of members are unbounded; subjectivity is okay; emotions are legitimate; sacrificing one's self-interest for the sake of the community is common; members associate with each other because doing so is valuable as an end in itself; knowledge is valued and learned for its own sake; and students are accepted and loved because that's the way one treats community members. These kinds of relationships among people create a unity that is similar to that found in families and other close-knit collections of people.

In a community of place, connections among people are keyed to a sense of place that comes from sharing a common location. The sharing of place with others for sustained periods creates a shared identity and a shared sense of belonging. Continuity and caring, Nel Noddings (1992) points out, go together. In her words:

> To meet the challenge to care in schools, we must plan for continuity:
>
> 1 Continuity in purpose. It should be clear that schools are centres of care – that the first purpose is caring for each other. This includes helping all students to address essential issues of human caring and, also, to develop their particular capacities in specialised areas of care.
>
> 2 Continuity of residence. Students should stay in one school building long enough to acquire a sense of belonging. Although I would prefer small schools, it may be possible to create a feeling of community in larger schools if community is made a priority. Children should be in residence more than three and, preferably, for six years.
>
> 3 Continuity of teachers and students. Teachers, whether singly or in teams, should stay with students (by mutual consent) for three or more years.
>
> 4 Continuity in curriculum. The idea is to show our care and respect for the full range of human capacities by offering a variety of equally prestigious programmes or specialisation, each embedded in universal curriculum organised around essential themes of caring.
>
> (1992: 72–3)

Key to community building is the principle that when teachers, students and parents are connected to the same ideas they become connected to each other as well. A community of mind emerges from the binding of people to common goals, shared values, and shared conceptions of being and doing. Becoming a community of relationships, place and mind involves the development of webs of meaning that tie people together by creating a special sense of belonging and a strong common identity (Tonnies 1957).

Although not cast in stone, community understandings have enduring qualities. They are taught to new members, celebrated in customs and rituals, and embodied as standards that govern life in the community. Further, they are resilient enough to survive the passage of members through the community over time. As suggested by Bellah and his colleagues (1985), enduring understandings create a community of memory. In time, communities of relationship, of place and of mind become communities of memory that provide members with enduring images of school, learning and life. Community of memory sustains parents, teachers and students when times are tough, connects them when they are not physically present, and provides them with a history for creating sense and meaning. The substance of a school's community of memory is often enshrined in its traditions, rights and rituals and in other aspects of the school's symbolic life (Deal 1985; Deal and Peterson 1991).

Perhaps the defining bench mark for identifying how deep community is emerging in a school is the presence of a community of practice. In ordinary schools teachers are involved in their own private practices. A school with thirty teachers is defined as a collection of thirty individual practices. The principal's practice is separated from that of teachers. In the learning community, individual practices are not abandoned but are connected in such a way that they constitute a shared practice (Sergiovanni 1994b). A single practice of teaching that is shared by teachers and principal alike exists. The faculty not only identifies with this practice but feels a moral obligation to help each other as connected members of this same practice. As the sense of shared practice develops, collegiality functions at a higher level than is normally the case. As the learning community continues to develop, the principalship too becomes a practice shared with teachers who accept responsibility not only for leadership roles but for the success of the school.

THE HEART OF SCHOOL LEADERSHIP

The story of community takes us to the heart of school leadership. Leadership is generally viewed as a process of getting a group to take action that embodies the leader's purposes (as is typically the case in ordinary schools) or shared purposes (as is the case in the learning community). Leadership in the learning community is different from commanding or bribing compliance in that it involves influencing others by persuasion or example, or by tapping inner moral forces. This influence is typically reciprocal. Unless followers are willing to be led, leaders can't lead. Further, groups naturally create norms that constitute a cultural order or way of life that provides them with sense and meaning. Leaders must be part of that order even as they attempt to change it, or their leadership will be rejected. Faced with either the fear or reality of rejection some leaders resort to commanding or requiring compliance. But when they do this, 'follower' commitment is sacrificed, and compliance is difficult to maintain over time.

For leadership to work, leaders and followers need to be tied together by a consensual understanding that mediates this pattern of reciprocal influence.

In the learning community leadership and learning go together. So do leadership and sense-making. Leaders and followers converse together, learn together and enquire together as they care together to construct a reality that helps them to navigate through a complex world. This reciprocal process of leaders and followers influencing each other to action not only involves issues of shared purposes, but involves roles that are connected to moral obligations. Just as teachers, parents and students have roles linked to moral obligations, principals are expected to meet the obligations that come from their role responsibilities as leaders.

It is through morally held role responsibilities that the principalship can be understood as a profession in the more traditional sense of what a profession is and means. Principals are bound not just to standards of technical competence but to *standards of public obligation* as well (Bellah *et al.* 1995). Standards of public obligation always override technical standards when the two are in conflict. It is in the principal's role responsibilities that we find the heart of school leadership – a commitment to administer to the needs of the school as an institution by serving its purpose, by serving those who struggle to embody these purposes, and by acting as a guardian to protect the institutional integrity of the school. The first roles of principals are ministerial ones. Key in cultivating a morally based leadership is to change the sources of authority for one's leadership practice.

THE SOURCES OF AUTHORITY FOR LEADERSHIP

The sources of authority for leadership help to answer the 'why?' question. Why should teachers (and students too) do the things that are required for schools to work well? In schools that are ordinary organisations the answers to this question are 'because they must follow the rules or else' and 'because principals know how to use the right leadership styles and to push the right motivation buttons'. In the learning community the answers to this question are 'because doing these things makes educational sense' and 'because doing these things is what is good and right to do'. The sources of authority embedded in these four reasons are bureaucratic, personal, professional and moral.

Bureaucratic and personal authority are the basis for expressions of leadership that rely on bartering. Bartering, as pointed out earlier in this chapter, is a story line from the narrative of social contracts, the constrained narrative and the narrative of formal organisations. Professional and moral authority are the basis for expressions of leadership that rely on bonding and binding. Bonding and binding are story lines from the narrative of social covenants, the unconstrained narrative and the narrative of social organisations. The first set of narratives tells the story of ordinary schools and the second set of narratives tells the story of learning communities. The sources of authority are summarised in Table 1.

Table 1 The sources of authority for leadership practice

Source	Assumptions	Leadership strategy	Consequences and type
Bureaucratic authority Heirarchy Rules and regulations Mandates Role expectation	Teachers are subordinates in a hierarchically arranged system similar to that found in formal organisations	'Expect and inspect' is the overarching rule	With proper monitoring teachers will comply. Their performance becomes narrow and predictable.
		Rely on predetermined standards to which teachers must measure up	
Teachers are expected to comply or face consequences	Supervisors are trustworthy, but you cannot trust subordinates very much	Identify their shortcomings and 'in-service' them	
	Goals and interests of teachers and supervisors are not the same; thus supervisors must be watchful	Supervise and monitor the work of teachers to ensure compliance	
			Teachers respond as required when rewards are available but not otherwise. Their involvement is calculated.
Personal authority Moti- vational knowledge and interpersonal skills Human relations and leadership practices	Heirarchy equals expertise; thus supervisors know more than do teachers	Figure out how to motivate them and get them to change	
	External accountability works best		Schools are formal organisations much like the other Gesellschaft organisations that dominate our impersonally experienced society

21

Table 1 The sources of authority for leadership practice *cont...*

Source	Assumptions	Leadership strategy	Consequences and type
Teachers will want to comply because of the congenial climate provided and to reap psychological rewards offered in exchange	The goals and interests of teachers and supervisors are not the same but can be bartered so that each gets what they want	Develop a school climate characterised by congeniality among teachers and between teachers and supervisors	
Professional and moral authority Felt obligations and duties derived from widely shared professional and community values, ideas and ideals

Teachers respond to shared commit-ments and feel inter-dependence | Teachers have needs, and if those needs are met at work, the work gets done as required in exchange

Congenial relationship and harmonious interpersonal climates make teachers content, easier to work with and more apt to cooperate

Schools are learning communities | 'Expect and reward'

'What gets rewarded gets done'

Identify and make explicit the values and beliefs that define the centre of the school as community

Translate the above into informal norms that govern behaviour | Teachers respond to professional and community values for moral reasons. Their practice becomes collective. Their performance is expansive and sustained. Schools are learning communities much like the *Gemeinschaft* communities that dominate our personally experienced society. |

22

Table 1 The sources of authority for leadership practice *cont...*

Source	Assumptions	Leadership strategy	Consequences and type
	Communities are defined by their centres of shared values, beliefs and commitments	Promote collegiality as internally felt and morally driven interdependence	
	In communities: • What is considered right and good is as important as what works and what is effective	Rely on the ability of community members to respond to duties and obligations	
	•People are motivated as much by emotion as by self-interest •Collegiality is a professional virtue	Rely on the community's informal norm system to enforce professional and community values	

Source: Adapted from Sergiovanni 1992

THE STORY OF LEADERSHIP

The story of leadership in the learning community includes not only narratives about sources of authority and ministerial responsibilities but narratives about learning as well. Capacity-building for teachers and capacity-building for students are strongly connected. For this reason learning for everyone runs deep. Leadership in the learning community is focused on transforming congeniality into collegiality and collegiality into a shared practice of teaching – a community of practice.

A vigorous and closely knit community of practice is critical to the development of any discipline or profession. Using science as an example,

Bronowski notes that 'what has made science successful as a social leaven over the last 300 years is its change from the practice of individuals, however great their ingenuity, to a communal enterprise' (1978: 123). He points out that during Leonardo da Vinci's time there was no scientific community: 'And one reason why prolific, vivid, imaginative, and inventive brains, like Leonardo's failed to make an imprint on the body of science was there were no colleagues...even that tremendous mind could not work in isolation' (1978: 123).

Leonardo had colleagues in painting, however, and because of his membership in that community of practice his paintings were undoubtedly better. Further, his work influenced the work of other artists and the discipline of art was advanced to new heights.

The story of community ends, then with the observation that the task of transforming ordinary schools into highly effective and caring learning communities across the globe awaits the development of a vibrant and energetic community of practice shared by teachers and principals alike.

References

Barth, R. (1990) *Improving Schools from Within*, San Francisco: Jossey-Bass.

Bellah, R. N., Madsen, R., Sullivan, W. M., Swindler A. and Tipton, S. M. (1985), *Habits of the Heart: Individualism and Commitments in American Life*, New York: Harper Collins.

Blau, P. and Scott, W. R. (1962) *Formal Organizations: A Comparative Approach*, San Francisco: Chandler.

Bronowski, J. (1978) *The Origins of Knowledge and Imagination*, New Haven, Conn.: Yale University Press.

Deal, T. E. (1985) 'The symbolism of effective schools' *Elementary School Journal* 85 (5), 601–19.

Deal, T. E. and Peterson. K. (1991) *The Principal's Role in Shaping School Culture*, Washington: US Department of Education.

Elkin, S. L. (1993) 'Constitutionalism: old and new', in S. L. Elkin and K. E. Soltan (eds) *A New Constitutionalism*, Chicago: University of Chicago Press.

Etzioni, A. (1988) *The Moral Dimension: Toward a New Economics*, New York: Free Press.

Hargreaves, A. (1989) 'Contrived collegiality and the culture of teaching', paper presented at the Annual Meeting of the Canadian Society for the Study of Education, Quebec City, Quebec.

Herzberg, F. (1966) *Work and the Nature of Man*, Cleveland, Ohio: World Publishing.

Hobbes, T. (1950) *Leviathan*, New York: E. P. Dutton.

Little, J. W. (1992) 'Norms of collegiality and experimentation: Workplace conditions for school success', *American Educational Research Journal* 19 (3), 325–40.

McLaughlin, M. and Talbert, J. (1993) 'Contexts that Matter for Teaching and Learning', Stanford, Calif.: Center for Research on the Context of Secondary School Teaching.

Noddings, N. (1992) *The Challenge to Care in Schools: An Alternative Approach to Education*, New York: Teachers College.

Oakeshott, M. (1975) *On Human Conduct*, Oxford: Clarendon Press.

Sacks, J. (1997) 'Rebuilding civil society: A biblical perspective', *The Responsive Community* 7 (1), 11–20.

Selznick, P. (1957) *Leadership in Administration*, Berkeley: University of California Press.

Sergiovanni, T. J. (1992) *Moral Leadership: Getting to the Heart of School Improvement*, San Francisco: Jossey-Bass.

Sergiovanni, T. J. (1994a) *Building Community in Schools*, San Francisco: Jossey-Bass.

Sergiovanni, T. J. (1994b) 'Organizations or communities? Changing the metaphor changes the theory', *Educational Administration Quarterly* 30 (2), 214–26.

Sergiovanni, T. J. (1996) *Leadership for the Schoolhouse: Why Is It Different? How to Improve It?*, San Francisco: Jossey-Bass.

Shils, E. A. (1961) 'Centre and periphery', in E. A. Shils (ed.) *The Logic of Personal Knowledge: Essays Presented to Michael Polanyi*, London: Routledge and Kegan Paul.

Sowell, T. J. (1987) *A Conflict of Visions*, New York: William Morrow.

Tonnies, F. (1957) *Gemeinschaft und Gesellschaft*, ed. and trans. C. P. Loomis, New York: Harper Collins.

2

MEETING THE CHALLENGE

Becoming learning communities

Neville Johnson

A recent book on leadership was titled *On Becoming a Leader* (Bennis 1992). The central idea in it was that leaders are always 'becoming' leaders in the sense that they have never reached the ultimate and can continually improve – become even better. In the same sense, this paper considers the ongoing journey of schools as they are meeting the challenge of 'becoming' better learning communities.

The idea of the school as a 'learning community' is not new. It has been usual for schools in their talk and documentation to consider their schools as 'communities of learners', 'centres of inquiry', and to view classrooms as 'learning centres'. In the literature similar notions have persisted over many years: schools as 'communities of inquirers' (Dewey 1938); 'centres of inquiry' (Schaefer 1967); 'learning enriched or impoverished schools' (Rosenholtz 1989); and 'learning academies' (Sparks 1994). A related term, 'learning organisation', is currently in vogue in the corporate world. I have observed elsewhere that:

> It is interesting to observe that it took a best selling book in the non-school arena (Senge 1992), and the acceptance of the concept [of 'learning organisations'] by business and industry, to legitimise and awaken interest in its applicability and use in schools.
>
> (Johnson 1996a: 6)

My interest in the possible resurrection of the idea for use in schools was partially triggered by the current context in schools. Schools have always been busy places, but like many other organisations, schools are even more 'intensified' workplaces than they were a decade ago (Hargreaves 1994; Johnson 1996b). School staff are being required to work longer hours; juggle an increasing number of more complex tasks and roles; meet significantly higher internal and external expectations of their performance; and accomplish this with fewer resources, or at best no increase in resources. In such a climate schools desperately need to have a focus that allows them to make priority decisions that de-intensify the workplace and provides a

26

vision for the future. My assertion is that in the light of this context, it is timely to reconceptualise or rethink the idea of the 'learning community' as a possible powerful vision for schools.

The story is told of the child who, when asked if she 'knew her colours', replied confidently that she was 'winter'. This child had rethought or reconceptualised 'colour' to include the fashion colours of winter, autumn, summer and spring. This paper rethinks the concept of the 'learning community' from the perspective of a number of challenges facing schools and their communities. The overarching challenge is to rethink the common, the usual and the comfortable. This involves making explicit and rethinking the beliefs and practices associated with terms such as 'culture', 'learning', 'staff professional development', 'teaching', 'collaboration', 'teams', 'leadership' and 'community'.

THE CHALLENGE OF RECULTURING

Over the past decade there have been persistent calls for 'improving' (e.g. Fullan 1993), 'restructuring' (e.g. Caldwell 1993) and 'reforming' (Sizer 1994) schools. More recently the importance of 'reculturing' schools has been emphasised as an approach to responding to the challenges being faced by schools (e.g. Hargreaves 1994).

The Autumn 1995 edition of *Theory into Practice* was on the topic of 'Creating learner centred schools', and in it Michael Fullan contrasts the dreams and realities of schools as learning organisations. He calls for a radical 'reculturation' of schools and asks what combination of strategies might achieve the clarity, skill and will necessary for systematic reform (Fullan 1995). It is clear that any approach to reculturing emphasises climate and spirit; motivation and morale; and the norms, values, attitudes and beliefs associated with the school.

In essence then, the school 'culture' is about the internal conditions of the school community in that, at one level, it provides information about: what is important in the work of the school (vision, goals, objectives and learning outcomes valued); how the school goes about doing this work (organisational structures, procedures and processes established); and how people in the school community relate to each other (nature and purpose of the personal relationships encouraged and maintained). In the words of Fullan and Hargreaves, culture is 'the way we do things and relate to each other around here' (1991: 37). The culture of the school has been the focus of much attention in recent years.

Current research on school and classroom improvement and change (e.g. Leithwood 1994) calls this cultural aspect the 'second order' dimension, and emphasises the need to address it if valuable staff energy and time are not to be wasted and schools are to improve. This research supports the practice of working on two fronts when implementing a change for improvement: Strive to bring about the curriculum, teaching and learning changes required (the 'first order' dimension), and at the same time, work to provide the culture that will support the implementation and continuation of the change (the 'second order' dimension).

As Hargreaves (1994) reminds us, reculturing (second order change) is not easy to achieve. It assumes that school staff acknowledge the value of the change; it may take too long to achieve if students and parents are excluded in the process; and it often runs up against structural and procedural constraints. In addition, the culture as envisaged, documented, enacted and experienced may not be congruent: there may be a tension between what is desired and what is practised.

The concept of a school as a learning community is focused on the culture of a school, and sees *learning* as what is important in the work of the school; the school goes about its work in ways that establish the conditions for effective *learning*, and in the school, relationships that enhance *learning* are encouraged between community members. As such, it is a promising vision for reculturing that can be taken up in different ways in different places. It is a vision that is capable of 'mutual adaptation', in the sense that each learning community exhibits particular shared characteristics, but can move to embrace these features in ways that are suitable to their context. What follows is a consideration of some of the features of a school that is 'becoming' a learning community, framed as further challenges to be addressed.

THE CHALLENGE OF SEEING LEARNERS AND LEARNING AS 'CENTRAL'

The identification of *learners* and their *learning* as central, as the core work of the school, is critical when schools are striving to reduce intensification and overload, and establish priorities for action. Initiatives, programmes and practices that have great potential to increase the effectiveness of student, staff and community learning should be given the highest priority. In fact, with many initiatives being 'dumped' on already crowded school programmes by systems, it is imperative that all external change proposals, and ongoing internal programmes, are subjected to what could be called the 'Big L Crap-Detector' test. That is, for each initiative it should be asked 'What potential has this to improve or produce more effective *learning* for all members of the school community?'

It comes as no surprise that in a learning community, learners and their learning are central to every aspect of school work and life. In a recent article, Julia Atkin (1996) identifies habit and custom, the desire for simple solutions to complex problems, the power of 'group think', and uncritical adoption of outside mandated change as forces that work against the creation of learning communities. She urges 'an essential shift in mindset' (1996: 3) to school communities defining, making explicit and evaluating what they value and believe about learning, and moving from there to principles and practice.

> If we are truly learning, it will be a dynamic interactive process but at any point in time a learning teacher or learning school, will be able to identify what values and beliefs are the basis for particular practices. They will be engaged in reflecting upon how particular practices help them achieve what they value and believe, and their values and beliefs will be continually revisited and refined.
>
> (Atkin 1996: 5)

Given this view, the focus of all effort by the school community should be, of course, to make the school a better place for learners and learning. However, this begs the critical question of 'What constitutes the school community's view of effective learning?' In some schools, each year teachers construct a concept map of 'learning', and use these to compare and discuss their changing conceptions of learning. In these learning communities it is expected that teachers may be required to rethink their basic beliefs and principles that guide learning a number of times during their careers, and that significantly changing or fine-tuning their practice is an ongoing reality.

Currently, as a result of rethinking learning, many teachers are moving from what could be broadly called 'transmissionist' to more 'constructivist' beliefs about learning. In part, this has required a number of basic realignments that include shifts:

- from the view that it is the role of the teacher to transmit clear and accurate information and the students role to learn it; to the view that it is the teacher's role to establish the appropriate learning conditions; to skilfully support, challenge and guide the student during the learning process; and to help make explicit this process to themselves and their students
- from the belief that students need to be extrinsically motivated to learn; to the belief that students have a strong desire to construct meaning of their world and are quite capable of motivating themselves if the learning conditions are suitable
- from a process driven by the teacher, basically passive in practice and focused on memorising material that the student has little commitment to, and interest in; to a process that is often driven by the learner who is engaged in 'moving back and forth between a domain of thinking and a domain of action' (Senge 1995: 20) in the pursuit of making sense of something they see the need to master

- from the conception of schools as distribution centres for dispensing and using the knowledge, information and orientations of others, and where students become skilled 'doers'; to the conception of the school as a centre of inquiry where students become skilled 'thinkers' as well as 'doers', and the producers as well as the consumers of knowledge (Schaefer 1967: 1).

In a learning community these shifts that indicate different views of the world, or deeply ingrained assumptions about learning ('mental models' in Senge's terms), are made explicit and critiqued through a process of systematic reflection.

In addition, in a learning community the aim is to maximise learning for all members of the community – principals and formal leadership teams, teachers and other staff, parents and adult advocates, not just children and young adults.

For principals and other members of the formal leadership team, this means that they should see themselves as 'lead learners' who model, demonstrate and make explicit the connection of school decisions to learning. This requires them to articulate for parents, staff and students the link between management/resource development initiatives and the potential for improvement in learning. Thus, a new structure, procedure or school facility is of value if its connection with increased learning opportunities can be defended and communicated to the school community.

In a learning community, parents and other adult advocates of students are seen as partners in student learning and encouraged to increase their understanding of the nature of learning and the complexity of schooling. They too are challenged and supported to rethink such aspects as student 'assessment' – its purposes, forms and tensions.

Students are challenged to be lifelong learners and to be committed to becoming increasingly confident, knowledgeable and skilled learners. Teachers and other school staff (including office administration personnel and teacher aides and assistants) are supported and urged by the school culture to make plans for their own learning and adopt an enquiry-oriented, systematic and reflective approach to their work. It is in this area of staff learning that a significant challenge lies.

THE CHALLENGE TO RECONCEPTUALISE STAFF PROFESSIONAL DEVELOPMENT

An important feature of the culture of learning communities is the significance of staff learning in ensuring that learners and learning are seen as central. Nias *et al.* claim that professional learning is 'the key to the development of the curriculum and is the main way to improve the quality of children's education' (1992: 72).

If a teacher learns to work in ways that improve student learning, s/he potentially reaches the learning lives of approximately thirty children in a primary school or hundreds of young people in a secondary college. Michael Fullan argues that 'the skills and habits of everyday teachers are central to the future of learning societies' (1993: 103).

It is important to note that 'staff professional development' is a concept that is given meaning by those who organise it, plan it, conduct it, and participate in it. I would assert that if staff development is to be a major lever for 'becoming' a learning community, it may need to be rethought and reconceptualised.

At present, staff professional development is often narrowly conceived as 'courses' and 'special activities' usually conducted off-site or after school. I would argue that such a narrow conception often increases the intensification of teachers' lives with little payoff for them or their communities. The challenge is for many staff and formal leaders to conceive of staff professional development more broadly as opportunities for learning that occur naturally in the workplace as well as outside on special occasions.

Therefore, in a learning community multiple forms and models of staff professional development as are appropriate to the particular requirements are selected, combined and embraced. (Johnson 1991). Use is made of forms such as short courses, action research, peer coaching and mentoring, case discussions, study groups, small group problem-solving, journal writing and professional networking.

Little reminds us that it is important to note that:

Teachers' central reasons and opportunities for professional development begin with the teaching assignments they acquire, the allocation of discretionary time, and the other work conditions encountered day-by-day.

(1993: 147)

Given this reality, it is critical that in addition to formal elements such as training and sharing workshops, learning communities make great use of informal elements using everyday work-related and embedded learning opportunities. These include activities such as planning meetings, watching each other teaching, and curriculum design and review occasions. During these activities it is important that the connection to staff professional development, that is staff learning, is made explicit.

A particularly interesting model of professional development currently being investigated (Johnson and Scull 1998) is the establishment in schools of professional 'learning teams' of staff that may be cross-faculty, based in faculties or year levels and coordinated by lead teachers, with a focus on curriculum projects and action research. These learning teams consciously use time when they are doing their work as learning occasions – professional development opportunities. More detail of this approach is provided later in this chapter when the challenge of developing effective professional learning teams in learning communities is explored.

For teachers, and other staff in a learning community, to be committed to career-long learning they need to be encouraged and supported by an organisation where there is a planned programme of appraisal connected to effective professional development that systematically and collaboratively builds quality practice. In such a 'learning enriched' culture (Rosenholtz 1989) teachers are more prepared to engage in the ongoing systematic reflection of the nature of 'learning', and assess if their teaching approach and practice provides the conditions for effective student learning. Teachers in a learning community take the action required to meet the challenge to improve their teaching performance, and in an intensified workplace this provides a considerable challenge.

THE CHALLENGE OF HIGHER QUALITY TEACHING

The word 'teaching' has connotations that limit the way we think about it, with some teachers restricting it to presenting, lecturing or delivering information, while others are challenged to provide a wide range of carefully stacked and integrated strategies and tactics that provide the conditions for effective student learning. In addition, we often use related concepts such as 'integrated curriculum', 'mixed ability', 'team teaching', 'outcomes-based education', 'cooperative learning' and 'assessment' without checking the meaning given to them by other members of the community. In a learning community, the challenge exists to rethink terms such as these and attempt to create a shared language to use when describing and discussing teaching, and to support the implementation of higher-quality teaching.

Schools that are well down the track to 'becoming' learning communities begin with a particular focus: the students they are teaching. They see the point of schooling as being the learning that students do, and thus the purpose of teaching is to ensure that students develop the understanding and abilities they need in order to respond to and shape the world in which they live. To this end, teachers are required to be career-long learners, working to master the multiple categories of knowledge associated with their work.

Lee Shulman (1987) suggests such a categorisation and examines what teachers need to be studying and thinking about in order to provide the best learning environments for students. It is interesting to note that he considers being expert and up to date in the content knowledge of disciplines we teach as necessary but not sufficient. He asserts that content knowledge is only one category of a larger number of possible knowledge areas. These include: general pedagogical knowledge – those broad principles and strategies of classroom management and organisation that appear to transcend subject matter; curriculum knowledge – the materials, programmes and design principles of curriculum; knowledge of learners and their characteristics; knowledge of educational contexts – ranging from the workings of the group or classroom, to the school's governance and finance, and the character of communities and cultures; knowledge of educational ends, purposes and values – the various platforms and philosophies upon which we build; and lastly and very importantly, pedagogical content knowledge – the knowledge of what strategies, tactics and skills to use, in combination, for supporting specified content learning in particular situations for specific learners.

In learning communities, students acknowledge the knowledge and expertise of their teachers, and are more likely to experience teaching that:

- offers a wide, carefully selected range of content, process and attitudinal learning outcomes that help them learn particular domains of knowledge in a more integrated and contextual manner
- values authentic assessment and reports student progress in ways that allow student and teacher reflection on learning and helpful feedback on both strengths and aspects to work on
- provides engaging and challenging learning experiences in the school, classrooms and other carefully selected learning environments, experiences that place a premium on student engagement and require them to work in a variety of ways
- demonstrates a wide repertoire of approaches to learning and teaching, and challenges and supports students and staff to actively engage in building meaning.

Thus, in learning communities teachers think systematically about their practice, learn from their experience, and draw on education research and scholarship to continually improve their practice. They see themselves as members of learning communities and contribute to school effectiveness by collaborating with other professionals and community members, and taking advantage of community resources. In this way the work of teaching reaches beyond the boundaries of individual classrooms to wider communities of learning, and beyond the pursuit of individual excellence to an involvement in building effective teams and engaging in collective learning.

Recent research (Crevola and Hill 1998) supports the assertion that the 'between classroom' differences are greater than the 'between school' differences when student learning is examined. Thus, in a typical school faced with the challenge of implementing a curriculum, learning and teaching change proposal, the response of the teachers could vary signifcantly, as could the learning gains of students in those classrooms. For example, Teacher A may already be practising in ways very like those required in the change proposal, and during implementation finds her/his teaching approach being legitimised and merely fine-tuned. In this case there may be a slight increase in already effective student learning. Teacher B's current practice differs widely from that suggested in the change proposal, but this teacher is very available to consider making changes in teaching. S/he embraces the new ways of working and actively implements them in the classroom. Quite significant learning gains for students result. When faced with the change proposal, Teacher C claims that s/he is already working in those ways in the classroom, but really isn't. This teacher rationalises her/his current practice and makes no changes in terms of classroom practice, and achieves no student gains. Finally, Teacher D is not available to consider the proposal to change her/his practice. This teacher may attack the change proposal as being unnecessary or poorly conceived, or may respond by 'nodding and grinning' but with no intention of implementing the required new ways of working in the classroom. Obviously, in this case no student learning gains are likely. This scenario provides an additional challenge for schools that are dedicated to 'becoming' learning communities.

THE CHALLENGE TO DEVELOP EFFECTIVE PROFESSIONAL LEARNING TEAMS

This challenge serves to address the problem of 'between classroom differences' in the implementation of teaching approaches that are aimed to result in higher student learning gains, and offers a powerful strategy for building even more effective learning communities. A study (Johnson and Scull 1998), mentioned briefly earlier, challenges learning communities to rethink the concept of 'team', and identifies important factors in the development of effective professional learning teams. In addition, the findings of this study, which was part of the Early Literacy Research Project (ELRP), have increased our confidence in the power of project-based/professional learning teams to reduce 'between classroom differences' and provide a structure that contributes significantly to a learning community culture in schools.

In the ELRP, professional learning teams were found to be a critical design element as teachers strove to implement a curriculum change that involved a comprehensive and integrated approach to literacy learning and teaching (Crevola and Hill 1998; Hill and Crevola 1998). The ELRP involved a total of twenty-seven schools in the Department of Education, Victoria (Australia), with twenty-three learning teams agreeing to participate in this complementary study. Extrapolating from the findings of this study, the characteristics of effective professional learning teams include the following:

1 Learning teams require a reason to learn and a purpose to engage in collaborative professional development practices. Projects provide such a reason.

Projects provide a 'vehicle' for integrating and achieving many school and system initiatives and goals. They can connect many improvement strands into a sensible weave. In addition, projects have a beginning and an end (even if they are in stages and are essentially ongoing). In workplaces that are becoming increasingly intensified with teachers feeling overloaded (Hargreaves 1994), it is essential that school staff have the opportunity to celebrate successes and feel a sense of reward and closure in their work. The failure of schools that work on too many unconnected fronts and use one-shot approaches to professional development are well documented (e.g. Fullan 1993; Johnson 1991). Projects, in contrast, provide ongoing opportunities for staff learning that are related to classroom practice.

2 The most effective projects for learning teams to be involved in are those that are focused on producing more effective learning for all students.

The projects should be selected because they have direct links to student learning outcomes and create meaningful learning opportunities for teachers, challenging them to develop their understanding and learn. Professional development undertaken as part of the real work of teachers allows teacher learning to be taking place while teachers engage in their normal work. This form of professional development is integrated, not added on, and therefore is less likely to further overload and intensify the teacher's worklife in the learning community.

A critical characteristic of professional learning teams is that the team collectively takes responsibility for achieving learning gains for *all* students regardless of their grade. It is this aspect of team work that is difficult to implement, as it demands a level of trust and cooperation that many teachers find challenging. When achieved, the impact on reducing the between classroom differences outlined earlier has been shown to be considerable.

3 Learning teams benefit from a combination of outside-provided and work-embedded support.

As mentioned earlier in this chapter, there is a need for those involved in becoming better learning communities to rethink their understanding of professional development and teacher learning. The ELRP demonstrated the effectiveness of a combination of work-based and outside-provided learning opportunities for teachers. More particularly, schools can no longer afford

35

the luxury of separating professional development activities from the ongoing realities of teachers' work. The two must be seen as integrated and interdependent to support school change and ongoing improvement efforts.

An appropriate combination of outside-provided and work-embedded support addresses the problem that work-based learning can often fail to be based on the best knowledge and strategies available to the profession, by tapping sources outside the school as necessary. It also responds to the possible poor transfer to the classroom of learning from outside school sources, by providing ongoing, systematic and reflective workplace support.

4 Effective learning teams practise many forms of collaboration and systematic reflection on practice.

Judith Warren Little (1990) introduced the notion of a continuum of collaboration, which involved teachers moving from isolation to different degrees of interdependence and collegiality. Effective learning teams are characterised by their use of a variety of collective learning opportunities, most of which involve routinised sharing and joint work.

Such opportunities for collaboration and collective learning often encourage learning teams to be engaged in critical reflection and problem-solving. Boud *et al.* describe reflection as 'an important human activity in which people capture their experience, think about it, mull it over, evaluate it' and argue that it is a process of such significance that it demands a specific allocation of time (1985: 19). Schon (1983) suggests the importance of critical reflection as an important skill in teaching; and according to Grant (1984) reflective teachers tend to adopt a more critical stance about their work and the social and political contexts in which their teaching is embedded.

5 A sense of 'personal productive challenge', and a balance between pressure and support, characterises the work of effective learning teams.

Baird (1992) introduced the concept of 'personal productive challenge' when considering effective teacher learning. In his view, 'challenge' comprises two main components: a cognitive, metacognitive demand component, and an affective interest component. When applied to teacher learning, the optimal situation is where a teacher has high interest and is faced with a high (but not too high) cognitive demand. In this case challenge is likely to be positive and productive and the teacher engages in the learning enthusiastically and effectively. Challenge is likely to be non-productive in situations where demand is high, but interest is low; demand is low while interest is high; and both demand and interest are low. It is interesting to note that Thelen's (1960) concept of 'discomfort' as a necessary component for new learning is a related idea to that of 'challenge'.

The ELRP demonstrated that effective learning teams get the balance between pressure and support right, so that a productive personal and team challenge results.

6 Learning teams are most effective when they have knowledgeable and skilled formal leadership, who work in supportive ways with the team.

The ELRP as a model for effective school improvement challenges schools to rethink the conditions of work for key people nominated to coordinate change projects in schools. For coordinators to support the process of change they must be both able and available to assist teacher learning, freed to work as learning partners alongside teachers as changes to classroom programmes are implemented.

For school improvement reforms dependent upon changing teachers' behaviours, coordinators of change projects must be able to work with teachers in the roles of coach and mentor, assisting teachers to develop skills which impact on improved student learning outcomes. They need to be able to assist in the development of resources to further support the implementation of the change project and work with the school community to establish and maintain the profile of the project. This study has shown that this could be achieved when coordinators of change projects were themselves provided with adequate leadership training, with their role valued and resourced with appropriate time allocations.

The learning team formal leader should be available to support teachers' learning, creating opportunities for strategies to be modelled and through providing additional coaching and support for teachers as required. An important role of the coordinator is as a 'linker' of team member with team member, of teacher with ideas, and of team members with materials and resources. In this role the formal leader often supports learning team members in seeing the big picture, thus challenging the limited view that often results from teachers working in isolation.

7 Successful learning teams address the tensions inherent in the formal leaders' role and in the personal and professional relationships within the learning team.

As demonstrated in the ELRP, learning team coordinators (formal leaders) often find themselves positioned between administrators and initiators of the project with their focus on the school and system goals and project outcomes, and the teacher members of the learning team with their focus on the practice and action in addressing the challenges of the classroom. Formal leaders have to be able to handle the tensions that often result, and it is essential that all learning team members strive to see the world through the eyes of the other stakeholders.

8 In effective learning teams all members consider themselves to be change agents and leaders.

Fullan's assertion that 'Change is too important to leave to the experts' (1993: 39) has serious implications for learning teams. The ELRP demonstrated the need for each member to acknowledge the role that s/he had to play in implementing classroom change. The view that each teacher is a change agent must underpin the discussion and action of the learning teams. In an effective learning team, the functions of leadership are distributed between all team members, while the responsibilities of leadership may reside with the formal leader.

9 When challenged by a change proposal, effective learning teams practise 'mutual adaptation' while implementing change for the purpose of improvement.

The ELRP demonstrated that the more effective learning teams never lost control of the improvement and change process. Effective learning teams realise that they need to stay in control as professionals and make use of the projects rather than be used by them. In addition, change for the sake of improvement must be embraced, but never change for the sake of change. To this end, 'mutual adaptation' (Berman and McLaughlin 1976) is often the best intention and outcome when learning teams are faced by an outside initiative and proposal for change. In this way the change proposal/initiative must be capable of flexing to be appropriate to the particular school and learning context without losing its critical characteristics and essence. Similarly, the teachers must be prepared to change their practices to embrace the critical characteristics and essence of the change proposal.

10 Learning teams implement change in ways and at rates different from one another.

The ELRP data supports the assertion that individual learning teams move through the curriculum implementation process in ways and at rates different from one another. It is to be expected that when faced with a proposal of curriculum change, different learning teams exhibit different concerns and different levels of use. Similarly, learning teams will exhibit different sophistication in the use of curriculum being implemented. Some learning teams will be satisfied with routine use of the curriculum in a passive management way, others insisting on refining, extending and challenging the ideas and practices of the curriculum. It is essential that learning teams in a learning community have realistic, but challenging, expectations and that they 'think big, but start small'.

THE CHALLENGE OF COLLABORATION, SHARED LEADERSHIP AND CONTINUOUS IMPROVEMENT

This challenge serves to integrate the five previous challenges. As illustrated in the challenge to develop professional learning teams, the evidence is strong (see also Glatthorn 1987; Little 1990), that teachers are more likely to change the way they work in classrooms, and continually improve their practice, if they are supported in their own working environment by a group of colleagues who engage in cooperative/collaborative professional development activities, and by a culture that values collaboration, shared/distributed leadership and continuous improvement.

One of the major misconceptions about teaching is that it is a relatively commonplace, easy-to-learn task. This assertion is challenged in the literature concerned with the implementation of change in learning and teaching which has revealed the necessity for ongoing, on-site collegial support in enabling teachers to acquire new and complex teaching strategies and to successfully transfer them into their repertoire of teaching practices (see for example Joyce and Showers 1995). A number of studies cited by Joyce and Showers support the position that unless adequate professional development and training is provided teachers do not acquire new teaching skills, and unless adequate follow-up support is provided implementation does not occur. It is the nature of this support that has been the focus of much recent work in teacher learning. As in child and young adult learning, much debate has taken place on the 'what' and 'how' of teacher learning, while there has been little discussion of the 'where' and 'with whom'.

An encouraginging development in schools is the interest shown in rethinking the 'where' and 'with whom' of staff learning. Discussion and exploration of cooperative/collaborative approaches to teacher improvement have resulted. Although not a clearly defined approach, it can be described as 'a process by which small teams of teachers work together, using a variety of methods and structures, for their own professional growth' (Glatthorn 1987: 31). It is often characterised by active teacher participation; focus on issues of concern, or work-related tasks recognised by teachers themselves; group self-direction, although the services of a consultant and/or critical friend may be negotiated; and systematic individual reflection on practice which is often structured by the group (Schon 1983; Wells and Chang 1986). It also acknowledges that what we learn is context bound.

Collaborative learning opportunities for teachers can take many forms, but as the professional learning teams project (ELRP) demonstrated, the main options include shared talk – regular and systematic talk among staff; shared work – where there is collaborative development of policy, programmes and activities; observation of teaching – teachers engage in regular and systematic observation of one another's classes; and collaborative problem-solving (action research) – which involves development and implementation of feasible solutions to teacher-identified problems (Little 1990). A few experts in the field advocate only one approach, but it seems more useful to conceive of collaboration more broadly so that teachers may begin with the option that is most comfortable to them.

The impact of peer coaching in enabling teachers to learn new ways of working in classrooms has been well documented (Joyce and Showers 1995). However, the evidence is still scanty for other benefits claimed, such as changes in teacher attitude and motivation. More recently, interest has been shown in the various forms of teacher collaboration. Terms such as 'buddying' (functional, collegial relationships of equal contribution, often short term and for specific purposes); 'preceptoring' (collegial relationships where one member is the 'teacher' and the other the 'student' – often as part of their job description); and 'mentoring' (long-term, intimate collaboration between colleagues where one is often given a leadership role by the other) are being used to describe these collaborative forms. Regardless of the form, each offers the opportunity to celebrate successes, address challenges and solve problems in a supportive environment, where there is a sense of a 'shared adventure.' (Baird 1992).

One challenge in a learning community is to break with the traditional, but often damaging, practice of collaboration being confined to teachers within particular grade levels, school level and subject disciplines. Collaboration across the boundaries of pre-school, primary, junior and senior secondary and tertiary levels of schooling, and across subject disciplines and departments, is essential for improved learning and school-wide improvement.

Such collaborative approaches with their focus on collective learning are supported by Prawat in an article titled 'Learning community, commitment and school reform' (1996). He argues that the learning-community approach to a school culture aims to build social and intellectual connections between people. He asserts that such a culture is based on engendering commitment in individuals and the collective, not by manipulating control over them. Such commitment strengthens action by transforming effort into value and meaning, which in turn leads to intrinsic motivation. Given this view, building a learning community is tantamount to developing a commitment to a shared direction and shared learning. Thus, collaboration, shared leadership and continuous improvement are major planks in the culture of a learning community (Johnson 1996b: 8).

A learning community is a community whose culture is characterised by commitment and professionalism. It is a community where the staff's voices are heard, their ideas are valued and they are viewed as professionals. In addition, these professionals are committed to collective learning. In Senge's (1992) terms, it is the notion of 'team learning' with individuals as a group continually learning how to learn and problem-solve together. Such a vision challenges the persisting view of the accomplished teacher as a stand-alone, self-sufficient performer who works and learns independently and values norms of privacy and non-interference. Little (1990) sees this as outdated practice when compared with the potential power of the collective capacity of a school, programme or group to serve student and staff learning. However, she warns us of the considerable habit and custom, structural and procedural forces marshalled against such a change.

There is, therefore, the challenge of becoming a learning community where each individual is valued, but so is the collective; where collaboration is built into the very fabric of the culture; and where the community has reasons to collaborate, and collaborates in particular ways for specific purposes that can be defended in terms of powerful community learning and continuous improvement.

The change process involves a delicate balance between pressure and support, and between individualism and collectivism. Pressure to encourage the school community to rethink/reconceptualise its current position, and support through a sense of connectedness between community members as they engage in joint work and meaning-making. Similarly, we are warned by Fullan that there are no one-sided solutions to individual isolation and 'group think'. He asserts that individualism and collectivism must have equal power, with the contribution of each community member and the group being honoured (1993: 33–6).

Confronting such tensions requires, and builds, commitment to 'becoming' learning communities. It is, however, a long-term and protracted process. Like any change process it is more a journey than a blueprint, and is often 'loaded with uncertainty sometimes perverse' (Fullan 1993: 24). The particulars of the culture for each school emerge through a process of community negotiation, guided by an overall sense of what one hopes to accomplish and the form of learning community one strives to become.

References

Atkin, J. (1996) 'From values and beliefs about learning to principles and practice', *IARTV Seminar Series* (May), no. 54.

Baird, J. R. (1992) 'Individual challenge and shared adventure: Two concepts for improving quality in teaching, learning and research', The John Smyth Memorial Lecture, University of Melbourne.

Bennis, W. G. (1992) *On Becoming a Leader*, London: Hutchinson Business Books.

Berman, P. and McLaughlin, M.W. (1976) 'Implementation of educational innovation', *Educational Forum* 40 (3), 345–70.

Boud, D., Keogh, R. and Walker, D. (1985) *Reflection: Turning Experience Into Learning*, London: Kogan Page.

Caldwell, B. J. (1993) 'The changing role of the school principal: A review of developments in Australia and New Zealand', in C. Dimmock (ed.) *School-based Management and School Effectiveness*, London: Routledge.

Crevola, C. A. and Hill, P. W. (1998) 'The role of reading recovery in a whole school approach to early literacy', paper presented to the 11th International Congress for School Effectiveness and Improvement (ICSEI '98), University of Manchester (January).

Dewey, J. (1938) 'Logic: The theory of inquiry', in *The Collected Works of John Dewey, 1882–1953*, Carbondale and Edwardsville: Southern Illinois University Press, 1962–67.

Fullan, M. (1993) *Change Forces: Probing the Depths of Educational Reform*, New York: Falmer Press.

Fullan, M. (1995) 'The school as a learning organisation: Distant dreams', in *Theory into Practice* 34 (4), 230–5.

Fullan, M. and Hargreaves, A. (1991) *What's Worth Fighting For: Working Together for Your School*, Hawthorn, Australia: ACEA Paperbacks.

Glatthorn, A. (1987) 'Cooperative professional development: Peer-centred options for teacher growth', *Educational Leadership* (November) 31–5.

Grant, C. A. (1984) *Preparing for Reflective Teaching*, Boston, Mass.: Allyn and Bacon.

Hargreaves, A. (1994) *Changing Teachers, Changing Times*, Toronto: OISE Press.

Hill, P. W. and Crevola, C. A. (1998) 'Developing and testing a whole-school, design approach to improvement in early literacy', paper presented to the 11th International Congress for School Effectiveness and Improvement (ICSEI '98), University of Manchester (January).

Johnson, N. J. (1991) 'Effective professional development: The key to quality teaching and effective learning', *IARTV Occasional Paper* (November), no. 23.

Johnson, N. J. (1996a) 'Reconceptualising schools as learning communities', *Reflect* 2 (1), 6–13.

Johnson, N. J. (1996b) 'School leadership and the management of change', *IARTV Seminar Series* (July), no. 55.

Johnson, N. J. and Scull, J. (1998) 'Rethinking staff professional development: Early literacy learning teams', paper presented to the 11th Congress for School Effectiveness and Improvement (ICSEI '98), University of Manchester (January).

Joyce, B. and Showers, B. (1995) *Student Achievement through Staff Development*, New York: Longman.

Leithwood, K. (1994) 'Leadership for school restructuring', *Educational Administration Quarterly* 30(4), 498–518.

Little, J. W. (1990) 'The persistence of privacy: Autonomy and initiative in teachers' professional relations', *Teachers College Record* 91 (4), 508–36.

Little, J. W. (1993) 'Teachers' professional development in a climate of educational reform', *Educational Evaluation and Policy Analysis* 15 (2), 129–51.

Nias, J., Southworth, G. and Campbell, P. (1992) *Whole School Curriculum Development in the Primary School*, Lewes, England: Falmer Press.

Prawat, Richard S. (1996) 'Learning community, commitment and school reform', *Journal of Curriculum Studies* 28 (1), 91–110.

Rosenholtz, S. (1989) *Teachers' Workplace: The Social Organisation of Schools*, New York: Longman.

Schaefer, R. I. (1967) *The School as a Centre of Inquiry*, New York: Harper and Row.

Schon, D. A. (1983) *The Reflective Practitioner*, New York: Basic Books.

Senge, P.M. (1992) *The Fifth Discipline*, Sydney: Random House.

Senge, P. M. (1995) 'On schools as learning organisations: A conversation with Peter Senge', *Educational Leadership* (April), 20–3.

Shulman, L. S. (1987) 'Knowledge and teaching: Foundation of the new reform', *Harvard Education Review* 57 (1), 1–14.

Sizer, T. R. (1994) 'Education reform in the USA and the coalition of essential schools', *IARTV Seminar Series* (November) no. 40.

Sparks, D. (1994) 'A paradigm shift in staff development', *Journal of Staff Development* 15 (4), 26–9.

Thelen, H. (1960) *Education and the Human Quest*, New York: Harper and Row.

Wells, G. and Chang, G.L. (1986) *Effecting Educational Change Through Collaborative Research*, Toronto: OISE.

3

PARTNERS IN LEARNING

School-based and university-based communities of learning

Shirley Grundy

> As Australian teachers and teacher educators face an increasing array
> of educational reforms and challenges, there is a constant call for
> provision of new forms of professional development. It is evident
> that more effective linkages need to be established between schools
> and universities to enhance the status of the teaching profession and
> to provide support for practitioners.
> Southern Cross Roundtable Portrayal Evaluation Team (1996)

In this chapter, the ideas and practices associated with the sort of professional partnerships advocated in the above quotation will be explored. The
particular form of partnership which will be explored is that between
school-based and university-based educators. The relationships between
these two groups of educational practitioners is not often viewed as a
'partnership'. More often, it is described in terms of separation and distance
between the two groups – the 'theory/practice gap', for instance. Where a
relationship is acknowledged as existing, it is often regarded as one of
superiority of one group to the other. On the one hand, teachers can be
positioned as subservient to university practitioners. They are the 'students'
of university academics in both undergraduate and postgraduate study and
they also become the 'subjects' of academic research. On the other hand
university academics are positioned as out of touch and irrelevant to the
'real' world of the classroom. The idea of partnership, then, will face an
uphill struggle for acceptance.

In the first part of the chapter, I explore some of the underlying conditions necessary for educational organisations, such as schools and university
departments, to become 'learning organisations'. These include issues to do
with the control of knowledge, the development of collegial dispositions and
orientations towards improvement. I then discuss the idea of partnerships as
a way of moving from individual 'learning organisations' to 'learning
communities'. Of course, learning organisations themselves need to be

44

communities of learners, but it is argued here that the learning can be enriched as the boundaries between learning organisations are permeated through partnership working relationships. I then discuss an experiment in partnership from the Australian context. This is the Innovative Links Project through which school and university colleagues from 130 schools and 16 university campuses formed research communities to support teacher learning. It is argued that for such partnerships to produce authentic learning communities, reciprocal learning must occur, where school-based practitioners also support the learning of university-based colleagues. Some examples of the way in which this reciprocal learning partnership was facilitated by the project are also provided.

CONTROL OF KNOWLEDGE

As noted above, our traditional view of educational knowledge is that university academics are its producers and custodians. Teachers and their work are the subjects of research, not the generators of research. Lawrence Stenhouse's seminal work *Introduction to Curriculum Research and Development* (1975) directly challenged this traditional relationship. 'It is not enough', he argued, 'that teachers' work should be studied. They need to study it themselves' (1975: 223).

In his advocacy of participation by teachers in researching their own work, Stenhouse was enunciating a fundamental principle of what we would now call the learning community school. That is, he was proclaiming the school as a primary site of knowledge production, and also clearly identifying who should be in charge of such knowledge production – teachers themselves.

The point which Stenhouse made so passionately in relation to the control of knowledge about a particular situation (in this case schools and the work of teachers) by those in the situation (in this case teachers themselves) was being made at about the same time in relation to other contexts. I recall that, while researching for an assignment during my undergraduate days in the early 1970s, I came across an article by Noam Chomsky. The paper was not directly relevant to my assignment on international diplomacy, so I did not note its reference details. The gist of the argument, however, stayed with me.

In the paper, as I recall, Chomsky asks and answers a number of questions with respect to Thailand:

> *Question:* Who has been investing the greatest amount into research
>   in Thailand?
> *Answer:* The United States of America.

Question: Who has accumulated the greatest amount of knowledge
about Thailand?
Answer: The United States of America.

Question: In whose interests has this research been done and is this
knowledge being used?
Answer: The United States of America.

The argument lying behind these questions relates to the knowledge/power
question, and it raises significant issues about the right to know and the
right to control knowledge, as well as the question of 'in whose interests is
knowledge produced and applied?' The implications of Chomsky's argument
could be paraphrased in Stenhouse's terms: 'It is not enough that Thailand
be studied. The Thais need to study it themselves.'

Of course, the knowledge/power relationship, either in the international
or in the educational scenario, is not as oppositional as the Chomsky
questions and answers suggest. Indeed, there are no doubt many examples of
where research and consultancy activity by an outside power has produced
benefit for the country which is the subject of the research. Moreover, as I
shall argue in more detail below, those from outside schools (for instance
university-based educators) can engage productively in research partnerships
which produce educational benefit. Nor is it the case that the only
legitimate, valid or reliable knowledge is that which is produced through
formal processes of research. Just as the inhabitants of Thailand clearly have
knowledge about living in that country which is every bit as important as
the knowledge produced by outsiders, so also the 'inhabitants' of schools
(administrators, teachers and students) possess knowledge about schooling
which is every bit as important as that possessed by researchers, consultants
and administrators from elsewhere.

This is, then, the point from which I wish to begin this discussion of
learning partnerships – from the assertion that not only do schools need to
be regarded as sites of investigation and learning, but those within the
school, particularly teachers, need to take an active role in the processes of
investigation and learning. This means that it is important to move beyond
thinking in terms of a technically proficient profession in which knowledge
about schools and what should be done in them is seen to reside elsewhere,
to be handed to competent though compliant professionals, who will
formulate plans and implement actions in the light of that 'elsewhere'
knowledge. The control of knowledge needs, as it were, to come home to the
profession and to the communities of schools in which these professionals
practise.

This leads me, then, to the first of a series of 'propositions' with respect to
schools as learning communities.

Proposition One: Schools which are developing as learning communities will be producers rather than consumers of professional knowledge

There is, however, an important corollary to this proposition which needs to be acknowledged in the development of learning communities in partnership. Here we need to extend the idea of university researchers as investigators of the practices of others. If university academics are to participate in teachers' learning communities, they will need to subject their own work to research and reflection. It is a sad irony that, while the work of teaching has been an important area of research for the last twenty to thirty years, the focuses of this research have been the practices of teachers in schools, not those of university teachers. To paraphrase Stenhouse: 'It is not enough that teachers' work should be studied. University academics need to study their own work as well.' The above proposition, therefore, needs the following important corollary:

Corollary One: University departments which are developing as learning communities will need to be producers of knowledge about their own practices

From individualism to community

Partnership and community, of course, challenge the individualism which has characterised educational work within both university and school environments. 'Individualism, isolation and privatism', Andy Hargreaves claims, 'make up one particular form of what has come to be known as the culture of teaching' (1994: 165).

Both university-based and school-based teachers have traditionally prized their autonomy. More recently this isolationism has been challenged within schools and we have seen strong advocacy of the need for teaching to become more of a collaborative profession. In a survey of school practitioners in which we were exploring the impact of various restructuring initiatives upon schools (Grundy and Bonser 1997), my colleague, Stewart Bonser, and I asked the following set of questions:

To what extent should a teacher working in isolation from colleagues have the discretion to make decisions about:

- learning outcomes? (F3.1)
- how the learning program is managed and presented to the students? (F3.2)
- the application of technological resources? (F3.3)

Responses across all of these questions reflected a continuing commitment by teachers and school administrative personnel to individual discretionary decision-making. Almost half of the respondents (46 per cent) believed that teachers should have discretion to make individual decisions about learning outcomes. Respondents were even stronger in their advocacy of individual discretion in relation to making decisions in isolation about the management and presentation of the learning programme and about the application of technological resources. Interestingly, teachers expressed stronger views in favour of individual autonomy than did principals.

Yet our data also indicate a strong commitment to collegiality and collaborative work practices. We asked:

> To what extent should the decision-making process in the school:
> - be consultative? (C4.1)
> - reflect collaborative approaches to decision-making? (C4.2)

and

> To what extent do you perceive that:
> - your decisions about teaching and learning involve colleagues? (F1.1)
> - teamwork is being used to share ideas in the development of student learning? (F2.1)

Responses to these questions provide evidence of a strong professional commitment to collegiality. Over 90 per cent of respondents advocated that decision-making should be consultative and reflect collaborative approaches. Similarly, the majority of respondents reported that decisions about teaching and learning involved colleagues to a considerable extent and that teamwork was being used to share ideas.

Hargreaves describes collaboration and collegiality as being 'pivotal to the orthodoxies of change' in schools (Hargreaves 1994: 186). Within organisations which are responding to the challenge to become learning communities, however, there will potentially be a tension between individual autonomy and collaborative, collegial work practices.

While Hargreaves might regard collaborative work practices as an 'orthodoxy' today, this was a reasonably novel insight two decades ago. Lawrence Stenhouse's advocacy of collaborative work practices in schools was fairly radical in 1975. He argued:

> I value highly the tradition of professional autonomy as the basis of education quality but it seems that this must now be negotiated at school level. Concessions must be made in individual autonomy in order to provide a basis for collaborative working, for the school

staff can no longer be seen as a federal association of teachers and departments: it must be a professional community. And it is with that community that professional autonomy must lie.

(Stenhouse 1975: 183)

Just over two decades on, the principle of collaborative professional work in schools is strongly advocated. For instance, in the Western Australian school performance indicators (Education Department of Western Australia 1997: 17), 'Leadership' is associated with a collaborative work culture. A school in which leadership is 'undeveloped' is one where:

Staff work independently in isolation.

A school in which leadership is 'establishing' is one where:

Team-work is evident in the school, with staff involved in management roles.

A school which is 'achieving' in the area of leadership is one where:

A collaborative approach exists in the school, with staff involved in leadership and management roles.

It is interesting, however, that while these school performance indicators give the imprimatur to collaborative work practices, the random sample of Australian teachers who participated in the study cited above (Grundy and Bonser 1997), while generally expressing agreement with the orthodoxy of collaborative and collegial practices, still value highly the possibility of expressing their individualism through independent, even isolated, work practices. In essence what professionals participating in this study appeared to be saying was that they valued opportunities to make decisions and work individually, but at the same time valued and expected to be able to engage in collaborative and collegial decision-making and team-based work practices.

Perhaps the distinctions that Hargreaves (1994) makes between 'individualism' and 'individuality' and 'collaboration' and 'contrived collegiality' are relevant here. Drawing upon Steven Lukes, Hargreaves identifies individualism with 'anarchy and social atomization' and individuality with 'personal independence and self-realization' (1994: 178). On the other hand, Hargreaves explores the characteristics of 'collaborative [work] cultures' and those that are grounded in 'contrived collegiality'. The former are 'spontaneous...voluntary...development-oriented...unpredictable', while the latter are 'administratively regulated...compulsory...implementation-oriented...[and] predictable' (1994: 192–6).

'Vibrant teacher cultures', he argues, 'should be able to avoid the professional limitations of teacher individualism, while embracing the creative potential of teacher individuality' (1994: 183). Moreover, while individuality is likely to be stifled in environments in which collegiality is contrived, obligatory and instrumentally created, collaborative communities are likely to provide room for generative joint work.

Harnessing this creative tension between individuality and collegiality will be one of the challenges for learning communities. This, then, leads to my second proposition with respect to learning communities:

Proposition Two: Learning communities will accept and foster a creative tension between individual initiative and expression and collaborative work and organisational practices

Organising for improvement in student learning

The question that arises now is the way in which the above two propositions are connected. The first relates to professional knowledge and the second to the organisation of work practices. In a sense, both of these propositions are 'means' statements. To make sense, they need to be connected to a proposal relating to 'ends'. Here, I make no radical propositions, but want to affirm the taken-for-granted (but underestimated) purpose of both schools and universities – that they exist for student learning.

Teachers, whether within school or university environments, can no longer be content to pass on to students bodies of knowledge, nor can teachers any more equate learning with teaching (or – to use the jargon of business – 'outcomes' with 'inputs'). Teachers, individually and collectively, are being held accountable, not only for students' learning, but for *improvements* to students' learning. The indicators of 'excelling' performance for a school, according to the Western Australian Education Department's performance framework, include the following:

> Planning for improvement and setting of targets for student outcomes are central for all staff and lead to deliberate actions at the classroom level.

> All human, financial and physical resources available to the school are allocated and used to maximise student performance...
> (Education Department of Western Australia 1997: 16)

Dimmock's reflections upon improved learning and the organisational structures of the school are apposite here:

If schools are to achieve improvements in student learning outcomes then new approaches to teaching and learning are required. These new approaches are unlikely to be effective if simply grafted onto present organisational structures and administrative, managerial and leadership practices.

(1995: 277–8)

Moreover, the above Proposition Two, which itself builds upon a substantial body of curriculum and school management literature and research, would suggest that the 'new approaches' which will achieve the improvements to which Dimmock refers are those which are grounded in a culture of community – the sort of community which privileges both collaborative practices and individuality.

Such practices do not work automatically or 'magically' to bring about improvement, however. Here we need to link organisational and professional work practices (individuality and community) with the knowledge production processes of inquiry to which Proposition One referred. In a paper collaboratively written with some of my former colleagues from the University of New England, we make the following link between collaborative work, improved student learning and processes of inquiry and knowledge production:

Because teaching practices are intrinsic to the curriculum that students experience...the examination and improvement by teachers, both individually and collectively, of their teaching practices is an important aspect of curriculum development. It should not be assumed, however, that collaborative work to improve practice is easy. The examination and critique of teaching practice is fraught with risk. Yet where groups of teachers engage in such critique in a spirit of trust and support, the resultant learning experiences for students [and teachers] are likely to be improved.

(Warhurst *et al.* 1994: 176)

Proposition Three, therefore, links the instrumental propositions referred to above (creating collaborative organisations and engaging in knowledge production through processes of inquiry) with the purpose of improving student learning.

Proposition Three: Learning communities will engage in processes of inquiry to investigate their organisational and work practices in order to work towards the improvement of student learning

Creating learning communities through partnerships

The three propositions presented so far have explored the idea of the learning organisation. Although the argument has proceeded from a consideration of schools, it has been argued that these proposals apply equally to university departments. However, I want to go further than proposing principles that need to apply to individual sites, be they schools or universities, as important as these might be. Just as we have moved away from considering the school or the department as merely the site within which individual teachers undertake their work, largely in isolation from their colleagues, so also, I will argue, we need to move away from regarding learning organisations as being situated within, but largely disconnected from, the environment in which they operate.

An implication of the argument of this chapter is that the learning interests of students are no longer best served by understanding learning as a one-to-one and one-way interaction between individual teacher and individual learner. Rather, we need to understand learning as a process of complex interactions between teachers and their students (students and their teachers) within and beyond the community of the school. Understood in this way, the school or university and the environment in which it is situated are no longer merely the sites of learning, they are rightly perceived as intrinsically connected with it.

Within contemporary society the boundaries between sites of learning are increasingly crumbling as virtual learning resources are created and accessed on the Internet, as the labour processes of learning and the labour processes of earning are brought together in vocationally oriented school programmes, and as teachers become learners themselves as they engage in career-long professional development.

All of this suggests that what is needed when we think about the teaching/learning process is an understanding of the complex ways in which the processes and places of learning are interrelated.

This, then, brings me to my final proposition regarding teachers for schools of the future:

Proposition Four: Members of learning organisations will need to explore ways in which networking and information-sharing possibilities can be utilised and to establish partnerships with other educational providers

Learning partnerships

I advocated above that both school-based and university-based teachers need to engage in knowledge-production processes about their own practices. In advocating a realignment in the control of educational research to teachers in schools, I was not advocating that university-based researchers should abandon research in this area. Even Stenhouse, who, as was noted above, argued that 'It is not enough that teachers' work should be studied. They need to study it themselves' (1975: 223), did not advocate the wholesale abandonment of school- and classroom-oriented research to teachers. Rather, he urged that educational research become a collaborative venture:

> Research in curriculum and teaching, which involves the close study of schools and classrooms, is the basis of sound development, and the growth of a research tradition in the schools is its foundation. Full-time research workers and teachers need to collaborate towards this end.
>
> (Stenhouse 1975: 223)

The opportunities for the development of productive, collaborative partnerships between members of school and university communities of inquirers have, in the past, been limited, but the potential is great. In Australia, during the period 1994–96, a National Professional Development Program (NPDP) was established. The NPDP was grounded in requirements of partnership formation for the funding of projects, so this programme has provided those of us in Australia with some experience of the benefit of such strategic alliances.

One of the NPDP projects, the Innovative Links Project, provided a rich experience of the benefits to teachers (both school based or university based) of a partnership approach to educational change and school improvement. The Innovative Links Project was an action-research based professional development programme designed to provide innovative professional development opportunities for teachers working within the professional community of the school, in partnership with colleagues from the university sector.

The project was organised through a series of 'Roundtables' located in sixteen sites around Australia, in both metropolitan and regional areas. The Roundtable consisted of teacher educators from a participating university and teachers from affiliated schools, together with union, employer and National Schools Network representatives. Participants included both primary and secondary schools from the government and non-government sectors. The Roundtables enabled schools to be networked at the local level and linked nationally.

The collaborative organisation and operation of the project provided a framework and strategies to enable members of school communities and university-based teacher educators, in association with other educational partners, to achieve the following objectives:

- develop schools as learning communities in which research, rethinking and renewal are regarded as normal and essential work practices
- examine and improve the work organisation practices of schools and enhance teacher competence
- provide participating schools with access to advice and expertise on current research findings and strategies relating to the area of concern for the school
- increase the skills of university-based teacher educators to develop, in partnership with schools and members of Roundtables, research-based processes of professional development
- enhance university-based teacher educators' understanding of school reform, national issues relating to schools, current classroom practice and the needs of educators and leaders in schools
- explore new possibilities for ongoing teacher education and professional development.

The intention to promote collaborative partnerships between educators from different sectors (the school and the university) was made explicit in these objectives and in all of the literature which described the modus operandi of the project. For instance, the following description of the operation of the project was provided in the Innovative Links publicity:

> In the Innovative Links Project, university based colleagues are teamed with school based colleagues to engage in action research around issues identified by the school. The expertise that each part-ner brings to this problem solving activity contributes to mutual growth and development. Time is provided through the project for reflection, planning, and evaluation. Conversations and learning take place, not only amongst members of the school team, but also amongst the schools and other stakeholders at the Roundtable and through special forums.
>
> Mutually rewarding collaboration requires commitments from participants to engage in joint work ethically and respectfully. The partners in the Innovative Links Project have made a commitment

to valuing the different contexts of each other's work, as well as being conscious of the need for trust and openness.

(Innovative Links Homepage 1995)

In one of the portrayal evaluation reports of Innovative Links, the evaluation team noted:

> The development of collaborative inquiry offers a way of allowing all organisations, including schools,...of aligning their internal values, philosophies, structures and operations through an aggregated perception of what constitutes...'reality'. The methodology of teacher research [in partnership with university academics] within the Innovative Links Project,...offers a working example of how this can be carried out to enhance both the effectiveness of the school and the professionalism of teachers.
>
> (Currie *et al.* 1996: 22)

It is not possible within this chapter to describe the variety of areas which schools and their academic colleagues explored as part of this project. The ways in which involvement with Innovative Links enhanced both 'school effectiveness and the professionalism of teachers' are well illustrated in a summary of involvement by teachers at Marsden State School in Queensland.

> As a result of involvement in the Innovative Links Project, professional development opportunities have been realised, both within the school and through Roundtable meetings. Within the school, members of the Innovative Links Committee have developed a whole school approach after gaining initial success through collaboration at a specific grade level.... Involvement in regular team meetings and Roundtable meetings has provided valuable opportunities for reflection. Activities have been well documented and teachers have realised the value of writing up their achievements and reflections in a formal manner.... Through the Roundtable meetings, teachers have gained personal contact with university-based researchers and coordinators of the National Schools Network. They have thus been able to place their own school reform and action research within a wider context.
>
> (Southern Cross Roundtable Portrayal Evaluation Team,
> 1996: 33–4)

In addition to the many accounts arising from the Roundtables as they documented their experiences, the two evaluations of the programme provide evidence that the principles for learning organisations which have provided the basis for the propositions in this chapter were abundantly supported in the work of the Innovative Links Project. Yeatman and Sachs

(1995), who undertook a formative evaluation of the Innovative Links Project, identified the 'learning organisation' and 'networking' aspects as two of the strengths of the project:

> Our view is that this is a brilliant project in design and execution. It has seized the time in its integration of two contemporary principles of organisational development: networking and a learning organisation approach to change and development. The beauty of the Innovative Links is that the boundaries of this learning organisation are so variable: both wide and narrow, both local and national, both across multiple industry partners and centred in the core partnership between schools and universities...In this context, the strategic value and pioneering features of Innovative Links as a project which institutionalises partnerships between practising teachers and teacher educators becomes clearly evident.
>
> (Yeatman and Sachs 1996: 5–39)

Such a complex, strategic project did not mean that the partnership work was without its tensions or contradictions or that the collaborative inquiry was easy to undertake. Embracing learning and development in partnership is particularly fraught. Indeed, the need for a set of ethical and pragmatic 'partnership principles' which would keep the work of the project 'on track' was identified again and again. We needed to be particularly and perpetually vigilant to ensure that the project operated as a partnership and the development of ascendancy of one partner over the other was avoided.

PARTNERSHIP PRINCIPLES

In a review of literature around issues relating to the reform of teacher education undertaken by Jennifer Gore for the Innovative Links project (Gore 1995) a number of principles for productive partnership were proposed:

- Democracy is required in partnerships, and hierarchical relationships, where expertise is seen to belong more clearly to one set of participants than another, are to be avoided.
- In the planning of the partnership, the distinctive interests of all parties need to be taken into account.
- Trust, communication and understanding of each partner's perspectives should be developed.
- Problems associated with a lack of, or limits on, rewards and recognition of individuals in universities and schools for collaborative activities need to be acknowledged and addressed.

- All involved in the partnership should be jointly responsible for and involved in the planning of the partnership from the very beginning.

In the Innovative Links Project we tried to address the sensitivities of this relationship by setting out sets of principles for participating schools and university academics. The principles for the participation by university academics in the project were stringent in terms of privileging the school site and teachers within the knowledge-production process. We were particularly concerned that the project should not be used to produce knowledge and rewards for academic colleagues to the exclusion of knowledge and rewards for teachers in schools. This is, of course, a somewhat artificial distinction, but our concern came from the recognition that the publication of research often has greater value in terms of recognition and promotion for academics than for teachers. The following principles, therefore, guided the participation of academics in the process.

Affiliated academic associates are committed to working with schools on a school's research and reform agenda. Academic associates are committed to:

- principles of teacher research which give precedence to the research questions generated within the school setting, rather than within the academic environment
- research grounded in principles of collaboration and democratic research processes, both in the development of research processes and in the interpretation of research data
- action-oriented research; that is, practical research intended to improve educational practice
- the ownership of research and the publication of the results of the research by schools, in the first instance
- publication of research results only with the approval of the participating school, and with due acknowledgement of the contribution of members of the schools, and with respect for confidentiality where appropriate.

These principles of participation incorporate the points made in the Gore (1995) study referred to above. Anecdotal evidence from the project suggests that these principles were respected by the university colleagues who participated in the project and that such adherence was vital to the development of collegial partnerships through the Innovative Links Project.

IN CONCLUSION

In this chapter, I have presented a set of propositions associated with partnerships in learning communities and have illustrated, by reference to the Innovative Links Project, how these propositions may be applied. These propositions acknowledge the fundamental professional responsibility of teachers to control their own professional knowledge (Proposition One). But knowledge production is not a solitary practice. The knowledge that we need now and into the future is that knowledge which is grounded in communities of inquiry (Proposition Two). Those communities of inquiry need to be seen as flexible and diverse, rather than static and site specific. Thus, partnerships among and within learning communities are and will be increasingly important (Proposition Four).

But all of this will simply be form without function if clear purpose does not underpin the operation and organisation of learning communities. This clear purpose must be the creation of diverse, quality learning communities for students (Proposition Three). The endeavour to constantly improve the learning experiences and outcomes for students must remain the principal focus of teachers and those who work in partnership with them in our schools.

References

Currie, J., Davey, S., Galagher, G. and Grant, M., (1996) *Reflection in Action: School Reform and Professional Learning through Collaborative Inquiry*, Murdoch University, Perth, Australia: Innovative Links Project.

Dimmock, C. (1995) 'School leadership: Securing quality teaching and learning', in C. Evers and J. Chapman (eds) *Educational Administration: An Australian Perspective*, Sydney: Allen and Unwin.

Education Department of Western Australia (1997) *School Performance: A Framework for Improving and Reporting*, Perth: Education Department of Western Australia.

Gore, J. (1995) *Emerging Issues in Teacher Education*, Murdoch University, Perth, Australia: Innovative Links Project.

Grundy, S. and Bonser, S. (1997) *Restructuring Australia's Schools: Changes to Organisational, Management and Pedagogical Practices*, Technical Report, Murdoch University, Perth, School of Education.

Hargreaves, A. (1994) *Changing Teachers, Changing Times: Teachers' Work and Culture in the Postmodern Age*, London: Cassell.

Innovative Links Homepage (1995) http://cleo.murdoch.edu.au/echalk/innovlinks/

Southern Cross Roundtable Portrayal Evaluation Team (1996) *Partners in Research: Teachers and Teacher Educators Learning Together*, Murdoch University, Perth, Australia: Innovative Links Project.

Stenhouse, L. (1975) *Introduction to Curriculum Research and Development*, London: Heinemann.

Warhurst, J., Grundy, S., Laird, D. and Maxwell, T. (1994) 'Curriculum Development', in E. Hatton (ed.) *Understanding Teaching: Curriculum and the Social Context of Schooling*, Sydney: Harcourt Brace.

Yeatman, A. and Sachs, J. (1995) *Making the Links: A Formative Evaluation of the First Year of the Innovative Links Project between Universities and Schools for Teacher Professional Development*, Murdoch University, Perth, Australia: Innovative Links Project.

4

TOWARDS THE LEARNING COMMUNITY

Working through the barriers between teacher development and evaluation

Richard Butt

INTRODUCTION

A successful learning community within a school consists of a rich, deep and complex set of intertwined structures, processes and relationships that is quite different from the culture of most schools. Moving from a more traditional school culture towards a learning community, as one of my colleagues from the field said, 'is like being suspended between "Army" and "Team" '. It's a difficult and new place to be, as schools strive to get beyond socialised dispositions towards authority, responsibility, accountability and professional relationships. It's so easy to slip backwards from the quest for a learning community into 'the old ways' – on the part of both school administrators and teachers. As schools grapple with these issues over the next several decades, it is important for researchers to identify and portray, amongst the myriad of processes which might constitute a learning community, those which lie at the core of the phenomenon and which represent key transformations which must be attained. In my work with schools and change over the last twenty-five years, the two processes which appear to be essential in the creation of the learning community are collaborative school-based professional development and the processes of peer and self-evaluation.

First, while attention to individual professional learning agendas is essential, a group of individuals does not become a learning community unless and until collective agendas are established and collaborative efforts are undertaken. Collaborative school-based development, while being part of the rhetoric of education for a number of years, has not been successfully implemented in many schools. The complexities associated with changing professional relationships from relative isolation, privacy and conservatism

60

(Lortie 1975) to collaborative and collegial interactions make changing school cultures difficult. The need to empower teachers to take charge of their own development and to restructure school time and space to permit collective efforts, while complicating the challenge, gives it the essential flavour of human development which lies at the core of the learning community.

Second, in a time when teacher and school accountability have become of paramount importance, the pressure on schools to engage in systematic forms of evaluation has increased. The current status of teacher evaluation is problematic in that it may be non-existent or at best intermittent; if it does exist, it is many times still perceived by teachers as ineffective, something to be endured. In many cases it causes regression rather than growth in teaching skills. Seldom have current practices in teacher evaluation been shown to be related in a synergistic way to teacher development (Butt and Townsend 1993; Butt et al. 1995). While these two phenomena – teacher development and teacher evaluation – taken separately, are important, it is their synergy which is the dynamic core of the development of the learning community. Without some significant progress in overcoming the barriers to the evolution of school-based development and evaluation as a unified process, the project of creating learning communities has little chance of success.

It was with these issues in mind that a group of colleagues from a number of Canadian schools and the university engaged in a year-long collaborative action research project which attempted to document case studies in which processes of teacher evaluation were integrated with teacher development. This chapter will document one case study and use comparative data from several others to illustrate the developmental hurdles we encountered while *doing* teacher evaluation within rich contexts for teacher development. We wished to discern what essential processes and structures (as described by Polkinghorne (1983: 24 *et passim*, 203 *et passim*, based on the works of Wilhelm Dilthey and Edmund Husserl respectively)) characterised teachers' perceptions in respect to how evaluation might or might not be related to development. Our final intention was to use the insights gained about worthwhile action to inform the development of policy which facilitates cycles of self-initiated, peer-assisted development (of which evaluation was but one part) which, in turn, creates the professional learning community.

METHODOLOGY

Establishing collegiality and finding partners

We define collaborative action research as a variety of stakeholders cooperating together to explore questions of mutual interest through cycles of action, experience and reflection, in order to develop insights into particular phenomena, create frameworks for understanding, and suggest actions which improve practice and inform policy. Relationships between university personnel, school administrators and teachers, however, are confounded by the fact that they have different work lives and roles and, therefore, different preoccupations and languages. Issues such as status, power and legitimacy enter the picture, making trust and mutual respect sometimes problematic. What each group will disclose to another group is sometimes severely constrained by these intergroup difficulties. Moving beyond verbal exchange to taking risks in action in mixed stakeholder groups is riddled with all sorts of difficulties. Indeed, collegiality and collaboration even among teachers in the same context is problematic (Butt, Townsend and Raymond 1992: 262). These problems question the value of data gathered by outside researchers who work within traditional research relationships and point out the desirability of collaborative action research. Simultaneously, however, they illustrate the difficulty of creating the sense of collegiality necessary for collaborative action research. These issues are further confounded within this project by the fact that *teacher evaluation* is one of the phenomena to be explored.

Bearing these concerns in mind, the establishment of good collegial relations with a sense of equality and mutual respect among stakeholder groups within our case study sites was essential. We chose, therefore, to offer the chance to participate in this project to teachers and administrators within two school districts with whom we had already worked for the past three to seven years on a number of projects related to teacher development. We felt that this enhanced the possibility that conditions conducive to collaborative action research existed or could be quickly recreated, as well as providing us with a pool of school personnel who had previously been prepared to take risks.

In Woodlands School Division, we chose Majestic Junior High School. In the previous year a group from this school had been particularly successful in its staff development efforts; teachers were very much involved in the process but the group also involved both administrators. This group developed a very high level of trust and mutual respect. Besides engaging in a series of activities for their own professional development, they also planned and implemented, with the remainder of the staff, activities which involved the whole school. The school staff worked collaboratively with each other, their administrators and university personnel in trying to create a set of processes for teacher evaluation which would work for them and be linked to teacher development. This process included, among other things, administrators team-teaching with teachers, interclass visitations, and peer evaluation. It is this project which will be described in this paper. Schools within Tamarack School District had been involved, over time, in projects similar to that described above. The group of volunteers in Tamarack School District included central office administrators, school-based administrators, experienced teachers and probationary teachers. Data from one case study conducted within this school district will be used for comparative purposes in this paper. It involved the deputy superintendent of schools and a group of probationary teachers who had experienced an intensive teacher development process prior to a summative evaluation for the purposes of permanent certification.

Data gathering and interpretation

At the outset of the study, in order to provide us and the reader with a sense of what might be usual practices in teacher evaluation, we solicited accounts from teachers in Woodlands School Division as to what they had experienced in teacher evaluation prior to any recent local innovations. We did this only in Woodlands School Division since its innovative efforts were more recent than those in Tamarack School District. The teachers provided us with anonymous written accounts of their experiences. These were subjected to procedures of content analysis in order to identify themes and patterns. Our case study at Majestic Junior High School involved four first-year and three second-year teachers, two veteran teachers and the vice-principal and principal. Following our initial organisational meetings at the beginning of the school year, periodic visits were made to the school approximately every six weeks to gather data as various aspects of the project proceeded. Data was gathered continuously from all participants regarding activities related to their teacher development and evaluation projects. Data reported in this paper is drawn from mid-year interviews which were tape-recorded and transcribed. Qualitative data was subjected to content analysis in order to identify patterns and themes, which have been illustrated, where possible, through the participants' own words or paraphrases therefrom. All interpretations have been validated by each group of participants. Interview transcripts have been edited to take out unimportant interviewer prompts. Interviewer and interviewee comments are in italics and ordinary type respectively.

MAJESTIC JUNIOR HIGH SCHOOL:
IN THE MIDDLE

The middle of the school year proved to be an opportune time to reveal the developmental challenges of linking development to evaluation for Majestic Junior High School. In examining the field notes and interview transcriptions from this time we were able to identify a number of themes related to the integration of teacher development and evaluation. The overall meta-theme was *collegial relations* among administrators and teachers and among teachers themselves. There were three themes within this meta-theme; one was a *context for teacher development* created primarily through intervisitation among teachers and by team-teaching with peers and administrators. Subthemes included *school-based development, collegial support* and *intervisitation*. Evaluation, then, took place as only one constituent element within the whole collective and cyclic process of teacher development. Even given this positive context of teacher development, however, Majestic Junior High School teachers carried with them deeply socialised perceptions and dispositions towards the purposes of evaluation, its processes, and the authority figures involved. They also exhibited different perceptions of self related to professional autonomy and efficacy which depended on both self-confidence and years of experience in teaching. These factors affected how teachers perceive opportunities for teacher development within the evaluation process. These issues all relate to the theme of their *readiness* to engage in evaluation as part of teacher development and are described as sub-themes in the thematic structure of the data.

The specific relationship which directly affected the quality of teacher evaluation was that established with the administrator who participated with the teacher in the evaluation process. This relationship was concerned with the nature of the administrator as a person, the way the evaluation was conducted, and the level of training and skill exhibited. These issues were reflected in the third theme of *collaborative evaluation style*. We will illustrate these themes, starting with this last one, to show their interrelationships, their cumulative effects, and how one might overcome challenges and facilitate a positive self-initiated peer-assisted development process which subsumes evaluation and contributes to the development of a learning community.

Collaborative evaluation style

When administrators who have a more collaborative style worked with teachers the negative feelings illuminated in the worst-case scenario diminished and teachers perceived evaluation in a more positive manner. Teachers perceived that they had the opportunity to co-design the evaluation process and that it was non-judgemental.

> *What about other things this year? Have you had a chance to be involved in determining more about your evaluation this year?*

> Greg had asked if I would like him to try a different evaluation method and I think I like the...system as it gives me a lot of feed-back, so I asked him to stay with that.

> *You didn't feel that he was being judgemental?*

No – it's the way he presents it, it doesn't seem judgemental at all. He's trying to help you become a better teacher – not 'well you did this wrong, you did that wrong'. He says things in a nice sort of positive sense, 'well if this happens how do you think that it went?' And then he'd talk about methods that he's tried and other teachers have tried and what he's read about whatever. It was never 'do this, therefore, you will be a better teacher'.

Teachers felt that administrators who created a collaborative evaluation relationship were more able to have a positive impact on teacher development. The quickest way to establish this type of relationship was through forms of team-teaching with the administrator. The following exchange highlights this point.

So Greg's going to team-teach with you again?

Yes. And also he brought in this time the idea of having a colleague's evaluation, like having...That's what I asked for, team teaching and then maybe a colleague.

So if you have to take the key things that helped you become more comfortable with it, three or four things, what things would they be?

Well just the one is the fact that he really talks to you about it, he doesn't say, 'I'm coming into your room on this day during this period and I'm going to evaluate you on this.' You know, I pick the time within the framework, basically I pick the class...and so that part, like, being involved in it, like I'm an active participant. I'm not just a person that's going to be sort of looked at.

So you're part of a process of negotiation.

Yes. So there's the pre-conference, and...I like talking about it afterwards and getting a sense of where I'm coming from as compared to...what he saw and what his perceptions were. Just that I feel more comfortable in the situation anyway. I mean, last year it was my first year teaching, I didn't know anybody on staff before I started working here. I like talking to other people this way [talking about what happened in each other's classes].

So this year...you are more comfortable with your teaching and with...having colleagues you can share with?

Yes. The main thing (is) feeling like an active participant.

Context for teacher development

Majestic Junior High School had designed its own approach to teacher development which provides a very positive and collegial context for the practice of teacher evaluation. There were three sub-themes which characterised this context: the school's focus on school-based staff development, the sense of collegial support that has evolved and teachers' classroom intervisitation.

School-based staff development

Well the school division is now into professional development, internal professional development in which each school does their own professional development. When we have some person from somewhere else paid big bucks come in and talk to you, they really don't know anything about your school situation, so I think that's how it started. Greg and Allan started this what they call [peer consultation].

There is not only a thrust to work on teacher development collectively but individual creativity and risk-taking is encouraged as well.

You've got some new courses this year. What are they?

Caricatures, animation. Well, we're halfway through the course right now. It's fun. The kids love it. And it's successful because we teach what they want to do. And I just decided that this would be something I would like to do. No one's been allowed to do that before.

Yes, so you designed this cartoon thing from scratch yourself?

Yes.

So you have more freedom within that?

Yes, it's still following the curriculum. I'm doing what they need to be doing, it's just done with a different approach. Like it's more specialised. And because they get a chance to take two of them in a year, like.

But you hadn't done it before because previous administrations...?

Wouldn't let me. They were too scared to try something different.

So you were able to take this risk because your administrators were willing to take this risk?

Yes. I don't really consider it a risk but, he did, the other guy did. And the kids just think it's great, the art enrolment keeps going up really well. That's why I'm teaching art, and I have two other teachers teaching art with me this time.

Collegial support

With all of the efforts related to teacher development made at the school level a strong sense of collegial support has evolved.

So what do you teach?

This year I am teaching grade 7 maths and science, grade 8 maths and grade 7 drama, grade 7 phys. ed. and health and visual arts.

So since you're teaching mostly outside your major that means you have a lot of preparation?

Yes, yes.

Very wide variety of courses.

And I'm lucky here with the staff, the departments are so strong that I can always get help in either, any subject so I don't feel that I'm stuck out there alone, I've got a lot of help behind me if I ask for it.

So you've got a nice feeling of collegiality?

Yes. The visual arts this year is a new course, so that one kind of, I'm on my own, but again like the staff any time that they find a paper or book or anything that they think might help me, it's in my mailbox or whatever with a note saying 'I found this, might help you or not, you know, throw it away or whatever.'

It's quite rare to find that sense of collegiality.

That's what a lot of people have told me 'cause any time I talk to other friends who are teachers I always rave about our staff, the stuff we do together and all the help that I'm getting, and they go 'I wish I was there, we don't have that in our school.'

Yes, so are there other things around this school that help you develop as a teacher? Other than the visitation process?

The help from other departments, other teachers, the other types of resources that other teachers have who have been here for a while and gathered all these things up. Right now for maths for grade 7s we're studying fractions. I think they've a different way of teaching fractions in the school so the department head had a meeting showing how they do it, so things like that help.

So how do you feel when you go to the head of the maths department and say 'How do I do this?'

OK. She's more than willing to help and I can do it my way if I want, they don't stop me from doing that. They suggest an outline, a course outline, and that's what most of the teachers are doing and if you want to do it your way then as long as it fits the curriculum it's fine.

Intervisitation

In our experience, getting teachers into each other's classrooms is a difficult barrier to break through, but once it's achieved it appears to open a floodgate of supportive feelings and learning about children and teaching. Many teachers in Majestic Junior High School confirmed this view. The following exchange is a fair example of many such confirmations.

Are you involved with this intervisitation business?

Yes, with two different teachers. A science class and a maths class. It's kind of neat going in and seeing someone else with [your own students]. When I went into the maths class I purposely went into a class that I teach. And that was kind of on purpose that we both are looking at the differences in how they behave and act in the two classes and kind of comparing kids in a way. He hasn't come into mine yet but he's going to, he just hasn't had time to fit it in. We're kind of using it to help each other out with comparisons of kids and better ways for seating plans and how to deal with certain kids that are repeat offenders in both classes.

So you've got a purpose and a focus for those visits and observations?

Yes. I don't know if that's exactly what we're supposed to do but that's what we're using it for 'cause we felt that's what we wanted it for, that would be best. We could use each other's tips and suggestions on how to handle certain kids, whatever.

And the science?

The science one was the one we were assigned to do.

OK. So one of them you pulled out of the hat and the other one you chose to do.

Yes. And I kind of just said, 'Who's got 9F this afternoon?' and he said he did and I said, 'OK. I'd like to come see your class' and he said 'OK'. We talked about it for a few minutes and I went and did it that afternoon. We decided what we wanted to look for, like, but after.

Do you feel your partner was stressed by having you in the room?

No. He's taught here for a long time, it doesn't bother him at all. He's one of the better maths teachers around, so that's another reason why I wanted to go and see him.

So do you consider that part of this whole thing, teacher development, that process of visiting each other?

I like it. I want to go in some more. I only have three preps this term so it's really difficult to be able to do it unless I have someone come in and watch my class. I can't do it otherwise.

Readiness

Despite the positive developmental context which the Majestic staff had created, various blocks or challenges to seeing teacher evaluation as part of teacher development were clear, as were various stages of teacher readiness to engage in collaborative teacher evaluation. These attitudes, we suspect, are largely the result of socialisation through life experiences as well as poor professional evaluation practices in the past. We suspect that continuous practice of collaborative evaluation over several years would help teachers break through these difficulties – but, as we can see from this case study, while we were relatively successful, it takes a persistently sustained effort to break through the dysfunctions of the past.

Despite the positive context in the school, two of our research group remained quite negatively disposed to evaluation even after a significant number of months of collegial activity. Even when the process was clearly communicated, while the researchers were present, they still couldn't 'perceive' and 'hear' the collaborative tone of the enterprise. This observation is not meant to be judgemental but is made to illustrate how 'far back' we will need to start with some teachers to develop trust and collegiality. Most other teachers, however, could engage to some significant degree with the process although there were various signs that some were more ready than others owing to a number of factors, including degree of expertise with the subject matter they were teaching, age and experience, self-confidence, attitudes towards authority, willingness to take risks, and perceptions of the purposes of teacher evaluation.

Purposes, taking charge, and teacher development

Despite the fact that the collaborative action research project had emphasised, early in the year, that teacher evaluation was to be part of the teacher development process and that it was collaborative, in some teachers' perceptions they were still separate phenomena. One teacher who had been doing exemplary individual development still saw accountability as the main purpose of evaluation. She had not seen or decided, therefore, to link evaluation to her agenda for teacher development.

Is this process useful?

The evaluation?

How can you make it useful to you?

Well, I suppose it keeps you on your toes, makes sure that you're doing what you're supposed to be doing. As long as you are it doesn't really matter but for some people I think it's a smart idea.

Have you got any special things you are going to do as part of this evaluation process?

I personally don't have a clue as to what things to do.

No?

I mean, all I've ever had is just someone come in and watch and write things down, so.

So I wonder how we can make this evaluation process useful to you and these new courses that you've designed?

Me too. I don't know. I just look at evaluation as getting that piece of paper that you can use when you want a new job or a reference, whatever.

Blocking/unblocking

Several teachers, when asked to describe their perceptions and feelings about evaluation, even within the context of the collaborative action research project, spoke of 'not being bothered by it' or 'not caring' because they just 'blocked the evaluation out'. Here is an example of that.

So, Greg coming in didn't worry you or threaten you?

No. I don't care, people come and walk into my class all the time, in and out, in and out.

How did it compare to student teaching? Better? Worse?

It doesn't bother me, I really don't care. I kind of block them out and don't really notice that they're there. I just do my normal routine and...

Given a positive collaborative and collegial climate, though, teachers eventually feel comfortable enough to 'unblock' and allow the relationship to begin even though the initial feelings are a bit scary. This teacher provides evidence of that change beginning to occur.

But I remember I was talking about something and the lesson went really well but I was really nervous and, at one point I looked to the back of the room and he was just sitting there, unsmiling. I was taken aback, 'cause you know it wasn't even the fact that he wasn't smiling, it was the fact that I noticed him and I never noticed him before. It was nice I had this knack of forgetting all about him. When I talked to him he said good things and things I could work on and I really, you know I learned a lot about stuff through evaluation, the way that they have it set up.

Fear of authority

When teachers frankly examine their feelings regarding evaluation instead of blocking things out, one realisation that might occur is that they have a deeply rooted fear of authority which goes way back in their lives. The following excerpt focuses on this fairly common theme.

Yes. Is Greg a threatening guy?

Not really, it's just the principal title I guess. I feel a little nervous and, again I always have this bad feeling that any time I'll get called to the principal's office, even though I know I haven't done anything wrong, I keep thinking, I'm always thinking about the bad things. It's something that's been drilled into my head. Each time you get called down to the principal's office it's something that you've done bad.

So, well, but, have these feelings got better over the last year?

No. Even though like I know that basically he's just going to try and help me out, and it's not going to be that awful it's just...I don't know what it is. I try to stay positive, don't worry about it, but it never happens. I think the only thing is I just have to get over my fear of being evaluated and like I said, after the post-conference I get a lot of information back on what I'm doing, I think it's helpful. So that part of it is excellent, it's just getting worked up the night before.

Contextual factors

A teacher's readiness to engage in collaborative evaluation is influenced by various contextual factors such as subject matter background and the difficulty of handling particular classes. Most of our teacher respondents talked of classes they hoped the evaluators would 'understand' and the additional worries they had when being evaluated in classes in which they did not have extensive subject area expertise. The following excerpt helps illustrate this point.

So, when it comes to this issue and process of teacher evaluation and teacher development, I mean it's nice to have that context of support but then in your case you've got all these different subjects that you maybe or maybe don't have the background for.

Yes.

So how does that make you feel? Like if somebody came in to evaluate you or observe you in phys. ed. would there be a difference between that type of occasion and anybody coming in to observe you in one of these other areas?

Definitely. I think just simply because I feel more comfortable in my phys. ed. class then I probably wouldn't even notice I was being evaluated and with worrying about, like my maths or science, I'm sure that I'd be thinking at the back of my mind, 'am I supposed to be doing this or that?'

So it's a matter of confidence.

Yes. I'm getting a little bit more confident with science 'cause the program that we use in textbooks, the materials are excellent I think, everything's laid out for you and I taught grade 7 science last year. You know I'll be reading over and going, 'Oh yes, OK. I remember this from last year...'

Very young teachers who are developing their confidence and teachers who need a permanent job feel especially vulnerable, as this teacher does, but the approach created by Majestic Junior High School helped teachers get beyond this.

So this is your second year?

Yes.

And you're saying it's different this year than last year. How can you expand on what that means?

Well first of all...last year I was more worried about whether I was going to be hired back again. It was a lot easier this year in a lot of ways you know in terms of I know more about the kids, I know how to respond to them more, like not perfectly obviously but more in that way. I know the staff better and know the evaluation procedures better than I did. I mean last year it was really clear and everything but I feel, I think I feel more comfortable with them. Like yesterday I had a student teacher come in and last year I would have gone 'Oh Oh'...

Just worried about having somebody in there watching you.

Yes, yes. But it was weird because I was taught with a partner but in university I never worried about that. I had my videotape and it never bothered me. I went out into the schools and did my student teaching, never bothered me at all having to come back here. And then last year I found it really did, probably because I was worried about getting hired back again and everything.

It's real now.

Yes it's real. So I kind of found that a little disconcerting at times. But this year I find that with Greg, the principal, I'm becoming more relaxed.

The barrier of intervisitation

If a collaborative evaluation process is to involve intervisitation and team-teaching it must be understood that despite teachers' isolation and need for support, their fear of 'being seen', their fear of criticism and their sense of vulnerability still make it a challenge for teachers to visit each other. This is a real block that all school-based activity has to break through. Many teachers reported experiences similar to the one noted here.

You talked about the sort of lessons you were doing and which ones would be appropriate, that type of thing?

Yes. And we sort of had a post-conference afterwards. But one thing is, it's nicer because last year there were ten new staff members and about six or seven of those were first-year teachers and we planned on coming in. We'd say, 'Oh we'd like to go in' and we didn't.

Why didn't you?

I don't know, well for one I was downstairs, like sort of isolated. It's really weird because down there there's sort of the science lab and then the library so you're really isolated. I'm upstairs now so it's easier but I think the general feeling...I mean everyone was open to it last year but we just never did it.

Do you think you avoided it? I mean all of you, I'm not talking just you.

I might have personally though I think because I, like some [people's] houses they would probably come to mine. Maybe that's at the back of my mind cause I find, it's starting to be better now. It's starting to be like I was in university, I don't mind people coming in.

It was weird because you know you have that sense that if some-one walked in your classroom and things aren't going well you go, 'Oh is it my fault?' But I find that ever since they kind of broke that barrier of having us into each other's classrooms...I don't know if Greg talked about it, but he set up a challenge where we had to have people in our classrooms...and I think since he did that it's become freer. I know yesterday I had two people say in the morning...'Can I just come in and watch?' Which worked out nice, it was nothing really, really.

COLLEGIAL RELATIONS: TOWARD
A LEARNING COMMUNITY

The overall meta-theme which subsumes all other themes in our data is that of providing a context of positive intercollegial relations where the focus is on mutually beneficial learning, well characterised, perhaps, by the notion of the school as a *learning community*. This was best illustrated, in the case of Majestic Junior High School, by the two veteran teachers. Besides illustrating how many of the negative attitudes and emotions might diminish as teachers gain experience, it also raises the question as to whether there could be or should be different processes of development and evaluation for teachers at different levels of development. Alternatively, it presents a model which we might try to evolve for teachers at all levels. This particular project shows how teachers can take more responsibility for teacher development and evaluation and work in a collegial way with administrators – but we must remember these teachers and administrators had been part of an active successful school-based development group for two years!

So I wanted to do something that would benefit me, being totally selfish. Connie and I went to Medicine Hat this summer and did the cooperative learning workshop and Allan's into cooperative learning and Connie was brave and started right away in September. Well, I was waiting for my kids to become perfect before I started so now I'm really reluctant because they're not perfect so I thought that if Connie and Allan, Greg and I could work together and they could help me get cooperative learning going with my grade 7s I would have something to work at. Like I'm the type that needs a change or something new every once in a while to keep going, and I twisted her arm and I talked to Greg and they seemed to think that [it would be alright].

So you're going to try that? But, was it your turn to be evaluated?

Yes. What are they going to say? We've both taught for so long, they know. So it should be something different. Something that will, maybe selfish, benefit me. And when we do the cooperative learning he'll obviously be able to see that we're both competent, we're both organised.

75

TAMARACK SCHOOL DISTRICT: INDUCTION OF PROBATIONARY TEACHERS

In the case of Tamarack School District we felt that the process of induction of probationary teachers merited examination and documentation, since it evolved out of seven or more years of careful training and development, including, at various times, members of the university-based research team. When the data was examined, it was clear that, as with Majestic Junior High, the overarching meta-theme was *collegial relations*, especially as it relates to teachers' learning, with their peers and administrators, more about their teaching and actually developing their personal professional practice. Tamarack teachers spoke a lot about the *collaborative evaluation style* they experienced, as did Majestic Junior High School teachers. The difference, however, lay in the richness portrayed by the Tamarack teachers through the four new sub-themes of *interpersonal support*, *understanding the whole teacher*, *continuity*, and *affirmation and self-development*. As with Majestic Junior High, there was a strong theme relating to a positive *context for teacher development* illustrated by similar sub-themes. There was, however, one distinctly different additional sub-theme related to *training* for Tamarack teachers. Surprisingly, given the potential power of previous socialisation for the neophyte teachers in Tamarack School District, issues related to *readiness* hardly emerged at all in comparison to the complexity in which it manifested itself with Majestic teachers as a major theme in its own right. It was spoken of lightly in conjunction with a major new theme, which did not emerge with Majestic Junior High teachers, called the *cultural ethos of teacher evaluation*. This theme included the sub-themes of *clarity and fairness of policy and practice*, *orientation and communication* and *readiness*.

INTERPRETATIONS, REFLECTIONS AND IMPLICATIONS FOR ACTION

Conclusions which may be drawn from the collaborative action research case studies, one of which was described in this paper, may, we feel, be confidently applied to the case study settings themselves. Whether and how these findings may be generalised beyond our case study situations will depend, of course, on the degree to which other contexts are similar to our action research sites and interests. The Majestic study involved most staff in one school, which was attempting something new, and four new teachers working through their probationary experiences in quite a stable and systematic process of teacher development and evaluation. Even though there were only four probationary teachers in Tamarack, the commonalties across their interviews were strong, especially with respect to the differences noted as compared to Majestic neophyte teachers. In total, approximately twenty educators participated in our enquiries – men and women at a variety of levels, teaching varied subjects, eleven of whom are fairly typical and representative of beginning teachers; each educator's experiences were studied in an in-depth way over time. For these reasons we might claim, from a phenomenological point of view, that the commonalties discovered probably apply, in some basic sense, to many teachers across many contexts. In this section we will try to discern and describe the essential processes and structures which are related to creating a link between development and evaluation, and what implications these have for the development of educational policy.

Understanding thematic structures

The thematic structure of the Majestic case was generally supported by the data from both experienced teachers and administrators from Tamarack School District. Tamarack's experienced teachers exhibited similar readiness challenges, though there were individual variations related to personal and contextual factors. In the schools where Tamarack teacher evaluation and development projects were active and healthy, there were fewer readiness problems than with their Majestic counterparts. Tamarack administrators perceived similar themes, including readiness, with regard to their experiences with teachers. It is important to note that administrators also saw those same themes with regard to themselves as participants. Their perceptions of their own readiness, however, related to their perceived levels of skill development, confidence, time and other such issues (see Butt and Townsend 1993: 232 and *passim*).

The fewer readiness challenges with experienced teachers in some Tamarack schools can be understood, perhaps, in terms of the number of years which Tamarack has been focusing on evaluation and development. It appears that, given time, and exemplary practice, previously socialised attitudes might change for the better and more healthy developmental and evaluative relationships result. The differences in thematic structure, however, between Majestic teachers (most of whom were probationers) and Tamarack probationary teachers bear a more detailed examination.

The added richness of the interpersonal nature of collaborative evaluation relationships, the clearer development and move towards self-development in Tamarack neophyte teachers (as compared to Majestic first- and second-year teachers), together with the lack of major readiness issues and concerns, speak loudly. The sub-theme of training related to Tamarack's ongoing project to provide all teachers and administrators with non-judgemental peer supervision skills is one ingredient which helps us understand these data. The investment of resources in the orientation, care and development of new teachers, however, as exemplified in the data by the theme of cultural ethos of evaluation, is also unique to this group. Those processes, in combination with training, appear to rapidly engage and overcome readiness challenges. They appear to represent key elements of policy and practice in integrating evaluation into ongoing cycles of teacher development and the building of learning communities.

Both Woodlands and Tamarack School Divisions have been at the leading edge of teacher development and evaluation over a number of years. Woodlands has invested heavily in school-based teacher development during the last five or more years. It has not, however, chosen the same approach to training for peer supervision as Tamarack School Division, which has invested heavily in this area since the early 1980s. Initially, Tamarack focused on administrative training but, over the years, this evolved to involve all teachers in reciprocal relationships with each other and administrators. It became more peer-oriented and informal, and moved from just focusing on summative evaluation towards facilitating teacher development in school-based ways through peer coaching. Later developmental efforts in the school system focused on initiating and strengthening school-based teacher development processes.

The school district has developed policies and procedures with regard to teacher evaluation, within a context of development, which are generally well followed, particularly with regard to teachers new to the school district (See Butt and Townsend 1993: 231–35). Because of length of time, provision of resources, training, policy development and consistent practice in most schools, the school district has had the chance to move further down the developmental continuum in regard to making teacher evaluation an integral part of the cycle of teacher development. Through the creation of layers of support among teachers, as well as with administrators, throughout the school district, these practices have begun to become part of the culture of a significant number of schools.

All of this policy and practice, however, has been particularly meticulously followed for neophyte teachers, under the coordination of the district's central office in conjunction with administrators and teacher mentors in schools. This group of neophytes showed, perhaps, the full impact of such activities. New teachers were not placed in problematic contexts and classes. If they were placed in contexts for which they were not prepared, they were given lots of ongoing support to adapt through peer and self-development. Given the right developmental environment, then, previously socialised attitudes towards evaluation and authority figures can be overcome for neophyte teachers, especially if they were not exposed to dysfunctional practices which results in cynical reinforcement of negative attitudes.

Majestic School staff, even though they had been part of a district-wide process for evolving school-based teacher development, were at an earlier moment in respect to the focus on teacher evaluation. The staff, including six of our teacher participants, had experienced the negative socialising experiences detailed in baseline data. Specifically, prior to their positive experiences with the school administrators in this project, they may have endured a number of years of extremely dysfunctional relationships with the previous administration and within the school. The four first-year teachers had not experienced these stressful events, but they also had not experienced the positive effects of the collaborative teacher development projects during the previous year. The positive sense of collegiality had only just been recovered following these events. Few teachers had received systematic training in clinical supervision or peer-coaching skills. It is not surprising, given this context and history, and that four participants were first-year teachers, that they experienced the readiness problems they did.

One significant way, however, in which the administrators in Majestic Junior High School, as compared to Tamarack supervisors, were able to provide for better progress in mutuality and reciprocity in the evaluation relationship was through investing time, energy and courage in team-teaching with teachers who were being evaluated, especially with difficult classes. This practice, perhaps, is a particularly powerful way of desocialising teachers from previous negative experiences with evaluation and rapidly changing the power aspects of the relationships and culture of the school. Data from both cases, however, are of value in that they point to the developmental challenges we might expect and can, therefore, plan for. The power of socialisation which needs to be overcome is clear, as are the sort of policies and practices which may be useful in evolving healthy evaluation processes integrated into the larger cycle of teacher development which is at the centre of the creation of the learning community.

THE POSSIBLE IN CREATING THE LEARNING COMMUNITY

In this section we would like to take the essential structures and processes evident in our data and stretch them just a bit further, not to the ideal, but to what we see as being possible in creating the learning community. Most of what we suggest has already been demonstrated in the case studies. We will just elaborate and extrapolate a little as we practise the art of the possible. What we recommend we feel applies equally to administrators as to teachers, or to the collective development of any other group of educators or professionals.

The turning point: relationship

The move from dysfunctional teacher evaluation separated from development to a process in which evaluation is integrated within the ongoing cycle of teacher development requires the creation of a continual experience of overlapping supportive collaborative relationships. These relationships among functional teams of peers, mostly within and sometimes across schools, would also include at least one administrator who practises reciprocity and engages, as far as possible, in group activities as a team member. The prime focus of these groups would be to provide collegial support and a safe environment within which they can engage in the risks of a continuing cycle of teacher development. This provides the context within which authentic evaluation can take place and be cyclically linked to development, particularly peer-supported self-development. This set of professional interactions constitutes a learning community.

Readiness and challenges: working through to the new culture

We have documented some of the various challenges and levels of readiness educators are likely to encounter in moving from dysfunctional evaluation towards the learning community. These phenomena are understandable in several senses of the word. First, we can understand and empathise with the teachers who do not want to subject themselves to the dysfunctionality of what they have experienced previously. We can also understand and empathise with the untrained administrator, rushed for time, who doesn't want to repeat those dysfunctional experiences. Second, we have enough data to understand how things came to be this way. It is of vital importance, then, that we work through these problems, collaboratively making sense of the various challenges and the states of readiness in a non-judgemental way. As we saw in our collaborative action research, part of the solution can be found in designing gradual developmental processes which are persistently practised over time.

It probably will take lots of experience of positive relationships to move educators to healthy organisational relations, development and evaluation processes. Some will take longer than others. It is possible that understandably cynical experienced teachers will not 'hear' talk of collaboration, but they may 'feel' it if they are involved, as part of the evaluation process, with their peers, in pursuing their own professional development agendas. Teachers' previously socialised fears of authority figures do not disappear quickly. As several examples in these case studies have shown, however, previous mistrust can be overcome when an administrator and teacher tackle a difficult class, an unfamiliar subject or a new curriculum together, in order to help solve a mutual problem. Teachers who are used to 'blocking out' the administrator can engage in partnerships in order to help them 'unblock' and engage in dialogue.

If the first question which teachers and administrators ask each other is 'What do we want to find out, what risks do we want to take for our mutual professional benefit, however modest the first efforts?', then the purposes of teacher evaluation are clearly focused on mutual self-development in a collegial relationship between co-learners as part of a community of learners. The first key, then, and the common element in this transformational process, is that all participants, in all roles, be involved as partners in a continuing effort to become co-designers of the whole process. Ideally, in the end, all would be equally exposed to mutual support and feedback by all.

Potential elements of policy

In order to move to the really functional level of useful teacher/educator evaluation which contributes to the development of the school as a learning community, as illustrated by our case study data, it is imperative that school boards move beyond having fair but isolated policies for teacher evaluation to having collegial and collaborative policies for teacher development which subsume and integrate, in a contributing way, policies of teacher/educator evaluation. Although these policies would be district-wide, they would focus on functional groups, that is, school- or curriculum-based groups of educators who would work collaboratively on their own individual and collective needs for development. Some elements of policy would be mandated, facilitated through the actions of leaders who are provided with the necessary human, material and physical resources. Much of the processes for development and evaluation, however, would be collaboratively designed by participants on the basis of mutually identified goals. One major aim of this process would be to increasingly facilitate self-development and evaluation through both self-initiated and peer-assisted efforts – the mutual and reciprocal relationships involved in these efforts being the core, not only of collegial appraisal and development, but also of the building of a learning community.

One core element of the policy for teacher development would relate to the continued facilitation of multiple forms of collegial relationships among peers and across role and stakeholder groups. It would deal with continued collaborative evaluation of all educators, not just teachers, and would take account of the possibility of mutual evaluation whereby, for example, peers could evaluate each other, and teachers could evaluate their administrative colleagues' skills in evaluation as those people, in turn, evaluate teachers. The basic principle here is reciprocity where everyone in every role is prepared to take risks in a supportive environment.

Policies would clearly acknowledge the difficult working realities of teachers and administrators and particular impediments to the realisation of collaborative teacher/administrator/school development. Policies should recognise that this type of transformation takes time (perhaps five to seven years) to deliberately and consciously develop. Potential impediments to development could be identified in a non-judgemental way and suggestions made as to how they could be overcome. The roles of existing teachers in the school district in helping with the transformation from more hierarchical and isolated forms of organisation to a more collegial and relational culture should be spelled out as far as possible. One major obstacle which must be overcome is the provision of space, time and resources to enable functional groups to work together. In some schools, while teachers have invested some of their own time for this process, administration and staff have also creatively changed the use of human resources, class sizes, timetabling, length of school days, use of substitute budgets and flexible staffing with teams of teachers to transform the way the school works and free up time for developmental activities.

Programmes of orientation for teacher/administrator/school development and collaborative evaluation are essential; they need to be continuously implemented and evolved. These actions are needed not just for transformation, and for the induction of neophytes, but for the continuing learning and development of all individuals and groups. Furthermore, knowledge of contemporary research on teaching and specific skills related to the implementation of new teaching techniques and curriculum changes can be integrated into these continuing programmes of professional development. In keeping with the findings of our case studies, we would say it is imperative that these new skills should be learned by cadres of teachers and others through peer teaching and practice across the school district and within functional groups. In this way, then, the school district can begin the process of becoming its own resource for teacher development needs and the creation of a learning community.

DISCUSSION AND CONCLUSION

Whereas the foregoing section provided some generic possibilities for policy development in regard to evaluation and its necessary developmental context, there are still broader contextual issues and implications to which we should make important connections, not only here in our discussion, but also with respect to policy design. In fashioning policy and actions for development and evaluation, it is clear that the process for each individual is intricately linked to that of one's peers. The logical and human extension of this process is to link it to staff and school development and evaluation.

The contemporary issues of facilitating site-based school development, collaborative decision-making, and the re-visioning of school staff, students and parents as learning communities provide a fertile context within which individual and peer development and evaluation can take place and to which it can contribute. In this regard, school districts can provide incentives and resources to encourage schools in the invention of creative ways of organising time and energy for collaborative projects of all sorts.

The development of school-based policies, collaborative decision-making related to curriculum innovation and implementation, instructional development, classroom management, school climate, school philosophy, school goals, or a school's vision for the future have all been shown by research to be related to teaching effectiveness, teacher and school development and in many cases student achievement (Butt *et al.* 1995). The key ingredient here is that the school staff be challenged to decide for itself (while taking account of parent interests, school district and governmental guidelines), where it is going, what it will do, and how it will accomplish its tasks. With regard to teacher and administrator development and school improvement, it must be the responsibility of the school staff to set its course as opposed to the school being directed from outside or 'drifting' with no direction.

The cultural transformation of the school and school district was compared earlier to moving from 'Army' to 'Team'. A symbolic transformation in school structure and use of time might involve something as basic as changing a proportion of staff-meeting time from large-group formal communication to small-group dialogue related to issues, agenda-setting and problem-solving, the results of which could then be reported back to the large group, discussed, and acted on democratically.

Regardless of any of the above, however, we would argue that very little will change with respect to the development of teaching skills generally unless more teachers risk themselves to try out, invent, practise and refine new skills in their own classrooms. To do this, most teachers need the interpersonal support of trusted colleagues; a sense of purpose that goes beyond the mundane; access to new knowledge and skills; dedicated time for purposive action and reflection; and a climate of encouragement. Even though teachers initially are resistive, school-based projects featuring such things as interclassroom visitation, peer coaching and the use of videotape on a continuing basis, are the sorts of activities which make it more likely that teachers will try new ideas and practise them effectively to make them part of their work lives and teaching styles. When teachers are able to make the teaching and learning that happens in their classrooms the focus of ongoing enquiry, they are able to live the part of the 'lifelong learner' or 'teacher as researcher' within the school as a learning community.

Besides the impact of school district policy and the roles, personnel and teachers themselves in facilitating the necessary transformation in personal and professional relationships, a key role still rests with school-based administrators. Their role in this particular project is imperative, not only for the success of the project, but also for their own success and development as administrators. To varying degrees, depending on current administrative style and the status of collaborative decision-making in the school, administrators will be challenged to facilitate the transformation of the school by transforming themselves and the way they work. This calls for clear policy and practices aimed at the development of administrators. The quickest way to collegiality, trust and collaborative relationships is through reciprocity on the part of the administrator. The degree to which he or she can engage in and model the process of development and evaluation with their staff with respect to their own teaching and administration is the degree to which transformation will occur. Teachers will, then, more readily take the opportunity and responsibility for peer and self-development and evaluation and be willing to respond to calls for documentation of their own competence as teachers. This will not occur through making a 'big deal' of teacher evaluation on its own, but through embedding it within a major investment in development. Evaluation might then occur as a natural moment in the grand cycle of development essential to providing both authentic affirmation and new directions for teachers and schools as well as evidence of accountability to stakeholders in education.

Note

I wish to acknowledge the courageous work that our teacher and administrator research partners did in Tamarack and Woodland School Divisions and the efforts of my colleague David Townsend in this project. This paper, however, is derived from research processes, data, interpretations and writings for which only I can be held responsible.

References

Butt, R. L. and Townsend, D. (1993) Case Studies of Woodland School Division and Tamarack School District, in M. Haughey, D. Townsend, R. O'Reilly and E. Ratsoy, (eds) *Toward Teacher Growth: A Study of the Impact of Alberta's Teacher Education Policy*, Edmonton, Alberta: Alberta Education.

Butt, R. L., Bryant, P., Chow, P. *et al.* (1995) *Facilitating Teacher Professional Learning*, Lethbridge: Southern Alberta Professional Development Consortium.

Butt, R. L., Townsend, D. and Raymond, D. (1992) Bringing Reform to Life: Teachers' Stories and Professional Development, *Cambridge Journal of Education* 20 (3), 255–68.

Lortie, D. C. (1975) *School Teacher: A Sociological Study*, Chicago: University of Chicago Press.

Polkinghorne, D. (1983) *Methodology for the Human Sciences: Systems for Inquiry*, Albany, N.Y.: SUNY.

5

ETHICS AND THE LEARNING COMMUNITY

Kennece Coombe

INTRODUCTION

In a recent monograph on ethics in educational reform, Burke quoted an unnamed colleague of his as saying: 'When it comes to doing the right thing...the race for the competitive edge has so overshadowed social justice and the common good...that now we operate from a sense of hit-and-run ethics no one has time for contemplation' (1997: 3). It is in the spirit of that type of sentiment that this chapter is written. While not seeking to downplay the benefits and advances of a concept in education such as the learning community, the discussion will range across an interpretation of the learning community as a force of educational reform, the theory and reality of ethics in such an environment and the needs and ethical responsibilities of stakeholders in the education process. Throughout, however, the underlying agenda is one of reflection upon the choices made and actions taken, both consequentially and non-consequentially.

THE LEARNING COMMUNITY

It is already clear from previous chapters that the language used to describe learning organisations and learning communities does overlap. While the former term is often used in the context of business and industry (Senge 1992), the latter is invariably applied to educational settings. As Blackmore (1991) points out, the emphasis in business, as well as in the school classroom, is often on the worker (student) being multiskilled, adaptable and creative to the extent of being an independent learner and creative thinker. As a development of this focus, terms such as 'total quality learning', 'organisational learning' and 'empowering the learner' are now part of the corporate landscape and convey how business and commerce images can so easily be intertwined with the language and principles of

86

education (Coombe *et al.* 1996). An overarching principle in the discourse of these corporate and educational worlds is that of the 'learning organisation'.

For many, especially those from a business background, the concept owes its heritage to the work of Senge, who defines it in these terms:

> A learning organisation is an organisation where people continually expand their capacity to create results they truly desire; where new and expansive patterns of thinking are nurtured; where collective aspirations are set free and where people are continually learning to learn together; it is an organisation that is continually expanding its capacity to create its future.
>
> (1992: 14)

It is easy to be seduced by Senge's turn of phrase and by those who have followed in the footsteps of his writings on the learning organisation (see, for example, Marquardt and Reynolds 1994). However, as Sergiovanni postulates, it should not be forgotten that organisations are generally driven by theories of economics: 'theories built on the simple premiss that as human beings, we are motivated by self-interest and thus seek to maximise our gains and cut our losses' (1994: 215).

It should be acknowledged that organisations also have a social history and as such are characterised by 'heritage, tradition, continuity and a consolidation of processes, practice and content' (Cocklin *et al.* 1996: 1), but, as Hargreaves (1995) warns, it is all too easy to slip into the pervasive business vocabulary of quality control and performance targets when referring to the learning organisation. In so doing, there is the real danger that the transformative, democratising and liberating aspects to which Senge has made reference are ignored or minimised. As Cocklin *et al.* show (1996: 2–3), such characteristics include, among others:

- leaders who model calculated risk-taking and experimentation
- decentralised decision-making and employee empowerment
- opportunities to learn from experience on a daily basis
- a culture of feedback and disclosure.

Watkins and Marsick (1993) make similar reference to these types of emancipatory characteristics associated with learning organisations. The imperatives of the learning organisation, in their view, relate to the promotion of enquiry, dialogue, collaboration and team-learning, and to establishing systems to capture and share learning and to empower people toward a collective vision. The end result is 'a group of empowered employees who generate new knowledge, products and services, network in an innovative community inside and outside the organisation; and work towards a higher purpose of service and enlightenment to the larger world'

(Marquardt and Reynolds 1994: 22). Thus, within this concept of the learning organisation, there is real opportunity for professionals to exercise what Considine (1994) refers to as the ideal of a commitment to public service and altruism and to counter the docility and conformity that often results from the negative deployment of power and knowledge by professionals working within organisations (Foucault 1980). In other words, the learning organisation has the potential to promote the ideal that professionals are:

> about the business of learning, questioning, investigating, and seeking solutions [and that the] basis for human interaction is no longer a hierarchy of who knows more than someone else, but rather the need for everyone to contribute to the process of asking questions and investigating solutions.
>
> (Kleine-Kracht 1993: 392)

While Senge and others are heralding the notion of a learning organisation as presenting the dawn of a new era, within the context of education, Kleine-Kracht reminisces that 'the idea of the school as a community centred on *learning* is not new' (1993: 391). Indeed she clearly articulates the position that the concept is readily evident in Dewey's philosophy of learning and teaching where 'teachers and students participate together in the process of learning and share experiences of learning. The shared work or learning holds the school together as a community and is the primary source of social control' (Kleine-Kracht 1993: 391). In a similar way, Retallick aptly summarises the essential differences in terminology:

> Whilst 'learning community' usually seems to refer to the roles that various participants might play in the education of young people, the idea of a 'learning organisation' is that of enhancing the organisational processes of the school to transform them into learning processes.
>
> (1996: 1)

In the context of this chapter, the concept of the learning community referred to by Retallick is used to draw attention to the pivotal, but often neglected, role of ethics in the educative processes involving young people and those who have responsibility for facilitating their learning. This notwithstanding, it is important to note from the outset that there is an ethical stance to be taken here in acknowledging that it is all too easy to advance the concept of the learning community as the panacea for educational ills or as an instrument of control in terms of directing thinking and practice into a particular rubric (Coombe and Newman 1997a). Such behaviour, though often well meaning, often destroys the professional scaffolding for the exercise of responsible autonomy of individuals. The danger here is that a narrow agenda of interests may be served without due consideration of the spectrum of the social life within learning communities and without due reflection on ethical responsibility for the teaching and learning needs within a particular educational context.

Political rhetoric from educational bodies (for example Hill *et al.* 1995) which support the development of learning communities in education tends to *prescribe* the practices and considerations to be included within the construct of a learning community. Although the language used is apparently benign, the coercive undertones are inclined to proscribe any variation from the one approved model. The application of a particular, ideologically driven, interpretation of learning communities can be seen in similar light to other policy directives for educational change and be subject to similar ethical scrutiny. Further, reliance upon a prescriptive form of learning communities may well lead to a situation where schools find themselves unable to 'measure up' on every one of the criteria which determine what a learning community is or where taken-for-granted assumptions of processes failed to produce the outcomes which are 'approved'. Where the 'rhetoric–reality gap' (Burke 1997) is too wide, blanket condemnation of the concept is a probability.

UNDERSTANDING ETHICS IN AN ERA OF EDUCATIONAL UPHEAVAL

Despite the rhetoric of empowerment, social justice, equity and human rights now being part of the common parlance in education, the findings from a recent study show the range of ethical and moral dilemmas that arise within education contexts (Coombe and Newman 1997b: 49–50). For instance, the following anecdotes convey the experiences of a group of neophyte teachers:

> In a small group situation, a child was singled out, pulled by his arm and made to stand in the corner while the teacher yelled at him in front of the other children...

> I did not believe in the way the children were criticised or put down by the teachers. Those children who were from different cultures or backgrounds were particular targets. The teachers continued the judgements, jokes, and their comments to me and expected me to feel the same and to treat the children in the same way...

A parent told me to hit his children when they are misbehaving and since I wouldn't, he questioned what kind of [teacher] I was for not hitting the children to make them do the right thing...

According to the authors of this study, these and other similar experiences show that the social and moral contexts of teaching and life in schools are never stagnant, that how sense is made of events does depend on context and, importantly, that the notion of ethics is never unproblematic. There is, nevertheless, a common-sense view among professional groups, such as teachers, that ethics is simply about commonly shared values relating to morality and 'proper' conduct. It is on this basis that a number of professions have actively pursued the development and implementation of symbolic codes of ethics. Such codes are seen by the community as important symbols that indicate that the association or group is one that values morality and integrity; and has a prescribed standard of acceptable behaviour which also serves as a validation for disciplinary action against non-conformity (Coombe and Newman 1996). Beyond this simplistic, generalised understanding, ethics and ethical behaviour remains difficult to define given the context-specific instances which often govern the behaviour of people.

Although the general idea of ethical practice is acknowledged within a range of professions, the constitution of ethical conduct as a professional standard can be seen as a construction of morality based on the cultural and professional biases of those in positions of power in that profession. An example used elsewhere (see Coombe and Newman 1997a) illustrates this point: it may well be considered as unethical practice if medical practitioners, say, were to advertise their professional services as medical practitioners; on the other hand, they are quite at liberty to advertise their availability and qualifications, where appropriate, to serve as lay marriage celebrants or biology tutors for upper secondary students. Thus, to advertise is not in itself regarded as unethical behaviour, except within particular constraints, and it is within the purview of professional organisations to determine which constraints, and what ethical principles, apply within a particular profession. These biases become the broadly based norms of behaviour, the ethical standards.

Many writers have attempted to define 'ethics', but none has done so better than Annis, who proffers the view that:

Ethics deals with what acts are morally right or wrong, what our obligations are, what the conditions are under which we are morally responsible for our acts, what moral rules or principles are justified, what traits or dispositions are morally good or bad, that is, virtues or vices, what things are desirable from a moral point of view, and related issues. Professional ethics deals with the same issues only it examines them in terms of one's professional role, what are one's professional obligations, etc.

(1989: 3)

The actions taken as a result of ethical practice fall into two main categories – consequential and non-consequential. Burke (1997) suggests that the ethical practitioner is one who takes action based on the consequences of those actions – the greatest good for the greatest number. He uses the example of a teacher dealing with antisocial behaviour in the playground who seeks to find a just outcome which 'promises an outcome for the greatest benefit for the most people connected to the school' (1997: 14). Such a teacher is making a consequential decision. Another ethical practitioner, who practises non-consequential decision-making, applies an 'uncompromising moral legalism' and would find a different solution based on a philosophy where adherence to the rules is considered 'more important than the consequences...in determining what is good, right, just and fair' (1997: 15). The latter probably suffers fewer moral dilemmas but lacks flexibility in taking into account the social context of the behaviours and the punishments where applied.

Although schools and educational institutions need to be careful not to 'fall into the crudely cultural relativist position of asserting that all cultural practices are equally good' (Coady 1994: 5), there remains the need to contextualise the ethical considerations socially. This is especially important when decisions are required about who decides what is 'good' or 'bad' and by whose values and criteria such determinations are made.

Within a profession, such as teaching, the pre-eminent values relating to ethical standards are most often a reflection of the biases of a particular, powerful enclave. Standards determined in this manner, however, may well be in conflict with the personal morality and ethical standards of individuals within the profession and with client groups. Thus, it is imperative that there is a shared understanding of what is ethically appropriate within a learning community and whether decisions should be taken consequentially or non-consequentially within the constraints of personal subjectivity.

For professionals who operate in the learning community, the impact of personal subjectivity is an important consideration in that this

represents the impact of spiritual power such as values, mindset and morals on the practitioner's operations. It is the criteria [sic] to which the practitioners refer when they wish to justify a decision. Professional ethics are objectively regulated by system rules such as laws, formal guidelines and societal norms, and are subjectively bounded by personal values, beliefs and cultural background.

(Liang et al. 1996: 434)

The notion of professional ethics being 'objectively regulated' is itself debatable. Instead the interpretation of what is considered to be ethical conduct needs to be contextualised to a specific organisation or profession or even to a specific situation at a particular point in time (Coombe and Newman 1997b).

Although Senge does not use the words 'ethics' or 'morals' when he discusses the learning organisation, he does refer to 'core values' in building a shared vision. He points out that:

> Core values answer the question 'How do we want to act, consistent with our mission, along the path to achieving our vision?' A company's values might include integrity, openness, honesty, freedom, equal opportunity, leanness, merit, or loyalty. They describe how the company wants life to be on a day-to-day basis, while pursuing the vision.
>
> (1992: 226)

He further asserts that 'A vision not consistent with values people live by day by day will not only fail to inspire genuine enthusiasm, it will often foster outright cynicism' (1992: 225). Coady (1994), similarly, suggests that it helps to think and reason about moral issues communally, especially where there are common moral challenges. She elaborates that communal consideration allows for personal judgements and intuitions to be tested 'not only against our own theories and principles, but against the theories, principles and judgements of others who have similar responsibilities' (1994: 4).

Both Senge and Coady are implying that there needs to be an understanding amongst members of the learning community that moral considerations and standards of ethical conduct are drawn from the values of those within the community. They should be neither coercive nor arbitrarily imposed. They should be seen not as mechanistically restrictive but as guidelines to practice and behaviour which are appropriate to the mission and vision of the community and yet still allow for autonomous decision-making and action by competent practitioners.

Within the broader context of education, the role, application and evaluation of ethics and ethical standards have received considerable attention in the literature (Burke 1997). The volatility of educational policy has much responsibility for this as teachers and educators are drawn to question what is happening in education and whose interests are being served. The caution and even distrust and outrage evidenced in embracing yet more innovative forms of educational interaction and relationships are symptomatic of the teachers' and educators' concerns. Within the wider society, there is equivalent outrage when decisions are shown to be made by those with political power, without negotiation between and amongst interested groups and ostensibly in 'the best interests' of those who are disempowered. Two well-known examples of such moral decision-making recently brought to light have been the 'stolen generations' of Australian Aboriginal children and the forced emigration of British war orphans to Australia. Both of these groups are now seeking some redress for the impact on their lives of decisions made 'in their best interests' half a century ago. To paraphrase Senge, this type of approach to reform has all the hallmarks associated with the 'dogma of planning, organizing and controlling' with little recognition of 'providing the enabling conditions for people to lead the most enriching lives they can' (Senge 1992: 140).

Sentiments such as these latter should be the pivotal consideration of educational reform, especially relating to the implementation of learning communities in schools. They shift the power base from those who 'know' what is right to others who choose 'what' is right for them according to the cultural and social contexts in which they situate themselves. Several authors (for example Marginson 1993) have highlighted mandated educational reform during recent years as a means of refocusing the direction of business and of education, and as such it is sometimes used as a tool of covert social control within those settings. The emphasis of recent times has focused strongly on aspects of technical rationality rather than any consideration of educational rationalism. Change such as this is driven by the agendas of those in positions of power and influence and, at times, it is useful for those who are involved in the development and implementation of the reforms to sit back and to take stock of what those agendas might be.

The role of 'education' in such a process renders a state of theoretical and ethical confusion. It appears to be strongly at odds with the classical interpretation of 'education' as having intrinsic value to the individual as enlightenment without needing measurable determinants of accountability. Instead it fits with the economically driven concept of education as a source of potential capital because education confers 'special benefits [and]...relative advantage over others' (Marginson 1993: 15).

Marginson indicates that economic rationalism in education began to develop strongly with an essay by Friedman in 1955 where he

> argued that all of the benefits of vocational and professional educa-
> tion were received by the individual who was educated. While some
> of these benefits might be non-economic in character, they could
> nonetheless be represented in economic terms. There were no bene-
> fits to society additional to these benefits already received by indi-
> viduals.
>
> (Marginson 1993: 36)

Indeed, Marginson goes on to cite Friedman directly as saying: 'Vocational and professional schooling...is a form of investment precisely analogous to investment in machinery, buildings, or other forms of non-human capital. Its function is to raise the economic productivity of the human being' (Marginson 1993: 36).

Correspondingly then, education can no longer be regarded, in and of itself, as an agenda of enlightenment or personal development. An axial shift, such as this, alters not only the role of the recipient of the education but also the role of the educator, and radically loosens the bonds between them. In this context, teachers do have the opportunity to 'contribute to critical dialogue with others. For example, they can challenge oppressive or "totalising" approaches which eliminate difference or which marginalise those who are less powerful....[although] forms of localised resistance are possible' (Garrick 1994: 130).

It is at this point that the opportunity arises for teachers to assume some responsibility for the application of professional ethics in the educational reform agenda. The ethics involved for the professional educator here are those of sifting and appraising proposals for educational reform. That is, there is a responsibility for the educator to protect the student from hegemonic control and infringement of professional autonomies; and to balance the needs or preferences of the organisation with the real interests of those whom they are educating.

In order to sketch ethical boundaries around these considerations, Lovat draws an analogy between educational reform and biomedical ethics. He reflects that 'four age-old ethical principles have come to be definitive. These are autonomy; justice; non-maleficence and beneficence [which] serve to guide proper conduct and action' (1998: 2). Ethical consideration of educational reform requires reflection of these four principles in relation to the major stakeholders in education: parents, children, teachers, school leaders and departmental officers. (It is not an oversight that employers have been left 'out of the loop' here.) In every political decision regarding education, and particularly educational reforms, there is potential for one or more of these groups to find themselves, at best remote, or at worst disempowered and disadvantaged, relative to these ethical principles. It seems timely then to reflect on the rights and understandings of stakeholders in the light of Walker's admonition that, 'virtually every important decision made by those in positions of educational responsibility reflects their degree of sensitivity to ethics' (1998: 5).

Such sensitivity to ethics is more than following rules as they are prescribed but includes positive and thoughtful relationships between and amongst people: in short, an ethic of caring.

THE ETHIC OF CARING

In a learning community, the ethic of caring should predominate, not as a fatuous, overweening delicacy or subservience, but as a genuine commitment to the well-being of others. Raywid (1993) identifies caring as one of six qualities of communities in schools: respect, caring, inclusiveness, trust, empowerment and commitment. Indeed, it could be argued that the notion of caring is inclusive of the other qualities identified, for it also encompasses 'engagement', which is a hallmark of caring, according to Noddings (1992).

Within an environment of caring, the views and opinions of all stakeholders should be recognised. This does not mean that the particular stance of one group should prevail over another but rather that concerns should be acknowledged, understood and treated with courtesy. Raywid points out that caring precludes 'rank-pulling' which enables one group 'to convey doubts about…integrity, capacity, goodwill, or essential decency' of another group or individual (1993: 33). Beck (1996) similarly emphasises that the notion of caring within a school community can be used productively to deal with social problems and to improve academic performance simply because children in particular feel valued.

A situation which gives import to respect for others and their convictions allows for inclusiveness of the community because it limits the degree to which any group or individual should feel excluded through a basic difference of opinion. Where respect is valued and opinions are appreciated, there would appear to be far less opportunity or predisposition to conflict based on disagreement, and there is a greater scope for the broad-ranging qualities of commitment, trust and empowerment.

These latter three qualities manifest themselves in a learning community in a variety of ways. The most obvious of these is that where there is a genuine commitment to the well-being of others, then all groups are likely to be inspired to gain increasingly greater competence (Mitten 1997). Mitten further points out that an awareness of power differentials that do occur between groups should be maintained so that the community is empowered to find ways in which the strong can protect or advance the weak without destroying their sense of dignity in the process.

A transition to a social order of this nature relies heavily on a sense of trust, at the most fundamental level, that a shift in power will not be abused and that participants from all groups are committed to the principles adopted for the learning community as a whole. Again, this is a situation where relationships between and amongst the groups of stakeholders are heavily interdependent. Teachers, for example, need to be able to trust each other to be able to share their work and ideas with colleagues for their personal and mutual development; school leaders need to trust teachers and parents in order to rethink organisational strategies and to consider ways in which the transformative ethics of caring, concern, and compassionate justice are to become realities within their particular learning community (Beck 1996).

The ethic of caring within the learning community is premised on the basic qualities of interpersonal relationships and justice outlined above, and in order for such transformative processes to be effective and sustained, the rights and understandings of all stakeholder groups within the community demand recognition and attention.

THE LEARNING COMMUNITY: RIGHTS AND UNDERSTANDINGS OF STAKEHOLDERS

It is in the attention to the rights and understandings of the various groups of stakeholders that it becomes imperative to apply what Lovat (1998) regards as the four guiding principles of ethical consideration: autonomy, justice, non-maleficence and beneficence. Reflection upon these principles can bring into sharp contrast the synergies and conflicts between and amongst the major stakeholder groups, particularly in the context of the learning community.

Lovat observes that autonomy, for example, is contrasted with heteronomy or 'rule by others'. He further points out that

> In ethical contexts, the concept of autonomy connotes independence and self-determination. It is a principle which assumes that the individual is responsible for, and most properly should determine the direction of, his or her own life, being essentially free of undue pressure or manipulation from external sources.
>
> (1998: 2)

In an educational setting then, such a consideration would serve to shift the locus of intellectual control from that of the teacher to one of negotiation with other interested parties, especially children and parents such that their own sense of autonomy is not imperilled. It is important to stress the aspect of negotiation here so that there is an accommodation between parents' cultural values and expectations of education with those of student needs and interests, the professionals' knowledge base and personal value system, and with the demands of educational policies.

The significance of these mediations is highlighted when combined with the demands of 'justice' which, Lovat says, 'refers to the expectations which a society holds concerning relations between the members of that society…[T]here are standards and mores which suggest how people should live up to their obligations to one another' (1998: 3). In the teacher–student relationship, Lovat suggests, this directs attention to the teacher's 'duty of care' for the child. In a much broader sense, however, it could also be seen to apply to the relationship between the home and the school in terms of mutual support and requiring both parties to meet their obligations in caring for the child, and to the relationship between the child and other children in terms of socially appropriate behaviour and accepting the rights and obligations of others.

'Non-maleficence' and 'beneficence' also can be seen as being closely linked. Lovat explains:

> Non-maleficence establishes a duty on all who would be ethical not to harm or injure, or impose risks of harm or injury, on oth-ers...[and] like all the other principles, *beneficence* has general ethical sense, proposing that every person who hopes to be ethical has a duty to engage in conduct which contributes to the good and well-being of others.
>
> (1998: 3)

In the school setting the application of these principles should imply careful attention to contributing not only to the child's intellectual, social and emotional development but also to the intellectual, social and emotional needs of all members of the learning community – including families, teachers and school leaders. In some learning communities, it may also be appropriate for the school's mission to include an emphasis on the spiritual needs of its members.

Overall then, for a learning community to function ethically, there needs to be a prudent acknowledgement of the similarities and contrasts of the expectations of all members of the community.

Parents

Previous research (Coombe 1995) has shown that the predominant concern of parents in regard to educational institutions is that their children are in a safe and secure environment. This concern is followed closely by one which focuses on the children's learning needs. These are the pre-eminent considerations of parents and form the basis of what they regard as their unwritten contract with the school. As the child grows, there is a shift towards education as vocational preparation. In the current economic and educational climate, parents tend to hold schools accountable for the gainful employment of their children. Within this scenario, then, it becomes clear that embedded within these parental expectations are the ethical considera-tions of beneficence and non-maleficence – that the school and teachers should be protective of the child and that the child will grow from the experience at school. Within the setting of a learning community, parents have a right to hold these same expectations for their own development as parents and as individual members of the community of learners.

Further to this, parents have the ethical right to expect that the school will not undermine the relationship parents have with their children or the cultural credos by which the parents live, and that the children will receive the same standards of care, attention and educational opportunity as other members of the school community. From the parents' perspective, these are simple issues of autonomy and justice for themselves and their children. From the teacher's perspective, they can be fraught with a myriad of ethical dilemmas, as the earlier anecdotes from neophyte teachers illustrated so vividly.

Children

Children moving through educational systems are in some ways the pawns of social change and the trendiness of educational policy. They can be seen as vulnerable in systems which do not overtly support them in their learning and emotional needs. Indeed, children have been treated as the *tabula rasa* upon which wisdom and knowledge are written over time. Their own needs and interests tended to be invisible. In a business setting, this approach would be tantamount to a highly counterproductive strategy of ignoring the needs and requirements of the customer base (Coombe *et al.* 1996).

The learning community, wherein the needs and interests of individuals are addressed on a personal level, promises much. Students are 'empowered, self-directed and committed learners' (Hill *et al.* 1995: 5). Such a learning community also reflects a policy through which 'students become members of a democratic society. In short [such schools] are likely to continue to be one of the few institutions that contribute to the moral and social intelligence of young people' (Kilvert 1997: 60).

Within that community, however, children, too, have responsibilities – to themselves and to others. Most importantly, they need to be aware of the impact of what they do individually upon the dynamics of the community as a whole. This would include aspects such as mutual collaboration amongst the learners with whom they were interacting; mutual respect for the ideas and values of others; and avoidance of behaviours which point to violence or intolerance.

The responsibility for children, too, is to be more aware of their own learning and that they can no longer be passive learners. They also must respect the rights of others to pursue their own learning goals. Knight refers to the experiences she recorded within a 'learning community classroom' where she was the 'teacher':

When students see themselves as critical members of a large community of learners and teachers, they also contribute to the learning of other children. 'When I see another child not understanding something, I first figure out the specifics and then think of a different way to show him', explains Catie. But Catie too has choices about her own learning...Learning is not the responsibility of the student.

(1994: 498–9)

Teachers

Nichols and Owens (1995) are mindful of three basic motivations which draw people into teaching. They summarise these underlying orientations as: 'a sense of calling, a service ethic, and a perceived legitimacy of teaching responsibilities' (1995: 47). Few neophyte practitioners are aware of the ethical minefields they will encounter as teachers. This has been highlighted earlier in this chapter. For now though, it is important to reiterate that even within the context of a learning community wherein there is a sense of collaboration, shared vision and mutual respect, the teacher cannot be oblivious to social and cultural concerns beyond the classroom.

It is not always ethically appropriate to accept the cultural norms of a child's family. Take, for example, the issues of corporal punishment and the attitudes towards education for girls in some cultural groups. It is neither whimsical nor culturally insensitive to decry such practices. Rather, these issues raise strong ethical concerns for teachers in terms of their protection of the child's rights to autonomy, justice, non-maleficence and beneficence. The teacher must decide what action to take. Within the learning community, such concerns can be addressed in a number of ways, first by dealing with the child ethically within the school setting and second by using the learning *community* to explain why things might be done differently in the school compared with the home environment.

For teachers, there needs to be an awareness of social justice issues and reflection upon the values they are passing on to children through both overt and covert curricula. In a learning community, it is essential that such reflection be continual. The results of such reflection may well result in teachers themselves deciding that they need to unpack and redesign teaching styles despite their cynicism about reform agendas in the past. For example, teachers may well realise that learning is a social act, and if this applies, then, as Prawat suggests, 'the criteria for judging teacher effectiveness shifts from that of delivering good lessons to that of being able to build or create a classroom "learning community"'(1992: 12).

School leaders

The school leader's role in a learning community is one of being a lead learner – one who works with others in the community to promote the community of learners.

The responsibility rests with the school leader to liaise between and amongst the various stakeholder groups of the learning community in such a way that the information is readily accessible and comprehensible to all. The leader then needs to operate in what Strike refers to as the 'public language...of a morally pluralistic society' (1995: 31). He points out that such a language would have three sub-languages which educators use to communicate in terms of public education:

- a rights language: 'talk competently about due process, equal opportunity, privacy and democracy'
- a language of caring or nurturance: because learners 'have needs and projects that must be respected, [the learners] need to grow and mature'
- a language of integrity about subject matter: 'teachers need to respect evidence and argument, they need to respect values internal to their subject matters, they need an ethic appropriate to the life of the mind and the pursuit of truth' (1995: 31).

Strike also suggests that thinking about relating notions of ethics to learners in terms of a language 'also allows us to connect [ethical] instruction...to important points about how people learn to see and interpret their worlds' (1995: 33). When this is overlaid on the day-to-day work experiences of practitioners within the learning community, the leader is in a position to foster professional development to assist teachers to consider ethical outcomes and implications in the practice of their profession and within the social contexts of their particular learning communities.

Hill and her colleagues have warned that 'Building learning communities requires us to redefine our mental models of teacher, parent, principal, leader and student and the relationship between them' (Hill *et al.* 1995: 5), and for many experienced teachers and school leaders this change in hierarchical base might well prove threatening – a loss of autonomy and respect. School leaders themselves have been shown (see Kleine-Kracht 1993) to express concern about being regarded as a learner within the community because it was seen as an admission of weakness. So the school leader too needs to depend on the support of other members of the broader community of learners.

It is also within the purview of the school leader's role to work with others to find alternative solutions for the successful development of the learning community. An example of one school where implementation required alternative strategies for ongoing development was reported by Everhart. He reflected that:

> Constructing a learning community within a school does not necessarily contribute to the social and intellectual skills necessary to build community. That requires exploration of and conscious commitment to interdependent links between the normative and value structures developed as part of the school community-building process.
>
> (1993: 207)

Where interactions between people are concerned, little is entirely predictable. Rather, there needs to be a sense simply of moving towards some common goal. This was recognised by the renowned educational philosopher, Dewey, in the early twentieth century. He reasoned that:

> There is more than a verbal tie between the words common, community and communication. [People] live in a community in virtue of the things which they have in common; and communication is the way in which they come to possess things in common...Such things [aims, beliefs, aspirations, knowledge] cannot be passed physically from one to another, like bricks; they cannot be shared as persons would share a pie by dividing it into physical pieces. Consensus requires communication...It may fairly be said, therefore, that any social arrangement that remains vitally social, or vitally shared, is educative to those who participate in it.
>
> (Dewey 1916: 4–5)

While learning is social and while it involves communication especially in terms of aims, beliefs, aspirations and knowledge, so too does it have an ethical dimension.

SCHOOLS AS LEARNING COMMUNITIES: SOME CONCLUDING REMARKS

In the period of rapid changes in outlook, attitudes, accountability and funding in education over the last fifteen years or so, public confidence in education has waned. Teachers' confidence in themselves has similarly been affected (Coombe 1998). It is not that teachers and schools have forgotten about learning, rather that the momentum of education has continually been disrupted under the guise of 'reform'. What is surprising is that, despite the disruption, the value of collaborative learning within schools and communities has been rediscovered to the extent that it offers an ethical advance in educational practice. In this way, learning communities not only promise autonomy, justice, non-maleficence and beneficence to each member of the community, they demonstrate the practice to support their claims of a collaborative learning environment which encourages the individual and collective learning of all.

References

Annis, D. B. (1989) 'Professional ethics in education: A neglected issue', paper presented at the Annual Meeting of the American Educational Research Association, San Francisco.

Beck, L. G. (1996) *Reclaiming Educational Administration as a Caring Profession*, New York: Teachers College Press.

Blackmore, J. (1991) 'Education in the marketplace', *Education Links* 41, 22–5.

Burke, C. (1997) 'Leading schools through the ethics thicket in the new era of educational reform', *ACEA Monograph Series*, Australian Council for Educational Administration: Melbourne.

Coady, M. (1994) 'Ethical and legal issues for early childhood practitioners', in E. J. Mellor and K. M. Coombe (eds) *Issues in Early Childhood Services: Australian Perspectives*, Dubuque, Iowa: Wm C. Brown.

Cocklin, B., Retallick, J. and Coombe, K. (1996) 'Learning communities in Australian schools: Case studies from rural New South Wales', paper presented at the European Conference on Education Research, Seville.

Considine, M. (1994) *Public Policy: A Critical Approach*, Melbourne: Macmillan.

Coombe, K. (1995) 'Child care: A study of policy, provision and women's ideologies', unpublished PhD thesis, Charles Sturt University, Wagga Wagga, Australia.

Coombe, K. (1998) 'The teaching profession: "A class act"', *Directions in Education* 7 (5), 4.

Coombe, K. and Newman, L. (1996) 'Ethics and the early childhood practicum: A pilot study', paper presented at the Conference on Australian Research in Early Childhood Education, Canberra, January.

Coombe, K. and Newman, L. (1997a) 'Ethics in early childhood field experiences', *Australian Research in Early Childhood Education* 1, 1–10.

Coombe, K. and Newman, L. (1997b) 'Ethical quandaries for neophyte early childhood practitioners', in V. Podmore (ed.) *Early Childhood Folio 3: A Collection of Recent Research*, Wellington: New Zealand Council for Educational Research.

Coombe, K., Retallick, J. and Cocklin, B. (1996) 'Beyond the horizon: Towards learning communities in education', in D. Lucardie, CPE [Continuing Professional Education] 96: *Beyond the Horizon*, Armidale: University of New England.

Darling-Hammond, L. (1993) 'Reframing the school reform agenda', *Phi Delta Kappan*, 74 (10), 752–61.

Dewey, J. (1916) *Democracy and Education*, New York: Macmillan.

Everhart, R. B. (1993) 'Community schools as enclaves', in G. Smith (ed.) *Public Schools that Work: Creating Community*, New York: Routledge.

Foucault, M. (1980) *Power/Knowledge*, Brighton, England: Harvester.

Garrick, J. (1994) 'Postmodern doubts and "truths" about training', *Studies in Continuing Education* 16 (2), 127–42.

Hargreaves, A. (1995) 'Changing teachers, changing times: Strategies for leadership in an age of paradox', Australian Council on Educational Administration Workshop, Melbourne.

Hill, J., Pettit, J. and Dawson, G. (1995) 'Schools as learning communities: A discussion paper', Sydney: Department of School Education.

Johnson, N. (1995) 'Schools as learning communities', paper presented at the Australian Curriculum Studies Conference, Melbourne.

Kilvert, P. (1997) 'Visions of the future: The school in the year 2007', in *Unicorn*, 23 (2), 57–65.

Kleine-Kracht, P. A. (1993) 'The principal in a learning community', *Journal of School Leadership* 3 (4), 391–9.

Knight, J. (1994) 'Learning in a community', *Reading Teacher* 47 (6), 498–9.

Liang, C., Schuen, T. and Neher, I. (1996) 'The reality of corporate education: Proceedings of selected research and development presentations', presented at the 18th Convention for the Association for Educational Communications and Technology, Indianapolis.

Lovat, T. (1998) 'Ethics and ethics education: Professional and curricular best practice', *Curriculum Perspectives* 13 (1), 1–7.

Marginson, S. (1993) *Education and public policy in Australia*, Cambridge: Cambridge University Press.

Marquardt, M. and Reynolds, A. (1994) *The Global Learning Organization*, New York: Irwin.

Mitten, D. (1997) 'The value of feminist ethics in experiential education teaching and leadership', ERIC Accession No. ED412045.

Nichols, T. and Owens, L. A. (1995) 'The role of teacher education in nurturing honorable and principled teaching', *Educational Horizons* 74 (1), 43–8.

Noddings, N. (1992) *The Challenge to Care in Schools: An Alternative Approach to Education*, New York, Teachers College.

Peters, T. and Waterman, R. H. (1982) *In Search of Excellence: Lessons from America's Best Run Companies*, New York: Harper and Row.

Prawat, R. S. (1992) 'From individual differences to learning communities: Our changing focus',*Educational Leadership* 50 (2), 9–13.

Raywid, M. A. (1993) 'Community: An alternative school accomplishment', in G. A. Smith (ed) *Public Schools That Work: Creating Community*, New York: Routledge.

Retallick, J. A. (1996) 'The school as a learning organisation: A case study of teachers and their workplace learning', unpublished paper.

Senge, P. M. (1992) *The Fifth Discipline: The Art and Practice of the Learning Organization*, Sydney: Random House.

Sergiovanni, T. (1994) *Building Community in Schools*, San Francisco: Jossey-Bass.

Sottile, J. M. (1994) 'Teaching and ethics', ERIC Accession No. ED378174.

Strike, K. A. (1995) 'Professional ethics and the education of professionals', *Educational Horizons* 74 (1), 29–36.

Strike, K. A. and Ternasky, P. L. (1993) *Ethics for Professionals in Education: Perspectives for Preparation and Practice*, New York: Teachers College Press.

Walker, K. (1998) 'Building on ethics in educational leadership', participant's manual for New South Wales Workshop, Wagga Wagga.

Watkins, K. E. and Marsick, V. (1993) *Sculpting the Learning Organization*, San Francisco: Jossey-Bass.

Part 2

LEARNING COMMUNITIES
Strategies and processes

6

TRANSFORMING SCHOOLS INTO LEARNING COMMUNITIES

Beginning the journey

John Retallick

INTRODUCTION

In April 1993 I was in the audience when Professor Tom Sergiovanni delivered an address at the annual conference of the American Educational Research Association in Atlanta, Georgia. The address, which was subsequently published (Sergiovanni 1994a), called into question much of the current thinking about how schools should be organised and administered. He spoke in a challenging way about 'changing the metaphor from organisation to community' as the basis for school administration. Since that time I have been intrigued by the notion of the school as a learning community; intrigued by what people actually mean when they talk of the school as a learning community; and most particularly by how they go about the process of change to transform schools into learning communities.

At about the same time I came across a developing interest in learning communities in the New South Wales Department of School Education, one of the largest school education systems in the world. The interest arose from a report of an international advisory committee appointed by the then Minister for Education in NSW which recommended that 'action be taken at all levels to promote schools as "learning communities" and to adopt policies and practices of training and development to such an end' (International Advisory Council 1994: 9). In the following year the Department issued a discussion document to all schools in the system (NSW Department of School Education 1995) with the aim of beginning the dialogue about schools as learning communities.

I also learnt of a significant initiative on learning communities in Catholic schools in the Wagga Wagga Diocese in NSW. Instigated by John Goonan, Primary Consultant, it started out as a Disadvantaged Schools Program initiative in 1994 when four schools became interested in cooperative learning. The teachers began meeting together on weekends to explore and share ideas. After some time the Diocese began sponsoring the weekend meetings, and the idea grew in importance to the point where, in 1996, the Diocese established a five-day 'Institute on Learning Communities' conducted by two consultants, Joan Dalton and David Anderson. Some thirty people – including principals and teachers – attended the first Institute, and since then five more Institutes have been held. Following each Institute, Joan and David visited the participants in their schools and worked with them as they began to translate ideas into practice. It has now become a major feature of schools in the Wagga Wagga Diocese, and some significant outcomes in terms of school change are becoming evident as schools begin to transform themselves into learning communities.

While this was going on I was developing an interest in the idea of teachers' workplace learning, and I, along with some colleagues, had been commissioned to conduct a national research project on that issue (Retallick 1994). One of our conclusions and major recommendations was that schools and education systems should give more attention to the idea of the school as an 'educative workplace' for teachers as well as students. Since then I have been further developing the workplace learning model of teacher professional development (see Retallick 1997), and I am now finding that there is a great deal of congruence between the notions of 'workplace learning' and 'learning communities'.

What I seek to do in this chapter is contribute to the development of theory about learning community, consider some of the major ideas and literature about learning communities, and provide a glimpse into two local schools which have recently started on the journey of transforming themselves into learning communities. Such transformations are not easy; they require a level of dedication, determination and long-term commitment that are difficult to find. Indeed, as Smith (1993: 11) argues, 'schools as they are currently constructed are poorly designed to foster the experience of community...they will need to be reformulated in ways that counter the disintegrative impact of their present organizational and governance structures as well as their curricula'.

TOWARDS A THEORY OF LEARNING COMMUNITY

As I will show later, schools start in different places in their quest to build a learning community and they go about it in different ways. However, one idea is fairly constant and that is that they are seeking something new, something different from what they have done before. As Sergiovanni puts it: 'Building community in schools is about a shared quest to do things differently, to develop new kinds of relationships, to create new ties, to make new commitments' (1994b: 153).

In any endeavour to build something new it is both important and helpful to have theory to guide strategy and action. Writers such as Raywid (1993) and Sergiovanni (1994a,1994b) have made a major contribution to building a theory of learning community through their advocacy of the sociological theory of *Gemeinschaft* and *Gesellschaft*. From the 1887 writings of the German sociologist, Ferdinand Tonnies, we are reminded that *Gemeinschaft* translates as 'community' and *Gesellschaft* translates as 'society'. Members of *gemeinschaft* communities 'have emotional ties to one another and are linked by shared values and beliefs, recurring interaction with one another, mutual dependence, and a shared commitment to a particular place – a neighbourhood or town or area' (Raywid 1993: 29). *Gesellschaft* groupings are not actually communities at all and have no such sense of connectedness; they are characterised by the separate and individual interests of persons in business or contractual relationships, where social patterns are governed by rules and regulations and bureaucratic controls.

In an attempt to advance that theoretical work I want to turn to another and more recent German social theorist, Jurgen Habermas, for some further ideas towards building a theory of learning community. Habermas is a major figure in social theory today and has written a great deal more than I can refer to here. I need to be selective of his work therefore, and I intend to draw only briefly upon his theory of communicative action and, in particular, his notions of 'lifeworld and system' (Habermas 1987). Habermas distinguishes between an 'organic form of social solidarity' and a 'market society integrated purely by systemic means'. He argues that in modern societies:

> The differentiation of a highly complex market system destroys traditional forms of solidarity without at the same time producing normative orientations capable of securing an organic form of solidarity...In one case, the integration of an action system is established by a normatively secured or communicatively achieved consensus, in the other case, by a nonnormative regulation of individual decisions that extends beyond the actor's consciousness.
>
> (1997: 116–17)

In making this distinction between a *social integration* of society and a *systemic integration,* Habermas calls for a corresponding differentiation in the concept of society itself. Society can be conceived from the perspective of the acting subjects as the *lifeworld of a social group.* In contrast, from the observer's perspective as someone not involved, society can be conceived only as a *system of actions.* Habermas proposes, therefore, that we conceive of societies simultaneously as systems and lifeworlds.

Language, culture and communication are the essence of the lifeworld. The concept of communicative action is central and complementary to the lifeworld and there are two aspects to it: The *teleological aspect* of realising one's aim, or carrying out a plan of action; and the *communicative aspect* of interpreting a situation and arriving at an agreement.

As Habermas puts it:

> In communicative action participants pursue their plans coopera-
> tively on the basis of a shared definition of a situation...the success
> of the action and the consensus brought about by acts of reaching
> understanding are the criteria for whether a situation has been dealt
> with successfully.
>
> (1987: 126–7)

Habermas's theory of communicative action helps us to understand some present trends in Western societies. He points out that impersonal systems such as bureaucracies and markets, via steering mechanisms of power and money respectively, are gradually colonising lifeworld contexts where cooperation and consensus are the keys to success. As 'economic rationalism' becomes ever more pervasive in our social institutions including schools, there is a need for educators who are committed to community-building to resist, to challenge and to create healthy alternatives to bureaucratic and market-driven approaches. One of the most robust of those alternatives for schools is the idea of the learning community.

THE SCHOOL AS A LEARNING COMMUNITY

Starratt (1996) reminds us that the idea of a learning community is a metaphor that helps us organise and pursue a new vision for education. He defines a number of characteristics of a learning community, as follows:

- Learning must be situated in a critical community of inquirers who accept that knowledge is always partial and fallible and who support the enrichment of knowledge through sharing of meanings, interpretations, and learnings among all members of the community.
- The learning agenda of the school must be continually related to something intrinsically human – to the exploration of questions important to human individuals and social life.
- The learning agenda of the school must be related to the large cultural projects of our current era as well as to the cultural projects of our history. Thus, school learnings are connected to a significant discourse about the making of history.

- School meanings must be continuously related to students' experience of everyday life.

(1996: 70)

Whilst Starratt acknowledges that every school which undertakes the task of remaking itself as a learning community will be unique, he argues that learning communities will manifest some common, core processes. He puts forward (1996: 71–81) a 'beginning listing' of those processes.

1 Learning takes place in a caring environment. This refers to all children and teachers feeling that they are cared for and that they care for each other. It also extends to caring for what is being studied in the curriculum through various cooperative learning processes.
2 Learning involves lots of storytelling. This is important both as a way of communicating and as a way of linking the lesson of the curriculum and the lifeworld of the student.
3 Learning in school is related to home and neighbourhood experiences. This idea connects the lifeworld of the school and the lifeworld of home and neighbourhood.
4 Learning should lead to some product or performance. This ensures students own their learning and demonstrates that learning is useful both inside and outside of school.
5 There should be periodic and continuous reference to an exploration of meta-narratives. These are the 'larger stories' concerning the central elements of our culture to which students need to have connection for meaning to occur.
6 The learning community should periodically explore the really big questions. Such questions include: What does it mean to be human? What is the meaning of life, of suffering, of death? What does it mean to be a community?

Another list of the shared qualities of schools identified as communities has been offered by Raywid (1993: 32–9). In this case the focus is upon 'alternative schools' where a strong sense of community has been accomplished. The author makes the helpful distinction between terms like *culture* and *climate*, which are descriptive constructs applying to all schools, and *community*, which is not evident in all schools but is rather an accomplishment of some schools. To assert that a school is a community means, for Raywid, that a number of qualities are evident:

- Respect: teachers and students treat each other with respect and authentic courtesy.
- Caring: encompassing but going beyond respect, caring is more particularistic and proactive in that it acknowledges the uniqueness of

111

each individual and reaches out to initiate positive interaction rather than being expressed only as a response to another.

- Inclusiveness: there are continual attempts to ensure that all participants are drawn into the whole range of interactions throughout the school and none are left as outsiders. What is different about a school as a community is that teachers and students are typically not separated by physical divisions; for example, they might share a lunch room or students might be invited to participate in teachers' meetings, and, perhaps more importantly, they share a common culture of assumptions and values in the school so that students and teachers are not pitted against each other.
- Trust: members of a genuine community trust one another to the point where they are prepared to disclose themselves and their work to their colleagues because they know that such disclosure will be beneficial to their relationships and improve their work as teachers and learners.
- Empowerment: both students and teachers feel empowered in a community because they know their voice will be heard and their feelings will count when it comes to expressing their concerns. This is especially important for students, who are often locked out of decision-making processes in schools and denied opportunities for influencing policy and practice.
- Commitment: a strong sense of attachment and a high investment of energy are features of a community; the school may be described as 'like a family' and there is particular attachment to the goals and values of the school which motivate members to achieve the best possible outcomes for all concerned.

THE CLASSROOM AS A COMMUNITY

While the school as a whole can be conceived as a learning community, it is just as important to think of each classroom as well. The work of Johnson and Johnson on cooperative learning underpins a good deal of the thinking about the classroom as a community. They suggest (1989: 4–7) that for a lesson to be regarded as cooperative, five basic elements are necessary:

- *Positive interdependence:* students are linked with each other in a way that one cannot succeed unless all succeed.
- *Face-to-face promotive interaction:* students orally explain to each other how to solve problems etc., and support each other's efforts to learn.
- *Individual accountability:* the performance of each individual student is assessed and the results given back to the group and the individual so that the group knows who needs more assistance.

- *Social skills:* skills of leadership, trust-building, communication and conflict management must be taught.
- *Group processes:* it is important that groups process how well they are achieving their goals and maintaining effective working relationships.

A research study by Whitmore and Crowell (1994) reminds us of the importance of context in considering the school as a learning community. This is true for the school as a whole and for each classroom where teacher and students work out what a learning community means in practice. They see the context of the classroom as a place of tension between the invention of the individual student and the conventions of the formal educational setting and the real world. As they say:

> The classroom exists within the realities of the historical, cultural, and political contexts of its school and community...the classroom rests in a zone where the tension between the forces of the social and personal is clearly visible. It is only in this nested perspective that we can appreciate the complexities of inventing a classroom community.
>
> (1994: 22–3)

Their study of a third-grade classroom, 'the Sunshine Room', reveals how students from a bilingual, working-class neighbourhood worked and developed together over a year as a community of learners.

Kohn argues that we have an obligation to specify what the idea of community means, and he defines it as:

> a place in which students feel cared about and are encouraged to care about each other. They experience a sense of being valued and respected; the children matter to one another and to the teacher. They have come to think in the plural: they feel connected to each other; they are part of an 'us'.
>
> (1996: 101)

He also cites research evidence for the increased effectiveness of schools which have emphasised community building. For instance, in one study (Battistich *et al.* 1995) it is reported that the stronger the community feeling, the more students reported liking school and the more they saw learning as something valuable in its own right. In another (Child Development Project 1991), it is suggested that taking the time to help children to care about each other might actually affect their enthusiasm about academic learning. Kohn comments:

That is an insight with the potential to reshape the whole enterprise of school reform...Students need to feel safe in order to take intellectual risks, they must be comfortable before they can venture into the realm of discomfort. Few things stifle creativity like the fear of being judged or humiliated...The moral is: if you want academic excellence, you have to attend to how children feel about school and about each other.

(1996: 103)

Dalton and Watson (1997) have developed a framework of understanding and practice which provides considerable insight into building learning communities in classrooms and schools. They provide 'four keys to classroom community': fostering caring relationships, teaching humane values, honouring intrinsic motivation, and learning for understanding. Their rationale for the learning-community approach is strongly grounded in constructivist learning theory and the view that children's development is an adaptive process that requires a supportive and challenging social context. They argue that it is also grounded in the changing nature of our present-day world which is losing some essential elements of community that can be fostered in schools. They say:

> as other adults in children's lives have less time to spend with them and as neighborhoods operate less as communities where people know and help one another, we as teachers have begun to more deliberately provide children with the experience of membership in a community – their school and classroom community – and more focused in helping them acquire the skills for maintaining community.

(1997: 5)

TEACHERS' PROFESSIONAL COMMUNITY

If it is important for students to care about each other in terms of improving academic learning, the research also reveals that teachers too can benefit from a strong professional community. McLaughlin's research in secondary schools revealed that teachers had a range of different responses to students but, importantly, teachers *within the same school or even within the same department developed different responses to similar students depending on the character of their collegial environment'* (1993: 89). What this means is that the quality of teachers' professional community has a significant bearing on how they respond to students in the classroom and therefore on student learning outcomes.

This research reveals that teachers who work in collaborative communities which are cohesive and highly collegial are more innovative, show higher levels of energy and enthusiasm and are more supportive of personal growth and learning. Furthermore, such teachers are more focused on meeting students' needs and devising strategies that assist all of their students to learn. Norms of collegiality and collaboration amongst teachers mean more than just healthy social relations; they mean that teachers are more effective in producing student learning.

A significant aspect of teachers' professional community relates to their workplace learning. As Sergiovanni points out:

> Few axioms are more fundamental than the one that acknowledges the link between what happens to teachers and what happens to students...the idea of making classrooms into learning communities for students will remain more rhetoric than real unless schools also become learning communities for teachers.
>
> (1996: 42)

One way in which teachers can develop a learning community amongst themselves is to regard their everyday work as an opportunity for learning. Workplace learning means just that – learning on the job. In a national research project in Australia I explored the idea that the workplace learning of teachers might be given greater recognition in their overall professional development. This exploration sought to achieve greater understanding of teachers' workplace learning and build a case for it to be regarded as a legitimate form of teacher professional development with university accreditation. This is not to argue that universities should no longer be involved in in-service teacher education, but as Hargreaves elaborates:

> In this postmodern world, many forms of knowledge are emerging as worthwhile and legitimate in ways that challenge the epistemological superiority of the academic establishment. Strong school cultures and vibrant professional networks create conditions where teachers can share their own practical knowledge and have independent access to other knowledge from elsewhere.
>
> (1996: 119)

Whilst learning on the job or workplace learning has long been recognised by teachers as vital to their success in the classroom, particularly in the early years of teaching, it is not usually regarded as professional development. Though it is highly relevant to their needs, the learning is seen to be informal and is generally uncredentialled. On the other hand, professional development is usually associated with attending formal courses or conferences outside the school workplace. The resultant learning may or may not be directly relevant to classroom teaching but there is explicit recognition of it in the form of a diploma or degree or at least a certificate of completion. The argument here is that this dichotomy should be abandoned in favour of a more seamless notion of professional development which is seen to encompass many forms of learning, one of which is workplace learning.

TEACHERS' WORKPLACE LEARNING

A model for understanding workplace learning in a broad sense has been put forward by Marsick and Watkins (1990). It includes three domains of perspective transformation. *Instrumental learning* is job focused and is aimed at skill development or improving individual productivity. This learning is behaviouristic and the focus of much human resource development. *Dialogic learning* includes learning about the organisation and one's relationship to it. It encourages individuals to enter into a dialogue with the organisation through emphasis on team relationships, coaching, mentoring, role modelling and the mission of the organisation. *Self-reflective learning* seeks to extend one's understanding of oneself in the workplace through increasing confidence and competence, dealing with issues of authority, analysing change in personal values or beliefs and clarifying one's orientation toward the job.

These ideas about workplace learning apply to all sorts of workplaces, including schools. However, for present purposes we need to see how concepts of learning can be applied more specifically to the school as a workplace. In a particularly pertinent piece of research, Rosenholtz (1989) examined the organisational differences between productive and unproductive schools and found far more collaboration in the former than the latter. Rosenholtz distinguished between 'moving' and 'stuck' schools and school districts. Teachers in moving schools had many and varied learning opportunities while those in stuck schools had few.

The significance of the notion of workplace learning for teachers' work is profound. The idea of the school as an educative workplace for teachers (as well as students) represents a considerable advance on thinking about teachers' work, and it provided the impetus for the national research project on teachers' workplace learning which I have previously mentioned.

The research project, titled *Workplace Learning in the Professional Development of Teachers*, began with the authors' definition of teachers' workplace learning as:

> an essential component of the overall professional development of teachers. It occurs largely in school settings and involves the trans-

formation of knowledge, values and beliefs into classroom practice. It includes both informal and planned learning, often involves input from others such as academics or consultants and has the intention of improving the quality of teaching.

(Retallick 1994: 1)

This definition points to the location of the learning as well as its nature. It does not deny the importance of 'outside' influences on teacher learning but insists that workplace learning is that which results from trying out ideas in the classroom, which is the central focus of teachers' work.

The design of the research project was based on the concept that teachers' workplace learning is shaped and determined by both individual and contextual factors. Teachers were viewed as active constructors of their own learning within contexts and structures that can support and enhance or impede their learning. The research sought to reflect that duality by gathering information on both the contextual and the personal dimensions of teacher learning. A questionnaire was administered to teachers in seventy-four schools and followed by case study research of ten teachers in their school context. The major outcome of the study was the development of a contextual model of teachers' workplace learning based on seven factors which help to explain the ability and willingness of teachers to undertake significant workplace learning. A brief overview of the seven factors is provided in the following paragraphs.

The context The context in which schools and teachers are situated was found to have greater significance than any other single factor in determining what and how teachers learn on the job. In a broad sense the context refers to the changing cultural mix of society and the changing family structures, economic circumstances and technological development of the society. The ideological responses to these and other relevant issues are reflected in government policies and initiatives on education which impact on schools in various ways. Such policies and initiatives very often have funding implications which either enable or constrain school activities and thereby affect the workplace learning of teachers.

The nature of the innovation/change For present purposes an innovation is defined as a 'product' and change as a 'process'. Some innovations, such as laptop computers, are clearly products and some changes, such as cooperative learning, are clearly processes, though that distinction is not always perfectly clear as in a new syllabus which is both a product and a process. The nature of the product and/or process is an important factor in *what* and *how* teachers learn, as is the question of who initiates the learning, i.e. teachers themselves or others. This question often raises the issue of ownership of the learning in relation to imposed or self-generated change.

117

The 'case study' teachers often made the point that for learning to be really effective it must come from within. That is to say teachers must want to learn before they will actually change their practices. The teachers often referred to the practical aspects of the innovation/change in relation to classroom usage. They tended to criticise professional development programmes which ignored the classroom application of the knowledge being presented. This practicality ethic is an important feature of workplace learning since the essence of it is the transformation of knowledge, values and beliefs into classroom practice.

The teacher as a person and learner   The question of *how* teachers learn is a complex one relating to the teacher as a person and learner. When teachers are studied as individual persons and adult learners, a great many differences emerge. The research revealed the most prominent in terms of workplace learning to be the career stage or stage of development of the teacher which is, of course, usually related to age. It was clear that beginning teachers, who were usually but not always the youngest on the staff, had different needs and concerns from those of more experienced teachers. The specific demands of the classroom provided the focus for beginners, whereas older, more experienced teachers were able to make connections between the classroom and the wider context which seemed to provide them with a clearer sense of purpose and stronger justification for their teaching.

The situations of teaching   This factor relates primarily to the question of where teachers' workplace learning occurs. Teachers work in different situations which impact on their professional development in distinctive ways. For instance, it was claimed by teachers who had worked in both primary and secondary settings that there are clear differences in the nature of the work and consequent demands on teachers. One of the case-study teachers, who had taught in both, reinforced this point by saying that primary teachers are more child centred than secondary teachers since the latter tend to be more subject centred. School size may also be relevant at this point, since most secondary schools are quite large whereas primary schools can range in size from one teacher through to very large schools. Teachers commented that in smaller schools they get to know everyone on the staff a lot better, though in larger schools it was evident that teachers work in manageable groups which form around particular professional interests and which can provide the basis for workplace learning.

Learning resources and support   The range of issues at stake here is concerned with the resources and support structures which facilitate or impede teachers' workplace learning. This factor also addresses the question of how and from whom teachers learn. Of crucial importance is the role of the principal in facilitating change and establishing structures within the school which enhance teacher development. In the research some principals were found to be strong agents of change and advocates for teacher learning while others were criticised by teachers for lack of support and recognition of what they were trying to achieve. Other executives (variously deputies, assistant principals, leading teachers, etc.) also had an important role in assisting and supporting teachers in their endeavours to improve their teaching, though most teachers felt that the support of their colleagues, i.e. fellow teachers, was the most important.

System recognition and reward   The notion that there might be system recognition and reward for teachers' workplace learning was relatively new and quite novel to most teachers at the time of the research. Teachers generally felt 'the system' was uncaring and unconcerned with their growth and development, and it was strongly criticised when resources, recognition or rewards were withdrawn. Since teachers view workplace learning as an essential element in their professional development and the major means by which they improve their teaching, it would make good sense for systems to give greater recognition and reward for it. This would enhance the incentives for teacher learning.

The culture of the school   The connections between the culture of the school and the nature of workplace learning appear to be fundamentally important. Some of the features of school culture which seem to have high salience for workplace learning relate to beliefs and values while others relate to organisational structures and functions. Of most importance is a strong belief by teachers in the efficacy of workplace learning. It is clear from the research that teachers believe that their most effective and useful learning occurs through on-the-job experience and reflection. They do not deny the need for outsiders to provide new knowledge and ideas but they are insistent that such new information is useful to them only when it has been tried in the classroom. Furthermore, many teachers believe that they learn most effectively from the students in their classrooms; i.e. their judgements about what 'works' are formed largely through interaction with students.

It is interesting to note the congruence of these research findings on teachers' workplace learning with ideas I presented earlier about schools as learning communities. Of central importance is the notion that building a learning community can start in different ways in different schools. One of those ways is for teachers to build a sense of community through their own collaborative workplace learning; another is through classroom interaction with students; and of course there are many more as I seek to show in the next section.

BUILDING LEARNING COMMUNITIES

Here I want to focus on processes and strategies employed by learning community consultants Joan Dalton and David Anderson, along with brief glimpses into what is occurring in two schools which have recently started on the learning community journey. Dalton and Anderson begin by arguing that

> we must prepare young people to live and thrive in tomorrow's world, one which enables them to:
> * grow and develop as whole human beings
> * live ethical values
> * maximise their talents to achieve their personal best
> * become responsible, contributing members of society
> * play an active part in shaping a better world for all.
>
> (Dalton and Anderson 1998: 1)

They then focus on 'the adults our children will need to become' in order to provide clear long-term goals for teachers and students upon which to align their teaching and learning. These goals are seen as 'the outcomes that ultimately matter', and

> can best be realised through membership of caring learning communities, where the spirit of support and challenge work in harmony together, where relationship is the glue that holds the community together, and where social–ethical values are the foundation upon which everything else is built.
>
> (1998: 3)

Six major principles of effective learning and teaching underpin the development of learning communities in the Dalton and Anderson approach. They suggest that these principles will help students achieve the mandated curriculum requirements as well as to become the kinds of adults who can function effectively in the future. The six principles are:

1 Constructivist learning that...
* immerses learners in 'hands on', concrete experiences
* accesses and builds upon what students know
* connects new learning to what students know and understand
* makes purpose and relevance clear to students
* actively involves students in constructing understandings
* focuses on significant ideas/concepts, questions and processes

- enhances pattern-seeing, connection-making, and relationship between ideas, concepts and processes – across curriculum, boundaries, systems
- is authentic in context
- helps students transfer/use new learnings in other situations, both current and future.

2 *Inquiry that...*

- encourages learners to pose, formulate and explore questions – their own, those of others; questions that are philosophical as well as practical
- involves learners in conducting research and using investigative processes
- encourages risk-taking and uses error as a learning experience
- builds in learners a sense of wonder.

3 *Communication that...*

- develops meaningful dialogue for peers
- uses different communication styles for a range of purposes, audiences and contexts
- uses multiple methods and a variety of media to represent thinking, ideas and information.

4 *Collaboration that...*

- engages learners in working with partnerships, small groups, and large groups
- is underpinned by a shared set of social–ethical values
- teaches students a range of interpersonal and collaborative skills, for example, listening actively, checking for accuracy, negotiating, managing conflict in a constructive manner
- fosters perspective-taking, developing an openness to others' viewpoints, ideas and opinions
- models and makes explicit a range of teamwork strategies
- builds students' commitment to contribute, to learn from others, and develop a willingness to work toward shared goals
- helps students learn to share responsibility with others.

5 *Self-responsibility that helps students learn to take increasing control of their learning and thinking, and...*

- focuses on understanding self as a learner, able to access different ways of knowing
- fosters on-going reflection on learning – what, how, why...
- helps learners to self-question, to monitor and reflect on their thinking/learning before, during and after action

- develops skill in using a range of creative and critical thinking processes, particularly macro processes such as decision-making and problem-solving
- teaches learners how to access, process and use information appropriately; use of context-appropriate learning-how-to-learn strategies and cognitive organisers
- helps learners to increasingly manage and organise their learning, for example, goal-setting, personal planning, choice-making, time-management, evaluation and assessment.

It also helps students learn to manage their behaviour, and...

- uses a constructivist approach and Christian, social–ethical values as the basis from which students construct their moral understandings and solve personal/behavioural problems
- fosters self-monitoring of one's own behaviour and accepting ownership of problems
- encourages responsible choice-making, learning positive ways of behaving, and choosing constructive strategies to resolve conflict.

6 *Human development that...*

- develops in students a lifelong love of and search for learning
- helps students learn to operate as principled, ethical human beings, displaying values such as respect, fairness, courtesy, responsibility, and kindness
- develops qualities such as initiative, resilience, flexibility, adaptability, imagination, persistence, confidence, and becoming enterprising
- engages students in visioning and developing preferred futures that have personal and global relevance
- has a focus on creating and publishing new products, data, writing, and modes (rather than reproducing simply what is known)
- develops in learners a global view
- develops in learners the ability to thrive with change.

(Dalton and Anderson 1998: 2–4)

STARTING THE LEARNING COMMUNITY JOURNEY

I want to move now to a glimpse into two schools where Joan Dalton and David Anderson have had a considerable influence in helping the schools begin the learning community journey. In both cases teachers attended an

Institute and on return to their respective schools initiated a process of change based on the above ideas and principles. In the first glimpse it is helpful to understand that the teacher, Frances Robertson, had been a primary school teacher until her recent appointment to Mount Erin High School, and she has had a long-term commitment to ideas about learning community. She spoke with me about her involvement in a 'cadre' of teachers who are taking these ideas to many schools and her particular strategy which she referred to as the Monday conversation.

The 'Monday conversation' at Mount Erin High School

JR: How did you get started on learning communities?

FR: I started on the notion of learning communities back in 1990 when I was working with the Beginning Teachers' Program for the Diocese. I was trying to think of ways I could improve the actual learning in the classroom and I experimented with some books and some support. Then three years ago, the Diocese employed Joan Dalton and David Anderson as learning community consultants to primary schools. They ran a series of weekend workshops which I attended and then they went into the schools to support those teachers.

Last year I was employed here at Mt Erin High School and I began using some of the learning strategies that I had developed through my contacts with Joan and David. Then I attended another Institute run by them that involved quite a few primary school people in the Diocese and a number of high school teachers as well. Again there was in-school support for those teachers.

JR: How have you worked with other teachers on ideas about learning communities?

FR: At the end of last year the Diocese decided to form a cadre; that is a group of people who could gently spread the ideas in schools. About twenty people met at the end of last year with Joan and David and since then we have had another three days together and we will have two more days together. In the meantime David and Joan are visiting the schools; David is visiting this school.

Now his role can be one of a hundred things. It could be just a simple talk to me about where I am going to support me or it could be to talk to the deputy or the principal. Last time he was here he talked to the principal and pointed out the possibilities of sister schools; one in Christchurch and another in Tokyo. Also David would provide an in-service if we asked for it but he would rather that I did things and he would support me. So that's where we are up to now.

Prior to the cadre being formed, when I came back from the Institute last year, I could see that there was no way I was going to be able to say: 'Hey everybody, perhaps we should all change our way of thinking'. So I initiated casual conversations on Mondays at lunchtime and just invited anybody who wanted to sit and chat about these sorts of things. Sometimes nobody comes because we've been busy with lunch duties or it's cold or whatever; other times out there on the verandah people will congregate and there could be a dozen people.

JR: So this is a regular Monday lunchtime conversation?

FR: Yes, it's always Monday lunchtime but there are lots of other times as well when people come and ask about the things I'm doing. It's casual conversation about cooperative classrooms; I call it the 'four Cs'. Now that was the way it was introduced one Monday morning at a staff briefing and I asked if anyone would like to come. It has been on the noticeboard once since then, just as a reminder.

The direction of those conversations has been: 'How are things going?' 'Have you have tried such and such?' I don't direct the conversation, it just flows. Another teacher who has been to one of the Institutes will often come and say: 'Gee I had a hard time, I was trying to do such and such with my maths class and it just didn't work' and then people start piping in and saying, 'Well what about trying this?' or 'Why did you do that?' We got to talking one day about grouping and ways of using groups; you know friendship groups versus teacher-organised groups versus random groups and that was really productive and it carried on for about three weeks.

JR: OK. So what you are really doing is establishing some dialogue about learning communities.

FR: Yes and at this stage it seems to be working because we have a network of about a dozen teachers who are at least oriented toward that kind of thinking. We also have another primary teacher who works here part time and she is part of the cadre as well, so there are actually two of us on staff. Now unfortunately she can't come to those Monday conversations but we have formed a fairly tight partnership.

I have also formed partnerships with other people and Sunday afternoons there is often half a dozen people in here. It's what I call the Sunday afternoon party; you come in to do some work and people start talking about all sorts of things to do with school. So a lot of it happens without any form of organisation but the result is some very healthy professional dialogue going on.

JR: Why is it that people are actually coming to you with these sorts of issues? Are you perceived as a resource person around here?

FR: Well I initiated the casual conversations, people are aware that I have been to the Institute, they are aware that I am part of the cadre but there has been no formal introduction or recognition of it, it has just happened. The other thing is I try to model things in my classroom. My classroom actually looks like a primary classroom; there are strings across the room with things hanging and everything is in colour including the noticeboard.

Last year I frequently found teachers in my room after school, just standing there looking, and I would walk in and we could have a conversation. So I am trying several different tactics. My approach is to be as casual as possible and build up networks of people in all departments. I specifically invite some people into a sort of loose partnership to work with me; I've tried to do things in the library and the librarians then comment on that to other teachers and I try to get people to share as much as I can and to make people feel they belong. They are all the different ways I am approaching it.

JR: What do you understand by this notion of learning community?

FR: A learning community is one where we are *all* part of the learning cycle, that is students and teachers. It's built on interdependent relationships: teacher to teacher, teacher to student, student to student. We use cooperative learning strategies to build up the learning community. We do things that enhance and enrich our own learning and we support one another in that. There is a sense of common purpose that permeates every level and each member is safe to take risks in an environment that prepares them for a lifelong journey of learning.

JR: So in what ways would you like to see this school change or develop to become more like a learning community? In other words, what is your vision of this school as a learning community?

FR: I guess my first goal is for teachers to recognise that they are learners too. We need to look at ourselves as learners, and we need to look much more closely at what actually helps students learn than just bombarding them with content. We would be aiming towards a vibrancy where all forms of learning would be accepted. We would promote a holistic development, recognising human needs for inclusion, interdependence and a sense of purpose. After all, today's children are tomorrow's adults, so we must promote skills and develop characteristics that will enhance future society.

In the second glimpse the teacher, Rod Whelan, presented a seminar on initiatives at Trinity Senior High School to which I was privileged to be invited. This school has also benefited from a five-day workshop conducted by Pamela Wells, who has particular expertise in cooperative learning (see chapter 7 in this volume). Three teachers attended the workshop and with

Pamela's assistance they began planning a study skills programme for Year 11 students which focused on student learning and self-management skills.

The 'Study Skills Program' at Trinity Senior High School

A major strategy at Trinity Senior High in becoming a learning community was the introduction of a study skills programme for Year 11 students in 1998. Four teachers attended an institute with Joan Dalton and David Anderson in late 1997, and by early 1998 the school had begun an important reorientation of culture and rebuilding of morale amongst teachers and students. The first stage was a good deal of discussion on what the school is really trying to achieve, i.e. the vision, and finally reaching consensus on 'the adults our children will need to become'. Following ideas presented at the institute, it was agreed that there should be certain characteristics and attributes of students who have been to the school, and they are summed up in the following words: inquirers, thinkers, reflective, adaptable, knowledgeable, communicators, principled, caring, global citizens and healthy people. Second, it was agreed that the school would adopt a 'charter' on relationships based on the theme of how teachers and students should treat one another. The charter includes the statement: 'We seek to treat one another with respect, fairly as equals without discrimination, as friends and with consideration and understanding.' A third focus for the reorientation was a commitment by a number of teachers to work towards the development of cooperative classrooms in practice.

With this framework in mind and following the Pamela Wells workshop, the staff agreed to construct a study skills programme. The programme is concerned about outcomes in the form of improved student learning, but perhaps more importantly it is also concerned about processes which will lead to the kinds of characteristics and attributes of students mentioned above. The first aspect of the process to be considered was the construction of the programme itself. Rather than teachers enforcing their expectations on students (a feature of the old culture) it was felt that it would be consistent with the beginnings of a learning community for teachers to negotiate expectations with the students and their parents. This involved some rethinking of teacher–student–parent relationships and the establishment of some common and agreed ways of relating to each other. It also meant some rethinking of the nature of learning and moving on from ideas about dependent/independent learning to ideas about co-dependent learning.

The following is an outline of the programme during the first school term in Year 11:

- *Lesson 1:* Getting to know you (as it is a senior high school all students are new to the school and are given a name badge); completion of the subject grid for the year; and an introduction to journal writing which is to be an ongoing feature of the programme. In the journal, students are asked to comment on three positive things they have discovered about the school and three things they would like to know.

- *Lesson 2:* Sharing of journal entries from the previous lesson and group discussion of problem-solving exercises; discussion on qualities and strategies of effective teachers, and reflection on the idea that you can be your own most effective teacher. In the lesson, students are asked to recall a teacher they found particularly effective in previous years and list the qualities and strategies that teacher brought to the learning environment. At this point the idea of co-dependent learning is introduced with reflection on the qualities and strategies that they, as students, can bring to the classroom.
- *Lesson 3:* Journal writing to review ideas on qualities and strategies of effective teachers; strategies for constructivist learning based on 'before learning reflection' (What do I already know? What do I need to know? How can I learn it?) and 'after learning reflection' (What have I learnt? How did I learn it? How will I use it? Any concerns, questions or issues?)
- *Lesson 4:* Introduction to the idea of a 'tool-kit' of skills and strategies for learning; mind-maps: principles, uses, purposes and advantages of mind-mapping for learners; constructing maps of subjects. There is discussion of strategies to help memory and stimulate connections across subject areas.
- *Lesson 5:* Reproducing mind-maps from the previous lesson; introduction to learning modality and learning style (visual, auditory, kinaesthetic); building up knowledge of self as learner.
- *Lesson 6:* Revisiting earlier topics to see what's working; pre- and post-learning reflections, mind-maps, range of learning styles and strategies.
- *Lesson 7:* Timetabling activities; weekly timetabling of negotiable and non-negotiable times; explanation of assessment procedures and regulations; planning an assessment booklet/calendar.
- *Lesson 8:* Writing assignments; referencing with the Harvard system, constructing a bibliography, appendices, abstract, editing drafts, presentation; question analysis, research strategies and dealing with the marker's response.
- *Lesson 9:* Individual work on an assignment to put the study skills into practice.

A second major aspect of building a learning community at Trinity Senior High was the creation of a charter of relationships. Rather than relying on rules and regulations (as in bureaucratic culture) an alternative approach is to promote a relationship-centred culture. The process is important here, and it involved students and teachers in inquiry into the nature of relationships that should exist in the school. The process began at an orientation camp with students in groups of about fifteen discussing and agreeing upon statements of how everyone in the school community should deal with one another. Back at school the charter was drawn up as follows.

At Trinity Senior High School we seek to treat one another:

With respect
by:

> having consideration for people and their opinions
> treating others as we would like to be treated
> being honest
> maintaining confidentiality
> making others feel comfortable and confident
> giving others the opportunity to speak
> listening carefully
> taking responsibility for our own actions

Fairly
As equals
Without discrimination
by:

> recognising individuality
> being tolerant
> valuing differences
> using authority fairly
> accepting mistakes as part of learning
> not judging others
> allowing everyone a positive input
> dealing with all in a friendly manner

As friends
by:

> listening
> letting others know they have been heard
> wearing a smile
> being approachable
> greeting people
> respecting opinions
> having a sense of humour
> making time for fun

With consideration
With understanding
by:

communicating in a friendly manner
being open
being positive
respecting privacy
accepting people as individuals
allowing people to be themselves
being receptive to suggestions and beliefs of others

CONCLUSION

What I have sought to do in this chapter is to contribute to a developing theory of learning community, overview some of the significant literature and ideas including our own work on teachers' workplace learning, and present two strategies in use in local schools at the present time. My hope is that readers will have found some useful insights and perhaps thought about some strategies which might help them undertake the exciting journey towards transforming their schools into learning communities.

Note

I wish to thank Joan Dalton and David Anderson for their helpful suggestions in this chapter, and also teachers Frances Robertson and Rod Whelan for their important contributions.

References

Battistich, V., Solomon, D., Watson, M. and Schaps, E. (1995) Schools as Communities, Poverty Levels of Student Populations, and Students' Attitudes, Motives, and Performance: A Multilevel Analysis, *American Education Research Journal* 32: 627–58.

Child Development Project (1991) cited in A. Kohn (1996) *Beyond Discipline: From Compliance to Community*, Association for Supervision and Curriculum Development, Alexandria, Va.

Dalton, J. and Anderson, D. (1998) 'Today's children: Tomorrow's adults', unpublished paper, Hands on Educational Consultancy (personal communication).

Dalton, J. and Watson, M. (1997) *Among Friends: Classrooms Where Caring and Learning Prevail*, Armadale, Australia: Eleanor Curtain Publishing.

Habermas, J. (1987) *The Theory of Communicative Action*, Vol. 2, 'Lifeworld and System: A Critique of Functionalist Reason', trans. T. McCarthy , Boston: Beacon Press.

Hargreaves, A. (1996) 'Transferring knowledge: Blurring the boundaries between research, policy, and practice, *Educative Evaluation and Policy Analysis* 18 (2), 105–22.

International Advisory Council on the Quality of Public Education in NSW (1994)

Johnson, D. W. and Johnson, R. T. (1989) *Leading the Cooperative School*, Edina, Minn.: Interaction Book Company.

Kohn, A. (1996) *Beyond Discipline: From Compliance to Community*, Association for Supervision and Curriculum Development, Alexandria, Va.

Marsick, V. and Watkins, K. (1990) *Informal and Incidental Learning*, London: Routledge and Kegan Paul.

McLaughlin, M. (1993) 'What matters most in teachers' workplace context?', in J. W. Little and M. W. McLaughlin (eds) *Teachers' Work: Individuals, Colleagues, and Contexts*, New York: Teachers College Press.

NSW Department of School Education (1995) *Schools as Learning Communities: A Discussion Paper*, Sydney: Training and Development Directorate.

Professional Development: First Substantive Report, Sydney: NSW Department of School Education.

Raywid, M. A. (1993) 'Community: An alternative school accomplishment', in G. A. Smith (ed.) *Public Schools That Work: Creating Community*, New York: Routledge.

Retallick, J. (1994) *Workplace Learning in the Professional Development of Teachers*, NBEET Commissioned Report No. 24, Canberra: AGPS.

Retallick, J. (1997) 'Workplace learning and the school as a learning organisation', in Faculty of Education, *Exploring Professional Development in Education*, Wentworth Falls, Australia: Social Science Press.

Rosenholtz, S. J. (1989) *Teachers' Workplace*, White Plains, N.Y.: Longman.

Sergiovanni, T. J. (1994a) 'Organisations or communities? Changing the metaphor changes the theory', *Educational Administration Quarterly* 30 (2), 214–26.

Sergiovanni, T. J. (1994b) *Building Community in Schools*, San Francisco: Jossey-Bass.

Sergiovanni, T. J. (1996) 'Learning community, professional community and the school as a centre of inquiry', *Principal Matters* (April), 1–4.

Smith, G. A. (ed.) (1993) *Public Schools That Work: Creating Community*, New York: Routledge.

Starratt, R. J. (1996) *Transforming Educational Administration: Meaning, Community and Excellence*, New York: McGraw-Hill.

Whitmore, K. and Crowell, C. (1994) *Inventing a Classroom: Life in a Bilingual, Whole Language Learning Community*, York, England: Stenhouse Publishers.

7

DIFFERENT AND EQUAL

Fostering interdependence in a learning community

Pamela Wells

INTRODUCTION

The traditions of learning together as a community by talking and doing have been a constant part of society through the ages. Whether it was the ancient wisdom of native cultures or the intellectual dialogues of Socrates and Aristotle, the focus was on the growth and thriving of the whole group whilst meeting the needs of, and extending the potential for, the individual. Though grounded in history the concept of learning communities is a current one, responding to the impact of the escalating rate of change, the necessity for effective interpersonal skills, an ever-expanding information database and the results of learning research.

In the last fifty years we have moved through the phases of the dependent learner and the independent learner, to the interdependent learner. The benefits of learning with, beside and from each other increase the individual's base control by providing greater options and flexibility for self-knowledge, interactions, acquisition and use of data and the development of a more global perspective. To collect a group of learners together and give them the label of community or team is, however, insufficient. The final potential of any group can be enhanced if time is spent on developing the skills and concepts of 'interdependency'.

In this chapter I will suggest a range of skills and related strategies that can be used to foster interdependence within a learning community. For each skill/strategy, I outline implications for the development of staff and I offer some processes that can be used for students as well. From my experience over many years as a consultant, I point out some indicators of achievement in successful situations and I consider some common causes and reasons for failure to become interdependent and learn as a community.

THE NEED FOR INTERDEPENDENCE

Past educational practices have left a legacy of stability, competition, labelling, learning in isolation and a strict focus on content. For future success, these need to be recognised and counterbalanced by a conscious commitment to working together, whilst recognising the valuable differences that exist within any human grouping. In an interdependent learning experience, the development of the key skill of perspective-taking leads to an understanding that difference does not mean inequality. This is crucial when we consider the elements of human nature, the challenge of communication in a group and the individual differences in learning modes. The goal of personal involvement demands that the whole group consider the establishment of a safe environment, opportunities for the development of trust and a commitment to equity. The expectations of individual responsibility need to be formalised and the individuals involved need to see benefit in examining their current beliefs and long-held mental models. Internal and external dialogue, the creation of networking strategies and the definition of a common language and vocabulary develop communication patterns which together form a framework for the formation, transition and sustained maintenance of community.

Learning about the differences in others enables us to examine the structures of our own thinking and modes of operation and practice, which in turn prepares us to become more effective members of the greater community. A learning community cannot grow from edict, neither can it be a forced change. An environment needs to be created in which people may wish to take advantage of the options and then the interdependence can be fostered. This is a nurturing process. The process needs to take account of the impact of the ideas on the individuals concerned and create strategies which will best suit the particular situation and bring these elements into a dynamic, living and evolving whole – a learning community.

THE SKILL OF PERSPECTIVE TAKING

In West Virginia a Cherokee elder told me to learn to listen; to listen and to think. It took a while to understand that this meant I had to listen: to turn down the internal chatter in my mind, to hear the words. To listen to the speaker – what do these words, coming from this person, in this place or situation, at this time, mean for me? Then I had to consider the gifts I was receiving, to think about the information, the modelling, the lessons and their relevance for me. This mode of listening is a far cry from the way we frequently engage in Western dialogue, waiting to work out the next polite time we can talk. Covey (1992) identifies this as an essential habit in 'Seek first to understand, then to be understood'. Understand the message of the speaker to you, so that your response can be relevant and therefore heard in true terms. Mackay (1994) suggests that the reason most people do not listen is that we are not talking to them, we are having a polite conversation with ourselves.

The skills required to take an exchange from the realm of listening to perspective-taking involve moving from ignoring, through pretending to listen, through partially listening, through active and reflective listening, to empathic listening. This high-order skill means a transfer of focus from I to thee, from me to we. It recognises that we need to value the speaker's rights to their thoughts, to listen in a non-judgemental way and to try earnestly to walk a mile in their shoes.

At this level of perspective-taking, we receive challenges to our deeply held values, a push from our comfort zone and an expanded database (because even if the thoughts concur with ours, the language expressed differently will enable us to hear the thoughts anew). We have an opportunity to affirm or to change our understanding partially or completely. We could believe more strongly in our original considerations; their validity could be reinforced. We could take into account the alternatives offered and create a new position for ourselves. We cannot lose in exchange if we understand the opportunities that perspective-taking offers and recognise it as an essential skill in all human interaction. It becomes paramount in maintaining the focus of learning together in a community when the blocks of threatening change, insecurity and obvious differences arise.

Strategies for perspective-taking

Exercises that encourage learners to give their natural response to a situation and then to hear or view the thoughts of others can be organised using the basic concepts that underpin the targeted project area as the topic. For example if a team is exploring the topic: 'the improvement of the availability of learning for all students', some concepts that will need delineation are learning, inclusion, difference, expectations. Taking an historical viewpoint and investigating the development of those concepts in society over the past fifty years can allow individuals to track their background and highlight the differences in personal attachment to the value or otherwise of certain practices and beliefs.

A strategy I used in one large community involved dividing the members into decade groups, relating to the major period of their own schooling. Individuals used the PMI (plus, minus, interesting) technique of De Bono (1986) to gather their memories, and then joined their decade groups which produced overviews of what they would keep from each era as being of value, what they hoped would have disappeared because these practices were remembered as harmful or now outdated, and what is presently in use that they admire. Discussions that followed the sharing of memories clearly showed the vast differences that exist between decades, and sometimes within them, given a variety of circumstances. New small groups were formed that included members from each period, and these visited each displayed report in turn. Lively explanations, sheer disbelief and debates arose. One outcome was a greater awareness of the background to members' education and the reasons for the definite differences in perspective that they take on any particular issue. Another was an awareness of the long-term influence our past experiences have in determining the strength of our convictions regarding certain issues currently under consideration, such as multi-age classes, integrated curriculum, technological interventions and the focus on lifelong learning.

Presenting someone else's ideas can also aid perspective-taking because the listening has to include monitoring for tone, and interpretation for commitment and priority. This type of sharing can have the whole community taking part in discussion in pairs, covering the same topics. This is followed by reporting in small groups, presenting one's partner's ideas rather than repeating one's own contributions. The task of being an advocate forces each member to consider anew the alternative viewpoint.

When we can verbalise both sides of an argument, presenting an even better case for the opposition, then we can come to better solutions. Johnson and Johnson (1995) emphasise the practice of creative conflict-resolution in detail, highlighting the power of feedback and restatement. Students need to practise these skills regularly, as they remain very self-centred (I, me, now) if the benefits and methods of interacting with others are not identified, modelled, used and reflected upon. One simple and short exercise is based on the current knowledge about a topic. It is better if the initial exercise is a creative-thinking exercise, to establish a common benchmark: for example, list as many uses for a brick as you can, using it for anything other than to build something. The students then share their lists, count the different responses and create a small-group total. Students quickly see that there is an advantage in joining their ideas together, that we do think differently and they become aware of the different pathways that were taken in interpreting the task.

CREATING A SAFE ENVIRONMENT

Educators know the importance for their students of risk-taking, and that it is okay to make mistakes in the learning process. This same balance of challenge and support needs to be applied to the members of any learning community, particularly one in which teachers are facing changes at conceptual, practical and professional image levels. Johnson (1995) emphasises the importance of the notion of intellectual integrity which translates as having the courage to say 'I don't know ...(that word), or...understand what you mean by that, or...but I got lost – can you go back to...'. As professionals we need to be more diligent and stringent about our use of language, especially as it pertains to our own learning about learning together. The establishment of common terminology, even if the meanings are group specific, is essential for common dialogue and the prevention of later experiences of confusion and division. Such a discussion also enables individuals a safe entry task, that is, to share their understandings and to be affirmed for their prior knowledge.

It may sound clichéd, but the thousand-mile journey really does begin with one step (Lao Tse). That first step should be a small one. Begin with the possible; begin with one step. There is always a limit; you cannot do more than you can. If you try to do too much, you will do nothing (Ouspensky 1989). The first challenges need to be timely, achievable, relevant and resourced. The importance of the last facet cannot be emphasised too strongly. Curriculum changes or the pedagogical development of teachers that begin as excellent systemic initiatives often fail to be transferred to the general school population in a homogeneous fashion, for lack of implementation and maintenance considerations.

The same imperative applies to smaller groups of educators working within schools or institutions. To take on one change project, or to consider one aspect of professional practice about which to learn more, is wise. The act of collaboration initially brings sufficient challenges without hampering a successful outcome by selecting an unwieldy topic of action research. The creation of a suitable pathway and/or a set of options to allow individual choice obviates many of the blocks to participation. Prior considerations of time, method and support mechanisms eliminate the responses 'When? I don't have the time!' 'How can I do that?' or 'Why doesn't the boss just tell us?' These considerations might also include a delineation of the boundaries of the project, that is, what are we not including, not covering, not considering. Such decisions give permission to stay focused, without inhibiting the making of connections to other areas or extensions within the field of study.

Strategies for a safe environment

It is important that each stakeholder in the learning community be involved in the planning and decision-making for a safe environment. If one is left out, then the community is already compromised. The most basic beliefs will often prove to be the starting or blocking point. If we proceed initially with caution and enable early success for each member, the momentum will build and motivation will become internalised.

In a case where two different institutions became one, there was a great need to affirm and validate the past and at the same time to create a common field of action and to define the future boundaries of operation.

One exercise that proved fruitful was the development of staff norms in specific terms for nominated situations. The first area examined was the staff meeting; the one, regular, weekly occasion when the whole community met together. Individuals began by answering the questions 'How do I wish to be treated?' and 'What are the meeting behaviours that annoy you?' With what could they be replaced? Replies such as respect, patience or kindness were required to be clarified as observable, behavioural indicators like 'Wait until the speaker has finished', 'Remember that we are discussing a procedure not personalities'; and 'Turn up on time and finish at the agreed-upon time'.

Students need to be involved in establishing the rules and goals for their participation. It seems sensible also to identify the types of celebrations that will work for the whole group when these rules and goals have been achieved. These could become a part of the classroom display, a permanent reminder of the reasons and ways we are working together.

BUILDING TRUST

Self-disclosure breeds self-disclosure which in turn breeds trust (Cooper 1992). Participants need to be given opportunities to share in pairs, and then in small groups within the learning community. One-to-one interaction has high levels of responsibility, and when coupled with the cross-sharing amongst four people provides a field to safely test the levels of trust established. The nature of the content of the sharing should be focused on the individuals' understanding and their own experiences, rather than an assumption of prior knowledge or the introduction of new material. The spiral of difficulty here is a continuum that works from the safe through challenging to personal, the latter being quite confronting in the workplace.

Initial sharing could be on expectations from the project or definitions of learning. In our current cultural climate as professionals one of the greatest challenges is to share our successes, the practices which positively affect learning and changes in student attitudes. A personal clarification of areas of concern or weakness in our practice requires a higher order of risk-taking to share, especially if those concerns relate to establishing a level of confidentiality within the group. This can be negotiated one to one in separate conversations, or it can be a whole-group decision according to agreed-upon guidelines.

Strategies for building trust

Working in pairs in a programme of observation of each other's work practices, and providing feedback on specific aspects chosen by the recipient, can be a means of developing trust. Recognising the effective practices of a colleague enhances mutual respect. It seems helpful if the members of the coaching pair can come from different roles or different areas of responsibility within the workplace, for this can diminish the potential for comparison or distraction.

In tertiary settings, the opportunities for objective feedback may be easier to organise in regard to time but more difficult in some areas where the underlying principles of adult education need to be explored in detail. Within a school system, this coaching can be arranged so that teachers from unaligned key curriculum areas in a secondary setting (such as English and science), or from separated grade levels in primary schools (such as Year 2 and Year 5), work together. If the backgrounds are sufficiently diverse regardless of setting, then when they visit each other's classes, the teachers are less inclined to be comparing the students' performances with their own, or making judgements on the content delivery or acquisition.

It is also suggested that the teachers in pairs have a basic respect for each other, but not necessarily a detailed knowledge, either personal or professional. Again, this keeps the focus of the observations specifically trained on the practice, on what can be observed and heard in the teacher's behaviour and the performance. The underlying message of the exercise is that we are working on improving practice, not the person. Affirmation of successful practice can be included in the feedback, to affirm and support whilst offering a challenge to change.

Another strategy to build trust is to construct a whole-group agreement and understanding that it is an advantage to make mistakes, for through this we explore and test reality freely. During the learning period, it is wise to offer students the opportunity to share their chosen methods prior to completing an exercise, to share their responses with others to check for options, to self-correct and to verbalise their final decisions. They should feel able to try in the first place, but also learn to trust their ideas with others without fear of retribution or put down. Students generally feel more confident to work totally independently in times of assessment, as they have established a feeling of self-worth.

ACCEPTING INDIVIDUAL RESPONSIBILITY

The individuals within the community have to accept responsibility for their own participation, for stating their needs, for delineating their goals and for representing their own points of view. If the establishment of a safe environment has been successful, then the willingness of individuals to raise difficult issues, or to respond objectively at moments of crisis, will be enhanced. Each needs to be aware of the potential for receiving support from others, and the co-requisite task of providing support when asked. If the goals of the current project are well defined and specific in terms, then it is easier for members to dialogue safely and in a non-judgemental way, as any discussions can be task oriented, objective and restricted to observable outcomes. Monitoring our own language, assessing whole-group needs, and discussing the processes of reflective listening and objective criticism all seem to minimise the need for conflict resolution.

Strategies for individual responsibility

Each learning community is organised differently, yet within each there should be a structure of partners, with each aligned to another pair, forming a small team, as in the cooperative learning structure, Think Pair Square. This means that each member has one person to talk with, another pair to turn to if their partner is absent, and someone who can update them if they themselves have been absent. These small teams are not necessarily homogeneous and could be formed by use of a random technique. We need to work beyond our comfort zones, in content, process and collegial networks if we are to grow through confronting difference. It sometimes occurs that, after initial explanations and discussions for all, a small community of learners forms within a larger group. Updates of information to the larger group as to the current progress or observations realised by the community alleviate the problem that the project could be viewed as separate or precious.

One of the more difficult responsibilities, regarding interdependence in a learning community, is to acquire the skill of representing your point of view assertively. Within a working establishment, people often fail to put forward their ideas, or if they have done so, acquiesce quickly and quietly to other opinions. Their reasons will usually be about the maintenance of harmony and the effective closure of an issue or meeting, though it is often an example of shelving participation and responsibility. At times of decision-making in a learning community, there is no room for omission or compliance if the whole is to be sustained. To be realistic about your goals, and the roles and tasks you undertake within a community, is another area for consideration. To be unclear, or to overcommit, only harms the objective and the potential for success, for the individual has to take small steps, as does the community. Constant monitoring for mismatch of theory, practice and goals should be an individual concern.

The community needs to undertake frequent pauses for evaluation. Reflection, whether on the part of individuals or the group, can be a part of all meetings, both at the beginning and at the end. The keeping of journals by members will aid the effective sharing at community times. In schools there are some teachers who still carry the dependent model within their experience and self-image as teachers and learners. For these educators some of these responsibilities need to be actively addressed by leaders, without denigration. For example, it is true but regrettable that many staff meetings, especially in secondary schools, still consist of the principal, standing near the doorway, reading a set of notices and making some forthright pronouncements, followed by announcements from a chosen few. Meanwhile the remainder wait in silence, compliance agreed to as the most expedient method of achieving a shorter meeting time. This valuable time is the only occasion where the staff meet, and yet formal agendas and such circumstances prevent their meeting at all.

Faculty meetings do not replace the need to share across curriculum divisions, for matters for whole-group consideration such as welfare, learning, management or community issues are universal. Information can be distributed in written form, either as paper notices or emailed to faculties. If 'they won't read it' is the response from a leader who needs control, then it will elicit that very reaction from staff, for the teachers know they are viewed in that light of irresponsibility.

The formats used by educational systems need to be revisited and to be examined with special regard to the underlying messages they are giving to all participants in the community. How much more effective would these brief, but optimum, times be if the whole staff engaged in dialogue and sharing in small groups, on issues of interest and impact for all? We know too much about leadership and effective performance management to depend on outdated models. The leaders need to predict the outcomes of continuing to use them, and the participants need to accept responsibility for demanding quality in their times together.

CHANGING MENTAL MODELS

Change takes time (Fullan 1991), and many educators in professional positions do not model the concept of self-as-learner. For some, like new teachers in large classes, it is a matter of survival, and they cling to the controls that they remember from their own schooling years. As in general life, our early experiences and initial training as educators set up expectations, standards and tenets that continue to influence our thoughts, responses and judgements, especially at times of change or challenge. My generation of educators trained at a time when the edict was definitely 'A quiet classroom is a good classroom'. At that time, a teacher's success was gauged by the presentation of obedient and compliant students, engaging diligently in data and content acquisition. The teacher was in turn working within their island, isolated from their fellow teachers, receiving decisions from a headmaster and affirmation of their ability from an inspector – a passive echo of their past life as a student.

Despite the enlarged knowledge base of the 1990s, the old mental models continue to influence, unless they are acknowledged and confronted as being inappropriate for this time. Yet is it surprising that teachers, working within a system of which they were a part as clients, find it difficult to join together and risk-take as a community of learners?

Teachers are often those who responded well to the school culture as students and were able to emerge as good products of the system. At a meeting with a school friend recently, we were discussing the challenges of education today, in particular the notion that teachers are often people who have never left school. In trying to clarify the power of past experiences, we remembered a particular teacher whose attitudes, modelling and pronouncements had impacted on our own self-images and our concept of education. Comments like 'The temperature dropped fifteen degrees when she came into the room', and 'She told me I was pathetic at poetry – and I believed her...until eighteen years later when I finally got the courage to take an English Lit. major', at no time denied the fact that she was an excellent teacher for the industrial era: product centred and label driven. The teacher's legacy was her formula for page layout: date, rule a line, leave a line; heading, rule a line, leave a line. Subheading, rule a line, leave a line. Begin. We both laughed as we began to recite it – very quickly, without pause for breath or thought after thirty years – for this had been dictated to us at the beginning of every lesson, six periods a week for three years. That this was the top class in a selective school, and that we were 16 years of age, did not deter the teacher from her assumptions. Her premise was that we would not know what day it was, nor the title of the novel we were studying, nor that, despite our so-called intelligence, we would remember the process. The tragedy arose from the fact that this was the same lady who gave us the phrase 'Flexibility is the sign of intelligence'.

This control, that undermined confidence to behave independently, disparaged individual thought or interpretation and represented a black and white view of right and wrong, left myths that impact today. Working together is cheating, there is a right way to do something, we all work one way, and the subjects of economic rationalism reign supreme – these are all beliefs that need confronting if we are to learn to deal with the world of today and the future. The classroom methods of the 1950s, 60s and 70s would be outdated for current student expectation, and yet many teachers return to the tried and true even when student behavioural responses fail consistently. The long-term power of these mental models is demonstrated when they prevent teachers from working together to solve the problems of inclusion and learning for all students.

Strategies for changing mental models

One exercise which requires teachers to look into the mirror of their mental models asks them to consider the legacy they would like to leave to their students. The whole group examines a list of current needs for survival in current and future times, both in the workplace and in the broader society, monitoring it for evidence of inclusion and successful completion in their practices. Such lists usually include learning how to learn, flexibility and adaptability, self-knowledge, interpersonal skills, the ability to work in teams, basic skills of acquisition of knowledge, creative thinking, problem-solving, decision-making, trend recognition and leadership for all. Students have the mental models of their early childhood already influencing their behaviours. With less to 'unlearn' or confront, they can be encouraged to identify the basic elements of their learning and self-management, and supported to adjust to frequent changes in routine and the people with whom they interact. Nearly everything in nature attempts to return to a state of stasis, and even in chaos there is order. Young children need to be given the dignity of safety and the challenge of change so they can realise the priorities of life. These do not include: 'What colour pen do you want us to use?' or 'How wide a margin do you want?'

DIFFERENT SITUATIONS – DIFFERENT PROCESSES

When we join a community, we do so usually from choice – sports clubs, community groups, places of worship, cultural groups or hobby/pastime classes. We know we do not have to be involved with everyone; we each have a clear purpose in joining and a goal in mind. Our actions and roles within the group will be to some degree set by its nature and our commitment or preparedness to participate. Learning communities exist in many different forms and situations, and each defines its strategy of process differently.

It is important to realise the fluid and evolving nature of a learning community. Often, an individual might be surging ahead as the group at large is taking two steps back, and vice versa. There might be a specific area of expertise chosen for investigation by the whole group, or a general commitment by each individual to select a facet of their professional practice for examination, reflection and action research. It is true that some schools survive where the staff have never had a discussion about learning, teaching styles, the recognition and the modelling of values or common expectations for students, teachers and parents. These are still learning communities, representing one end of the continuum.

Strategies for different situations

How can a learning community be created in a large staff? In one secondary school, a team of teachers volunteered to be trained to work with Year 7 on a thinking skills programme which would be timetabled and considered as part of the assessment and reporting process. Later the remainder of the staff asked to be given an overview and some joined the programme in following years. The initial cadre found that the project developed to include consideration of teaching strategies, transformation of the programme to maintain its current relevance, the needs of pupil preparation and links with the primary feeder schools, and involvement in a university/school programme. In this case, an ongoing expectation of learning and development for small groups of staff became a norm. The size and membership of the learning community varied with changes in the focus areas though the role of the leaders and facilitators has remained fairly constant. The whole school population has supported the community by giving it permission to exist without interference, and the original programme continues, many years later.

How can a learning community be formed if people work on different sites? Understanding the difficulty and the necessity of galvanising a regional team of consultants all working in different fields and from different sites, one director chose to make their learning community a priority. Regular sessions (one or two days) were scheduled in which together the director and the consultants confronted values, personal mental models, expectations and the micro- and macro-contexts for their work. The planned continuity allowed for complex sharing of information, an increasing scale of challenge, and a change from opportunity for participation to expectation of commitment. Given a specific timeframe of two years, as much time was devoted to team closure and celebration at the end as to team formation and building in the beginning.

INCLUSION: HONOURING DIFFERENT STYLES OF KNOWING AND LEARNING

Many teachers have realised the importance of extending their teaching styles to cater for a variety of individual differences (Butler 1996). They are aware of the need to ensure that in each unit of work they have: linked to prior knowledge and instigated goal-setting techniques; allowed entry for the visual, auditory and kinaesthetic learners; and offered a range of activities that will engage the multiple intelligences. They have recognised their one preferred style of learning, whether it be 'concrete sequential', 'concrete random', 'abstract sequential' or 'abstract random', and challenged themselves to provide their students with a balance across the options.

This last area of knowledge needs to be considered as paramount when we focus on inclusion in community. By personally studying learning style, individual teachers can come to know many of the conscious and unconscious biases and prejudices that guide their thinking and decision-making. This variance in operational mode creates the basis of our value judgements of others as we work and learn together. A 'concrete sequential' will look at the work space of a 'concrete random' or the regular responses to deadlines of an 'abstract random' and wonder how they have the gall to collect their pay. In turn, 'abstract randoms' (themselves seen as away with the fairies) view the 'concrete sequential's' dependence on schedules and regulations and think, 'Life – get one!' An 'abstract sequential' who loves to think and learn but cannot value the practice exercises of playing silly games is often viewed as not working as hard as everyone else. The 'concrete random's' challenges to the status quo and seeking alternates or the unexpected are seen as divisive rather than evolutionary.

Each of us has a preference for the way we operate or manage our tasks, and each has the choice to vary that mode in different situations. Each mode has gifts to bring to the group; each has areas of annoyance for others who are strongly operating within a given style. Each learning community must be aware of this fundamental potential for good and for conflict.

Strategies for inclusion

This important aspect of learning communities impacts highly on the development of interdependence, for its essence is respect. The ability to learn from, with and by each other will depend on the participants' ability to walk side by side, even if their thought processes and practical modes of operation are not directly linked. Some practical activities where the process enables the members to see that problems can be solved in different ways, but still come to the same or an equal conclusion, are valuable in the initial stages of community development. Taking on a new project which will involve learning for all members can also reveal the strengths and weaknesses of various approaches. This also places everyone on an equal footing and diminishes the insecurities of the meek and the overconfidence of the known experts or vocational blockers. In several schools we have used the introduction of cooperative learning structures and the teaching of social skills to achieve this end.

The promise of more effective classroom management and easier access to assessment for teachers and students creates interest, whilst the external focus on the students allows the principles and beliefs about working together as a team to be discussed with ease. The realisation that the community of teachers as learners needs to model these behaviours and beliefs for students does not take long to eventuate. The maintenance of the state of commitment requires consistency, persistence and in some cases insistence by the team as a whole.

Yet the final rewards can be far greater than imagined in the beginning. One principal shared with me after a two-year period of collaboration: 'When you suggested we deal with the conflict between the teachers, by starting with a focus on students, I thought this to be avoidance, and yet now the whole school's culture has changed, teacher welfare being the greatest achievement. It's a different place to be!'

INTRODUCTORY STRATEGIES:
THE FACILITATOR'S ROLE

A leader would do well to consider the use of an external facilitator in the forming and norming (i.e. coming together under a commonly agreed-upon framework) stages of a community as this enables all members to participate equally in the process. Regardless of their ability to complete the strategy, the leader needs to take part in the initial discussions as an equal. Once they take the central role, they create and reinforce distinctions. With the use of a facilitator, no one member is outside the dialogue. Taking Max DePree's (1992) leadership task of 'define the reality, say thank you at the end and be a servant in between', it is important for the implementation and maintenance of the community that a leader explore the servant/facilitator role in detail.

After a five-year period in Australia and the USA debriefing adult postgraduates who had attended long-term workshops and courses, I have found that the following list of impact factors is seen by the participants as essential to the successful creation of a community of learners.

The facilitator:

constantly encouraged us
listened and responded to each person
accepted all responses as valid
called everyone by name
let us give answers from our own expertise
gave personal experiences, was accessible
stated rules and norms at the beginning
allowed the level of task to match our performance
always told me the expectations of exercises/projects
kept us on task with time reminders (prior and during exercises)
modelled work with me, not for me
let us be responsible for our own learning
gradually increased the level of difficulty
provided a logical procedure and opportunities for constant review
gave us a tremendous sense of belonging
was committed to an outcome, but flexible about the final format
was consistent and patient
devolved responsibility
connected with people as humans

interacted individually through journal sharing

was caring, sympathetic, sensitive to individual differences/needs

had real fun – lightened the tension

modelled behaviours

provided safety with the use of a partner first, and then a small
team, then the larger group

used random grouping

made available expertise in small chunks at appropriate times

gave us frequent and lengthy opportunities to talk about what we
had learned together and as individuals

catered for all learning styles and modes through instructions and
activities

brought people in from the periphery, each in a different way

was respectful re closure, waiting for the speaker to finish

sharing grounded us in our similarities

made us consider our judgements

allowed individuals to think on their feet

kept living records of our discussions – publicly available for later
reference or adjustments

increased/decreased the pace

monitored our performance – gave personal feedback in private

monitored/physically moved around to visit each member

intervened rarely, then to clarify/redirect

observed us in groups and gave feedback (often humorous) on the
process

provided synthesis and closure at the end of the day

demonstrated with prior knowledge, previous experiences – real-life
examples

encouraged us to take risks, and to stretch

modelled techniques for inclusion/conflict resolution

gave each of us special recognition (from peers and facilitator)

customised the process for us

was the continual questioner, stimulated our thinking.

Implementation and maintenance strategies

Process is different in each new learning community situation. Common
factors that have high impact are membership (whether it be voluntary,
systemic or Machiavellian), leadership, size/composition, long-term
goals/short-term objectives, timeframe and expectations. These differences
should be influential in the selection and adaptation of implementation
strategies for learning community projects because they will be impacting
on the interdependent nature of the group.

Identifying real-task challenges provides a relevance that motivates and gives meaning to the work. Most of the topics for these can come from the current management plans of schools or long-term goals from schools' vision statements. One successful theme has been the provision of services to the students or student learning. This allows the initial focus to be away from the teachers' own practices, but very quickly the inevitable link is made and the terms of reference expanded.

Experiences that push participants out of their comfort zones highlight the need to deal with change and alter their perspective on basic precepts. Having staff switch areas of expertise or swap roles whilst staying within their general domain can aid this. For example, the person in charge of sports can swap roles with the school production director, or someone who has spent most of their career in one part of the Kindergarten to grade 6 school can change to another.

The introduction of an experience that is new for everyone will allow all to consider their own learning modes and those of their colleagues. Several have realised the benefits of this when they have undertaken new approaches that included catering for the multiple intelligences, cooperative learning or philosophy for the younger students. Regardless of the topic it is important that there be identification of a specific project with an identified timeframe and a small-steps plan for its implementation.

Maintenance strategies that support the individual and whole group will need to cover the continuation of implementation themes with some new considerations. The team formation within the community needs to be regularly changed, perhaps on a term or semester basis. Team-building over time needs to continue, but not to the same degree as at the beginning of the year. Reflection techniques can become more complex and personal with the passage of time, and the sharing time for this can be extended with the development of trust and commitment to the process. Interdependence requires that solutions for the resolution of conflict be included as both internal and external differences become apparent.

The mark of a successful classroom involvement with cooperative learning is a request for further work on conflict resolution. When the class is teacher directed and teacher controlled there is little room for conflict, and only when the safety nets have been released do the conflicts arise. Once students understand that they own their own choices, then heated debate can ensue. Remember how well-behaved students suddenly misbehave, if their own teacher is replaced by a casual for any reason? A myriad of reasons can explain this phenomenon, but chief among them would be the sudden release of control factors that leave the previously docile students without mechanisms for choice and order. Their former good behaviour was not an internalised understanding nor a set of options to be used in a variety of situations.

Evaluation markers can sustain a community if the indicators of success were initially established collaboratively. Flexibility in timeframes and outcome delivery seems to prolong commitment. Using honest appraisal as individuals, pairs or the whole group, evaluation goes beyond assessment to focus on what has been achieved, why or why not, and how the next step needs to be altered. Celebration of early small successes, celebration of persistence and more celebration of accomplishment at the end can be positive steps in the fostering of interdependence. Teachers are so involved with the outline of the next goal, they know the individuals and lesson content in such detail and are for the most part so orientated to the welfare of others, that they rarely take the time to stop, turn around and see how far they have come. Keeping records of early attempts, journal entries and ad hoc conversation snippets can support the realisation of progress if these are revisited at well-spaced intervals throughout the year.

We need to strive for a balance, both as individuals and as a group. The greatest test of cooperation or valuing comes with meeting greater difference. It is easy to include students who love your lessons as they are; it is not so easy when students have different expectations and require you to change your methodology.

When it comes to adults learning together in large groups such as a secondary school staff, this tolerance level is tested in the extreme. I have seen four definite responses – acceptance, lip-service, backbiting and confrontation. Without tolerance, a project may as well fold before beginning (and often does). The understanding that different is equal, and that the meeting of difference is the magic that forces us to react, think and perform at a higher level, is the real meaning of interdependence in a learning community.

References

Butler, K. (1996) *A Teacher's Guide for Learning Styles*, 2nd edition, Melbourne: Hawker Brownlow.

Cooper, C. (1992) 'Principals and effective leadership', keynote address to NSW Principals' Conference, Wollongong, April.

Covey, S. (1992) *The Seven Habits of Highly Effective People*, Melbourne: The Business Library.

De Bono, E. (1986) *CoRT Thinking*, New York: Pergamon Press.

DePree, M. (1992) *Leadership Jazz*, New York: Bantam Doubleday Dell.

Fullan, M. (1991) *The New Meaning of Educational Change*, New York: Teachers College Press.

Johnson, D. and Johnson, R. (1995) *My Mediation Notebook*, Edina, Minn.: Interaction Book Company.

Johnson, N. (1995) 'A celebration of teaching and teachers as learners', keynote address to South Coast NSW Principals' Conference, Wollongong.

Mackay, H. (1994) *Why Don't People Listen?*, Sydney: Pan Pacific

Ouspensky, G. (1989) *The Fourth Way: The Teachings of G. I. Gurdjieff*, London: Penguin.

8

PURPOSE AND PROCESS IN EFFECTIVE LEARNING COMMUNITIES

Paul Shaw

Why do good ideas about teaching and learning have so little impact on educational practice and student learning? In a recent article, Elmore argues that there is a 'significant body of circumstantial evidence that points to a deep, systemic incapacity of U.S. schools, and the practitioners who work in them, to develop, incorporate and extend new ideas about teaching and learning in anything but a small fraction of schools and classrooms' (1996: 1). Here in Canada, for instance, after six years of developing curricula, presenting workshops featuring local consultants and renowned outside experts, a large school authority found little evidence in an evaluation that a new writing curriculum was implemented effectively in all but pockets of classrooms and a very few schools (Worsnop and Hannon 1988). We live in times of ubiquitous change, yet paradoxically we have had little success in bringing about change in the learning of students in all but a few classrooms or schools.

Perhaps it's the way that we have approached change. Linda Darling-Hammond tells us that:

> Two very different theories of school reform are working in parallel and sometimes at cross-purposes...One theory focuses on tightening the controls: more courses, more tests, more directive curriculum, more standards enforced by more rewards, and more sanctions. These reformers would improve education by developing more tests and tying funds to schools' test scores...A second theory attends more to the qualifications and capacities of teachers to developing schools through changes in teacher education, licensing and certification processes...professional development schools, efforts to decentralise school decision making while infusing knowledge, changing local assessment practices, and developing networks among teachers and schools.
>
> (1992: 22)

This first view asks teachers to comply with new procedures, standards and a narrower, less compelling curriculum. The difficulty here, as McLaughlin (1990) explains, is that you can't mandate what matters. You can't mandate the creative problem-solving, the collaborative learning and the engagement that is necessary for a school full of teachers to adapt and create a more effective programme. The second view, although fraught with difficulties, holds much more promise. It is about developing the capacity of teachers and schools to fulfil their agreed-upon purposes. Capacity is about building the knowledge, skills, norms, habits and values necessary to adapt, renew, rethink and inform our classroom practice with respect to improving the learning of all students. These reflective capacities are the outcome of sustained, rigorous enquiry and dialogue with curious and committed colleagues leading to informed strategic thinking and action. In short, it is the enactment of a learning community.

The promise of learning communities is the hope they provide in ensuring that good ideas about teaching and learning will indeed have an impact on educational practice. In a recent paper, Fullan (1997: 228) argues for schools to attend to teaching and learning in a sophisticated in-depth manner by:

1   building greater organisational capacity; and
2   developing greater external support.

Although this is a complex undertaking, he views effective schools as those having vibrant internal learning communities plugged into two-way relationships with external networks. Fullan is careful to point out that the support both internal and external embodies socio-emotional as well as technical (intellectual) factors.

Successful learning communities enact and bring meaning to the nature of community. Clear and common purposes, that guide shared decision-making and the day-to-day work values, ongoing support mechanisms and collective action are all defining characteristics of community.

The learning organisation holds out the promise that:

- What is learned will impact on the organisation as a whole. From the student's perspective the potential to experience strong and consistent messages with respect to what counts as progress, the value and nature of enquiry, and expectations and skills of working cooperatively, amongst other learning traits, is significant.
- The commitment to and preoccupation with reading, experimentation with practice, enquiry, reflection, and assessment of progress and continuous improvement will become embedded in the way the organisation does business.

- Learning will be collective and therefore not person dependent. As such the potential to tackle issues of succession of staff and/or leadership can be addressed.
- The organisation will have a built-in means of remembering, and thus opportunities for the development and enactment of guiding ideas over the long term are possible.
- An infrastructure for learning can be embedded in the work of teachers and schools, and thus the potential for an adaptive self-renewing organisation is strong.
- The learning infrastructure that provides for more formal learning will provide powerful spin-offs in terms of the creation and support of school culture that values and engages in the many opportunities that accrue for informal dialogue and learning.
- Classroom practice and student learning will be affected in systemic ways.
- The in-depth learning in one area of learning will be more easily transferred and applied to practice in other areas of the programme.

With this much promise it is hard to imagine why it is so difficult for schools to embrace the school as a learning organisation. But the learning organisation presents many threats to the current work of the school. It asks school personnel to work in new ways, to form closer and more collaborative working relationships and networks; it requires a new and more pervasive infrastructure including a serious rethinking of the use of time in schools; it presents a paradox of more responsibility and collective action on the one hand versus a loss of independence on the other. Schools that choose to become learning organisations will need to develop processes that will acknowledge and minimise the threats while maximising the promise of such significant change.

The concept of colleagues learning from one another runs counter to much of our experience as teachers. Typically, our training was short and often we were left alone by and large, to sink or swim in our first years of teaching. We discovered that our workplace fosters isolation and professional privacy (see Hargreaves 1994 and Little 1982). Indeed the recent Royal Commission on Education in Ontario (Begin and Caplan 1994) which devoted an entire volume to the professional learning of teachers, found that the way in which schools and school days are organised supports the isolation and professional privacy of teachers who tend to work, plan and teach individually (vol. III: 3). Their recommendations with respect to the professional development of teachers included ongoing professional development as a requirement for continued certification. How the newly formed College of Teachers achieves this, whether their requirements will go beyond personal learning expectations in valuing and supporting the collective learning of school staffs as they develop their own capacity with respect to the work of the school, remains to be seen.

In Ontario, much of teacher learning has taken place outside the workplace in discrete and isolated activities such as workshops and additional qualification and graduate courses. Whereas these experiences may or may not be well received by the individual and may or may not affect the individual's classroom practice and procedures, it is clear that they do little to contribute to the schools' collective capacity to adapt and respond to the diverse and changing needs of students and society in general. These experiences are based on a set of assumptions (see Fullan and Stieglebaur 1991) that suggest an expert is required in order for teachers to learn; workshop and course designers know best about what teachers need to learn; learning can occur in contexts isolated from the teachers' work; teacher learning takes little time and new innovations can be learned in one or two workshops; and follow-up to the more formal learning is either not required or will occur spontaneously.

In contrast, job-embedded staff development, in bringing the collective learning of participants to bear on the work of the school, is a necessary condition for organisational learning, and focuses teacher's learning predominantly on and about their classroom work. Job-embedded learning is predicated on very different assumptions that include:

- the purpose of the learning being critical if participants are to engage in the process
- acknowledging and using the collective wisdom, range of experience and needs that participants bring to their learning
- participants learning and practising what they perceive to be relevant to their personal and professional needs
- recognising that learning takes time and involves ongoing examination of, questioning of and reflection on present practice
- teachers needing to put into language their theories, concepts and perception of classroom practices and procedures; valuing and building relationships with other participants
- the values, norms and skills that underpin the school as a learning organisation permeating the entire work of the school.

This set of assumptions more closely aligns with our knowledge and understanding of adult learning principles and therefore is more likely to succeed.

CONDITIONS AND CONTEXTS FOR CREATING LEARNING COMMUNITIES

In a recent paper, Peter Senge identifies three conditions that are necessary in order for an operating environment for learning to be built. The first is the emergence and articulation of guiding ideas.

> The power of guiding ideas derives from the energy released when imagination and aspirations come together...the promise of learning organisations is, at least in part, the promise that the power will become deeply and widely embedded in a way that rarely, if ever, happens in traditional authoritarian organisations...Guiding ideas are arrived at gradually through much reflection on the issues and opportunities with respect to context and purpose. They are insightful, informed, and emerge as shared intent. They are fostered by leaders who lead as teachers, stewards and designers.
>
> (Senge 1996: 51–2)

How schools and school systems develop these guiding ideas is a troubling issue. Schools in Canada are overwhelmed with the pace and the complexity and, at times, conflicting nature of the changes. Disenchantment with educational reform is a natural outcome when the system is experiencing giant ideological shifts in purposes and directions that undermine the values and practices that have previously been embraced. Add to this the overload and fragmentation that characterise today's schools and we begin to understand the context for dealing with any kind of change (Fullan 1997).

The development of guiding ideas in schools is hampered not only by such overload and fragmentation but frankly because schools are simply not organised in ways to permit the adults who work there to bring imagination and aspiration together. For what we aspire to for our students is not a question that can be answered quickly or lightly. It's a question that requires considerable ongoing thought, debate and information; that can only be answered collectively, when the diversity of views, experiences and passions that surround the work of the school are made known in constructive and informed ways.

Many schools with which I work have never considered the question, whilst others have simply discussed it at the occasional staff meeting and drafted a mission statement that adorns the classroom doors. Purposes for schools are arrived at through the process of action, of working together to make a difference for our particular students in our particular community. The uncovering of purpose is informed by the learning experience of the student. This means that data are constantly collected and examined by colleagues, not only of achievements and outcomes but also of classroom practice and procedure. Senge (1996) sees these guiding ideas as arriving gradually over time through ongoing reflection. But the purposes of schools are many, so, as Fullan (1993) tells us, the morally compelling purposes have to be uncovered and acted on. Most teachers will commit time, energy and passion to the new, if they see that this commitment will help their students in terms of their knowledge, competence, sense of well-being and social justice.

Guiding ideas, when informed both internally in terms of the work of the students and the school and externally by the modelling of best practices and the learning from current research, can produce powerful purpose and commitment to the work of the school. An important component to the development of guiding ideas then is to network broadly. Teachers must realise they are part of a wider environment that they can influence but also one that can inform and contribute to the purposes and work of the school.

Senge (1996) identifies the conscious attention to learning infrastructure as the second component required to build operating environments for learning. This begs the question as to what these learning processes would look like, how they might be implemented, studied and emulated in other schools. With few exceptions, this infrastructure simply is not present in schools. The infrastructure necessary for teachers to enquire, question, examine and evaluate classroom practices and procedures, particularly from the perspective of the learner, is complex and in many ways quite unlike how most schools presently operate.

Time and its use are key to the infrastructure. The time necessary to build the depth of understandings needed to enable teachers to make informed judgements in complex situations is more often than not completely underestimated. During the past three or four years, schools in Ontario have been implementing a new approach to the education of grades 7 to 9 students called Transition Years. Although loosely thought of as 'destreaming' by some, the approach to transition years suggested by the Ontario Ministry of Education and Training is far more complex. For instance, the approach requires knowledge of adolescent development (physical, emotional, social and intellectual), multiple intelligence, new forms of assessment and new classroom practices and procedures. A prime assumption of transition years is that curriculum, teaching and services can be delivered based on adolescent needs and characteristics (Hargreaves *et al.* 1996).

In a secondary school I visited recently, a number of subcommittees had been appointed to investigate the developmental needs, classroom pedagogy and assessment procedures, etc. These committees had six weeks to gather their information. Each of the various subcommittees reported to the Heads Council (department heads plus principal) but not to each other. A few weeks later the heads published the recommendations they had chosen. Teachers were appointed to teach the grade 9 students and the timetable was written. It comes as no surprise that, in not attending to the requirements of professional and organisational learning, the grade 9 transitions year programme has been perceived as unsuccessful from day one.

The amount of teacher learning required to implement the transition year programme effectively is enormous and more often than not seriously underestimated by participating schools. A description of the knowledge, disciplines, assessment and evaluation procedures, classroom practices and skills would likely far exceed the requirements of a Masters degree. Yet, year in and year out, schools take on complex change initiatives without any possibility of those involved having the time to learn the new programme well. With respect to transition years, I would be surprised if more than a few teachers had even ten hours of time to learn to make the informed judgements necessary for the programme to succeed.

Recently, some of the schools in Ontario have developed a pact with their community to enable the teachers to have a half a day a week for the joint work of the school. Their concerns and willingness to restructure their use of time raises the question as to how most other schools can continue to assume responsibility for major changes in practice (e.g. new curriculum, outcome-based assessment procedures, technology) without ensuring that the teachers responsible have the necessary time to learn to do the work well. In a time when the work of the school and the learning of students is falling under ever closer scrutiny it seems foolhardy to take on major innovations without ensuring that we have the capacity of infrastructure required to succeed. I am arguing that schools require at least a hundred hours per year for the shared learning and work of the school. Such a modest proposal will require schools to rethink how they structure their school year, week and day.

A second component of the infrastructure for learning is the school organisation itself. Is the school organised in ways that permit, promote and enhance the opportunities for teachers to plan, to share responsibility and to evaluate jointly the programme for student learning? Does the school organisation both permit and foster students of different ages to work together? Is the school organised in ways that both enable and encourage teachers to learn about their craft and to observe each other engaged in the practice of teaching? Many teachers speak of the schedule or timetable as if it has a life of its own. Schedules and timetables can be made to do just about anything. It really depends on the purpose and commitment of those who construct them. Likewise we are still building schools based on assumptions that have underpinned teaching and learning in times past (e.g. classes will consist of approximately thirty students who will meet regularly in an isolated classroom with four walls, a chalkboard and a door). But can existing and new space be configured to help make teaching and learning more visible to all; to enable technology to be used effectively; to enable teachers to share and respond to practice; to plan, teach and evaluate collectively?

A third infrastructure component comprises the roles, relationships and responsibilities by which we feel constrained or empowered. Often traditional roles and the expectations that surround them truly inhibit the development of the kind of enquiring collaborative work that characterises the collective learning that is the underpinning of the learning organisation. Adaptive organisations can redefine roles and related relationships to accommodate the evolving purposes of the school. For instance, recently in Ontario, several school districts have replaced the traditional subject department head role with multidisciplinary team coordinators and/or facilitators. This facilitative role is seen as eliciting more participatory enquiry, learning and decision-making. As a result, teachers are becoming comfortable with roles and responsibilities that include the collective examination of classroom practice across grades and subjects.

Senge's (1996) third way of building an operating environment for learning is the building of a domain for taking action. In the school this domain is very much about roles, relationships and processes. The degree of commitment by one's colleagues to move to action is greatly enhanced when in fact they perceive that they are stakeholders in the enterprise. In larger schools, this means that the work of the school (by which I mean work whose core is teaching, adult and student learning) has to be designed, nurtured and moved to action by a stakeholder representative team. Who are the stakeholders? How will they be represented? What roles will representatives play? How will each staff member be able to participate? How will leadership emerge and be shared? These are important questions, the answers to which in part will be determined by the roles, relationships and processes.

Commitment is about ownership and participation. Participation is about equity, about being valued for one's ideas no matter how diverse, and about contributing to significant decision-making. It is therefore inherently about building mutually trusting relationships among and between all stakeholders. In the context of the school, this requires administrators who listen; who model, demonstrate, encourage and value curiosity, inquisitiveness, diversity in ideas and openness; and who are adept at designing and facilitating a process of participation whereby participants contribute in an informed manner to the core decision-making and learning of the schools. For teachers, it is necessary to value, model, demonstrate, encourage and engage in the same kind of behaviour. It is very much about assuming a collective responsibility for student learning and the work of the school.

Process is a significant obstacle for schools in building an operating environment for learning. How do you engage a hundred teachers in a meaningful ongoing dialogue with respect to student learning? How do you sample frequently the learning of students and efficacy of classroom practices and procedures across the school? How do you tell if the latest innovation has made any difference for the students? Can ongoing assessment become a tool for adult as well as student learning? Can teachers make craft knowledge visible to themselves and colleagues? How will good ideas be identified and be able to permeate the entire organisation? How will we know if we are doing better? These are the kinds of questions schools have a great deal of difficulty answering, in part because of the traditions of our workplace culture discussed above, but also in attempts to re-culture, because of the lack of knowledge, skills, norms and values about how to engage one's colleagues in a substantive and sustained process. Process obviously requires design for which training is available. But it also requires certain kinds of relationships, perhaps the most difficult aspect of which is the building of trust among participants.

The culture of isolation referred to above is pervasive, and to participate in a learning community requires the development of high levels of trust, support, tolerance, shared purpose and values, openness, respect and inclusiveness. Recently, I have had the opportunity to create new projects between the university and a local school board. In answering the questions of potential participant teams, the bottom line for them was 'Will this require us to share our practice with colleagues?' The representative teams saw this aspect of the project as being the most difficult for their colleagues to embrace.

In summarising the above discussion on context and conditions, I draw on the work of Watkins and Marsick (1993), who identify the features of learning organisations as:

- culture that is learning oriented, with beliefs, values and policies that support learning; for example, tolerance for mistakes as opportunities for learning and problem-solving (within well-defined financial limits); a surfacing of hitherto undiscussable topics; empowerment; and policies that reward knowledge and the sharing of knowledge as well as rewards for performance
- structure that is decentralised, lean, and focused on team relationships
- strategy that is entrepreneurial, focused on innovation and learning
- enhanced slack or reserves in the form of employee knowledge, literacy, and willingness to learn and to solve problems; technology that frees people to learn and to work more productively; information systems that permit the widespread collection and sharing of data and sharing of learning gained; and financial reserves dedicated to learning.

STUDYING SCHOOLS FROM WITHIN

What are the experiences of the learners in our schools? How and to what extent do they solve problems? (Or do they solve problems?) How do they use texts? In what contexts do they read and write? For what purposes and audiences? Do our students work independently? Interdependently? Are they becoming lifelong learners? What are the practices that help or hinder the above? How would we know? How will we know if the new curriculum or innovation positively affects some or all of our students? These are often troubling questions to school practitioners and yet the answers are readily available, right in our classrooms. The capacity that Elmore (1996) seeks, in order for schools and practitioners who work in them, to develop, incorporate and extend new ideas about teaching and learning can be developed through deliberate and systematic gathering, examination of and reflection on evidence that informs questions of student learning and/or classroom practice. Cochran-Smith and Lytle support this position when they state that what is missing from the knowledge base for teaching are the voices of teachers themselves, the questions teachers ask, the ways teachers use writing and intentional talk in their work lives, and the interpretative frames teachers use to understand and improve their own classroom practices (1992: 292).

This form of enquiry has been called practitioner research (Anderson, Herr and Nihlen 1994), action research and classroom enquiry to name a few. It can take many forms but one helpful definition is provided by Kemmis and McTaggart:

> a form of collective, self-reflective enquiry undertaken by partici- pants in social situations in order to improve the rationality and justice of their own social or educational practices, as well as their understanding of these practices and the situations in which these practices are carried out. Groups of participants can be teachers, students, principals, parents, and other community members – any group with a shared concern. The approach is only action research when it is collaborative, though it is important to realise that the action research of the group is achieved through the critically ex- amined action of the individual group members.
>
> (1982: 6)

One significant part of evidence-gathering is the ongoing assessment procedures used by teachers across the school. By assessment procedures, I mean something other than marks, grade point averages and percentiles. As Earl and Le Mahieu suggest, the true meaning of assessment suggests images of teachers observing students, talking with them, and working with them to unravel their understandings and their misunderstandings – transforming assessment into an integral part of learning that offers detailed feedback to the teacher and the student (1997: 162). As people learn and move from neophytes, to novices, to experts, assessment can give them models of performance and can clarify the assistance, experiences and forms of practice that they need to improve and extend their performance.

The challenge for schools is to create the infrastructure described above to ensure that the time, commitment, value and passion required for this work is in place so that the work is meaningful, morally compelling and truly addresses the core issues of teaching and learning. For as Anderson, Herr and Nihlen remind us, the promise of practitioner research is also subject to misuse (1994: 7). It has the potential to bring to light important theories about practice that have been too long discredited as informal theory or 'teacher lore'. It can empower school practitioners by helping them discover their voices and resist attempts at de-skilling. It can build collegiality and a common community of learning among practitioners, which in turn provides a model of enquiry for students. On the other hand, it can also become one more teacher in-service scheme that can be packaged and taken on the road; another implementation strategy cooked up by management to 'build ownership' in schools for the latest centrally mandated reform. It can become just one more expectation – one more thing teachers are expected to do.

PRINCIPLES AND PRACTICES OF A LEARNING COMMUNITY: ONE SCHOOL'S APPROACH

A recent study (Shaw 1997) of one learning community illustrates many of the key principles that underlie their success. This particular community was a 500-pupil, K–6 (kindergarten to Grade/Year 6) school located in a lower socio-economic suburban area that is unique in terms of cultural diversity, transiency of the population and the need for instruction in English as a second language. The entry point for the shared work of teachers was to address issues of literacy. There was a formal structure created for the teachers with respect to their professional learning that was called 'professional growth'. The design and focus for the professional growth sessions was established by a planning and design group (of seven stakeholders including the principal) who were responsible for both representing the views of their colleagues and setting direction for the work. Staff dedicated seventy hours a year to engage in the process. A focus for the sessions was agreed to and would at times be sustained for many months. Approximately one week prior to each session an agenda was published that would include:

a   a focus question for the session

b   a request for participants to gather some data, e.g. student work; an audiotape of a teacher/student writing conference to bring to the session
c   a professional reading, pertinent to the focus question, e.g. a paper from *Language Arts* or the *Reading Teacher*.

Sessions lasted for two hours. The time for these sessions was created equally from in-class and out-of-class work time. Each session involved teachers of all subjects and grade levels.

Typically, each session began with a sharing of the data (artefacts, stories, students' work, etc.) brought by each participant. Teachers would talk about matters such as their interactions with students, the design of their programme and the responses of students. Within the first few months the focus of the conversation had shifted to the conferencing process that occurs between teacher and child(ren) with respect to the learner's writing. Teachers shared audiotapes and videotapes of their interaction with students. The professional dialogue identified such issues and opportunities as whose talk dominated the conversation; how the teacher might respond to content and critique conventions; when and if it was appropriate to encourage revision; when and if it was desirable to broaden the range of genre; how to support the students' skill as writers without assuming ownership for the text; how to help the students find their own voice as writers and build an appreciation of authorship and audience. As each session proceeded the nature of the dialogue would turn to the implications of the experiences shared. Often preferred practices were identified and a general agreement reached for the faculty to collectively try a new technique or procedure. During the first year, where issues surrounding trust and purpose had to be clarified and developed between the participants themselves and between participants and the new principal, each session closed with time to reflect on the process.

A key element of professional growth in our case study was that teacher talk was informed by current research through relevant reading, periodic interaction with acknowledged experts in the field, and regular opportunities to attend conferences and to visit exemplary classrooms. With respect to the professional readings, the selection of relevant papers that would inform the dialogue was important. It was not uncommon to free a participant to spend an afternoon in the university library searching for an appropriate text or to call Canadian and/or out-of-country professors to recommend material. One of the impacts of the professional reading was to create a 'reading culture' within the school.

A second component to informing the dialogue was the interaction with local, national and international university faculty and other educators. Important here was the role that visiting educators were asked to play in the process. This role was one of equal participant, who would listen and respond when their experience or research would contribute to or clarify the dialogue. The use of audio (telephone) conferencing, where a distant educator could listen to questions from the staff and respond for all to hear, is another illustration of this relationship.

The final component of informing the dialogue was to reach out to view and learn about best practices through classroom visitations and attending conferences. As described above, teachers brought some form of data from their classrooms for each session. This process of evidence-gathering was at times spontaneous and varied and at other times deliberate and systematic. Spontaneous and varied approaches would occur when the participants were asked to bring evidence with respect to the focus question or general topic. Deliberate and systematic data-gathering was less common; however, when used, it appeared to provide a compelling basis for action. Clearly one of the outcomes of gathering and sharing evidence across all classrooms and programmes was making classroom practice transparent and visible to one's colleagues.

THEMES EMERGING FROM THE CASE STUDY

This case study points to ten themes which I believe help us understand the conditions necessary to participate and what it means to participate, teach, learn and renew ourselves within an enquiring community of practice.

Shared purpose

It is clear from the data that teachers in our case study were strongly committed to improving the literacy learning of all students. It can be argued that the frequent gathering of data made the needs of the students extremely transparent and thus subject to description, assessment and reflection. It may also be argued that in an inner-city-like community, addressing issues such as literacy development was morally compelling to the participants (Fullan 1994). One might speculate that the high degree of commitment to the enquiry process and collective refinement of practice was deeply influenced by the perceived importance of the work. The major preoccupation for all participants was the examination and learning about classroom practice and student learning.

Craft knowledge became visible

Regular gathering and sharing of classroom practices, procedures, student work and observations through audiotape, videotape, artefacts and narrative clearly made the craft knowledge visible to the entire staff regardless of role or position. The observable nature of the data enabled participants to question, examine, discuss, refine and reflect upon their own and other professional practice. The focus on the observable (behaviour) as opposed to belief was perceived by participants as enabling difficult issues to be examined with safety and comfort.

Collective responsibility for the programme led to consistent experiences for learners

The professional growth planning team (a vertical stakeholder team) steered and evaluated the process, created the focus questions and set priorities for programme implementation across the school. Participation in the professional growth process ensured that responsibility for the schools programme was jointly shared by all staff. Clearly, the collective learning of the participants impacted on all classrooms and all students in systemic ways. One of the perceived benefits of this collective responsibility was that it is not person dependent. As all were involved in the construction of a shared reality some members could leave, but the knowledge, values, norms and passion remained with the group.

Honouring adult learning principles

Participants in setting the agenda, choosing their data, developing focus questions and reflecting on process and practice were able to experience self-directed learning in a process that recognised their wide range of previous experience, skills, interest and competencies. They were able to participate in a supportive environment that was free from personal criticism or threat with respect to competency. Participants made reference to feeling calm and/or safe, to recognising that each held a different position with respect to the practice under examination and that this was okay.

Networking broadly

The ongoing focused dialogue was informed by best practices (visitations, workshops and conferences), relevant current research (readings, expert visitations, audio (telephone) conferences) and data collected from classrooms across the school. This professional dialogue continued throughout the work day but also included interactions with pre-service teacher candidates and the many visitors (some 4,000 plus) who visited the school and were curious about classroom practices and procedures. Of note is the relationship with outside experts. They were university professors, researchers, authors, etc. Their role was to fit into the inquiry process. They were asked to observe the data, listen to the conversation and respond, if they were able, to the questions that were asked of them. This relationship placed the outsider in the role of participant, as an equal member of the group.

An enquiring collaborative workplace culture

There is an ample evidence that the professional growth process described above contributed significantly to the creation of an enquiring collaborative culture. This manifested itself outside the professional growth process in the form of continuing dialogue and reflection on practice, a natural questioning of school policy and procedures, a spontaneity in the formation of representative groups to problem-solve and manage the business of running the school, and a confidence in taking risks in classroom practice. This commitment and preoccupation with reading, experimentation with practice, enquiry, reflection, assessment of progress and continuous learning became embedded in the way the school did business.

In-depth learning in one area of enquiry transferred readily to other areas of the programme

Visitors to our case study site wondered, as did the participants themselves, at the efficiency of focusing on literacy for such a long period. But literacy pervaded the entire day for students and teachers. When the Provincial Ministry of Education mandated a new science curriculum, this was seen by the professional growth planning team as an opportunity to explore the genre of enquiry through the mediums of reading, writing, speaking, listening, presenting and reflection.

Principles and practices underlying the learning process permeated the work of the school

The professional growth process required a high degree of trust among participants; norms and skills of collaboration, enquiry, reflection, self- and collective examination; and the valuing of the purposes and work of people with a diversity of viewpoints. The trust, norms, skills and values necessary for this process to succeed could not be developed in isolation from the entirety of the school's work. Whether it was building the budget or timetable, planning and implementing the creative arts programme or developing a collective problem-solving approach to discipline, the same norms, skills and values had to be used if the trust and the process was to be developed and sustained.

Transforming our view of teaching

The interviews clearly illustrate the shifts that teachers made with respect to how they viewed their work and thought about classroom practices and procedure. For many, the 'discovery' of the intellectual nature of the task of designing and enacting a child-centred programme brought a renewed

163

passion and optimism to their teaching. For experienced others, comfort with a newfound 'tentativeness' surrounding their practice replaced a more concrete or definitive view of how they proceeded in the classroom. Most spoke of the confidence to take risks and the security of knowing that you were not alone in the dilemmas faced daily. Troubled children were seen as a joint responsibility as opposed to 'my problem alone'. All spoke of the shared vision, shared practice and common language and experience. In addition, many spoke of a new, more trusting relationship that emerged with their colleagues as well as their students. For all, the opportunity to participate professionally not only in the learning community but also in the decision-making and work beyond their own classroom was valued.

Building capacity within the organisation

One perspective on this job-embedded professional growth process was that it was about capacity-building. The process itself was viewed as building the knowledge, skills and attitudes of the participants to deal effectively not only with literacy issues but with future change issues. The capacity of an organisation to respond to needs is dependent on the collective will and learning of the people who work there. This case demonstrates both a process and something of the experience of those who worked collectively to continuously improve their practice and the learning of the students. This continuous capacity-building included improving know-how (the sharing and processing of knowledge and information) and was not done in isolation but included strong ties with universities, authors and professionals in other contexts.

WHAT IT MEANS TO BE A MEMBER OF A LEARNING COMMUNITY

In retrospective interviews, teachers who participated in the case study summarised above had very strong feelings about their experience in the learning community. They spoke of the evolving commitment and satisfaction in building common understanding, language and practice; about the intrinsic excitement and value of discovering, some for the first time, the reflective and intellectual engagement that accrues from examining one's practice with a view towards designing and implementing, in an informed manner, classroom practices and procedures that were perceived to be more responsive to the learner's needs. They came to value having frequent access to current and relevant research (information) and the sense of control that emerged with respect to their work.

Sergiovanni (1992) argues that in any organisation what is rewarding (i.e. intrinsically) gets done. This sense of control extends beyond one's practice.

Faced with overload and fragmentation as described above, the collegial control that emerges through the development of shared purpose (Senge 1996) with respect to the work of the school and the ongoing change agenda ensures confidence and reward in one's work. Participants also spoke of the importance and challenge of building the trust that was necessary in making their practice visible to others.

Trust is about respect; it is about feeling free to share one's accomplishments and failures without fear of criticism. It is very much about participating in relationships with others that are predictable. It was helpful in the case study above that participants were able to discuss the issue of trust and find ways of acknowledging and accepting the differences within the group. Differences were acknowledged as positions with the clear understanding that no one position was better or worse than another. Over time there was a sense that 'we are in this together' and it was acknowledged that the gradual development of a 'shared reality' was extremely important to the development of trust. Also important was the predictability of the process. Participants came to trust the process as they knew that the purposes, sequence of events and expectations would not change from time to time. Participants also spoke of the subtle pressure within the developing culture to engage in the shared work. One teacher spoke in a positive way of the 'gentle coercion' to participate and share their practice.

There can never be enough time for the learning community to gather data, share, respond and reflect about their work. The extension of the teacher's role by way of the examination of practice and student learning, by engaging in various teams to establish priorities, design activities, create new and more supportive structures in order to support the work of the professional community, leads to a serious intensification of the teacher's and school's work. It has been argued elsewhere (Hargreaves 1994) that intensification creates chronic and persistent overload and the potential de-skilling of the teacher. However, in the case of the learning community, the subsequent empowerment with respect to classroom practice and control with respect to the purposes of the school suggest more positive opportunities and outcomes. Ultimately the participants in our case study saw the experience as an 'opportunity to grow' that was unlike anything they had experienced in other contexts.

ISSUES AND OPPORTUNITIES IN CREATING LEARNING COMMUNITIES

In recent collaboration with colleagues (Hargreaves, Shaw and Fink 1998) we have developed seven frames or lenses through which to examine the work of schools. It is helpful to use these perspectives when considering the issues, opportunities and required strategic thinking and action with respect to the creation of learning communities. The perspectives are purpose, passion, politics, culture, structure, leadership and the learning organisation itself. Practically, successful learning organisations are not added on to existing school practices but rather are pervasive ways of thinking, acting and learning that permeate all aspects of the school's work.

Learning communities become effective and sustain when the purposes are evident and owned by all participants. In schools this means getting at the very heart of teaching and learning, that which is morally persuasive to all. Getting at the core work of the school requires the ongoing, collaborative examination of classroom practice and student learning. It requires an enquiring, trusting, collaborative culture where the norms, values and behaviour of the participants embrace open, honest and sustained dialogue about the purposes and work of the school. Such a professional culture can only succeed when it permeates the work of the entire school, and thus it has serious implications for how the school is structured, how decisions are made, and how opportunities for leadership emerge.

Schools that are successful learning organisations structure themselves around the professional learning of teachers and students. This manifests itself in the real time and processes that are developed to engage in job-embedded learning. But it also requires a structure that is adaptive and fluid, where the artificial boundaries of grades, divisions, departments and/or status have at least been diminished to such a degree that they do not impinge on the construction of a shared reality that will come to pervade the work of the entire school. This requires a thoughtful and honest response by all to the political reality that surrounds the work of the school. Whether it is building the capacity of and working with parents, or ensuring the board office consultant or superintendent has a commitment to the work, it is important to include and be responsive to all stakeholders in the community.

Learning communities flourish when the passion and diversity of views and experience are embraced and valued by all. This requires a high degree of trust which will develop over time with the emergence of more participatory roles and relationships. Authentic opportunities for leadership abound in the job-embedded learning school, particularly where the norms, values and processes required pervade the entire work of the school. Thus the traditional lines of authority diminish or disappear to be replaced by more collegial work and decision-making. Particular practical issues include the following.

Developing and supporting the ongoing dialogue

My colleagues call it good, honest, open, safe, talk (GHOST). Creating the conditions where adults learn best means developing contexts that are free of criticism, where the wide range of experience is valued and built on, where a diversity of views is encouraged and accepted and where participants are able to retain and use what they perceive to be relevant to their personal and practical needs.

Informing the dialogue

The quality of the dialogue is ensured by a focus on the learning experience of the students which is clarified and made cogent through access to current research and models/demonstrations of best practice. Access to current research can often be facilitated by working in partnership with individuals from faculties of education, perhaps through technologies such as audio conferencing and email.

Networking broadly

The idea that schools, staff developers and faculty members who share similar passions and desires, organised around powerful visions or themes for improvement, would build support networks to share their experiences is compelling. Technologies such as audio and computer-networked conferencing can produce very focused and relevant conversations and may shift both time and place for the ongoing learning.

Gathering data from the classrooms

If the engine of the learning community is dialogue then the fuel for the engine is data: data consisting of the student's work and behaviour and teacher interaction/intervention in the learning process. Communities of enquiry are constructed when participants are able to gather, question and reflect on similar data from across classrooms and a diversity of students. For instance, what is the experience, range of genre, nature of audience and quality of writing across a school on a given day? Such a slice of student learning from all classes and subjects in representing teachers' practice and procedure can, when shared, examined and collectively reflected upon, become a compelling vehicle for changing practice across the school.

Authentic data has a power and a reality that often will avoid the seemingly endless debates that occur when the dialogue focuses on teachers' beliefs and assumptions about teaching practice. More often than not the collection of one sample of data will raise many more questions and the need to gather other kinds of data. The challenge here is in building the capacity, i.e. the skills, procedures and processes, norms, values and structures necessary to do this work.

Documenting the journey

It is important that the ongoing conversation, data representation, pre-ferred practices and current research be documented over time. It is through this process of documentation, which can be both a collective and a personal one, that the collective learning and reflection over time occurs. The documentation also helps in organising, interpreting and evaluating one's data, learning and progress over time. It is through this process that participants can ensure that their collective work makes sense, is consistent and reliable, is valued and found credible by others, and is relevant to the work of the school and the questions that are being raised. It is when ideas are 'fixed in writing' that contributions can be critically reflected on, revised and extended.

Reflective practice

The United States Army call it after-action review (AAR); Marcel Proust said that 'the real voyage of discovery lies not in seeking new landscapes, but in having new eyes'; and Argyris and Schon argue that 'Reflection is essential to educators' capacity to think not only about their practice but also about how they think, their implicit theories, and the sense they make of their experiences' (1978: 38). Little-understood and hard-to-define reflective practice occurs when we have the opportunity to examine our practice, over time, through the benefits of different lenses and the experiences of others. Often, it manifests around the artefacts we collect, through lingering conversations and the time to distance ourselves and relive and re-examine our own behaviour and the behaviour of others. What is clear is that the links between instruction and outcome remain obscure and are anything but linear. The opportunity to reflect, through ongoing oral and written discourse, enables that which is inherently personal and pragmatic to be examined and to some degree to be replicated and experienced by others.

CONCLUSION

The learning organisation holds out the promise that schools might indeed be able to impact educational practice and student learning through the collective examination of and action about good teaching and learning ideas. However, for this promise to hold, it will be necessary for schools and educational authorities to rethink teacher development in the light of the importance of the collective examination of classroom practice within the school. The shared enquiry with respect to classroom practice described in this chapter requires attention to the guiding ideas that underpin the work of the school, the creation of the necessary infrastructure for on-site learning, and effective domains for moving easily and relatively quickly to action. The attention to process required in successful learning organisations demands the development within the faculty of the norms, values, knowledge and skills of participation and action.

References

Anderson, G. Herr, K. and Nihlen, A. (1994) *Studying Your Own School: An Educator's Guide to Qualitative Practitioner Research*, Thousand Oaks, Calif.: Corwin Press.

Argyris, C. and Schon, D. (1978) *Organizational Learning: A Theory of Action Perspective*, Reading, Mass.: Addison Wesley.

Begin, M. and Caplan, G. (1994) *For the Love of Learning: Report of the Royal Commission on Learning*, Ontario: Queens Printer.

Cochran-Smith, M. and Lytle, M. (1992) 'Communities for teacher research: Fringe or forefront', *American Journal of Education*, University of Chicago (May), 298–323.

Darling-Hammond, L. (1992) 'Reframing the school reform agenda', *School Administrator* 49 (10), 22–7.

Earl, L. and Le Mahieu, P. (1997) 'Rethinking assessment and accountability', in A. Hargreaves (ed.) *ASCD Yearbook 1997*, Alexandria, Va: ASCD.

Elmore, R. (1996) 'Getting to scale with good educational practice', *Harvard Educational Review* 66 (1), 1–26.

Fullan, M. (1993) *Change Forces: Probing the Depths of Educational Reform*, New York: Falmer Press.

Fullan, M. (1994) 'Co-ordinating top down and bottom-up strategies in educational reform', in R. Elmore and S. Fuhrman (eds) *The Governance of Curriculum*, Alexandria, Va.: Association for Supervision and Curriculum Development.

Fullan, M. (1997) 'Emotion and hope: Constructive concepts for complex times', in A. Hargreaves (ed.) *ASCD Yearbook 1997*, Alexandria, Va: ASCD.

Fullan, M. and Stieglebaur, S. (1991) *The New Meaning of Educational Change*, New York: Teachers College Press.

Hargreaves, A. (1994) *Changing Teachers, Changing Times: Teachers' Work and Culture in the Post Modern Age*, Toronto: OISE Press.

Hargreaves, A., Earl, L. and Ryan, J. (1996) *Schooling for Change: Reinventing Education for Early Adolescents*, London: Falmer Press.

Hargreaves, A. Shaw, P. and Fink, D. (1998) 'The Change Frames Project', report to the Ontario Ministry of Education, Toronto.

Kemmis, S. and McTaggart, R. (1992) *The Action Research Planner*, Geelong, Victoria: Deakin University Press.

Little, J. W. (1982) 'Norms of collegiality, and experimentation: Workplace conditions for school success', *American Educational Research Journal* 19 (3), 325–40.

McLaughlin, M. (1990) 'The Rand Change Agent Study revisited', *Educational Researcher* 5, 11–16.

Senge, P. (1996) 'Leading learning organizations: The bold, the powerful and the invisible', in F. Hesselbein, M. Goldsmith and R. Beckhard (eds) *Leader of the Future*, San Francisco: Jossey-Bass.

Sergiovanni, T. (1992) *Moral Leadership: Getting to the Heart of School Improvement*, San Francisco: Jossey-Bass

Shaw, P. L. (1997) 'Creating a community of practice: A case study', paper presented at the 6th National Conference in Educational Research in collaboration with International Network (PACT), Faculty of Education, University of Oslo, Norway (May).

Watkins, K. and Marsick, V. (1993) *Sculpting the Learning Organization*, San Francisco: Jossey-Bass.

Worsnop, C. and Hannon. E. (1988) 'Report on the implementation of K-6 Language Arts', Peel Board of Education, Ontario.

9

THE ROLE OF COMMUNITY IN ACTION LEARNING

A Deweyian perspective on sharing experiences

Garry Hoban

The notion of a community has commonly been used in educational literature over the last ten years to emphasise the importance of social interactions for learning in various contexts. In professional development schools, Darling-Hammond (1994) identified ten features which encourage the establishment of a 'learning community' for practising teachers: mutual self-interest and common goals; mutual trust and respect; shared decision-making; clear focus; manageable agenda; commitment from top leadership; fiscal support; long-term commitment; dynamic nature; and information-sharing and communication. Many of these features are consistent with Senge's (1990) features of a 'learning organisation' to foster collaborative workplace learning in the context of an ever-changing business world: systems thinking; personal mastery; mental models; building a shared vision; and team-learning.

In the context of a classroom, Bereiter and Scardamalia (1993) argued that children should act like research teams and be organised as 'knowledge-building communities' with the following eight features:

- a desire to research real problems; the use of new information produced from research
- a sustained period of engagement
- enquiry is driven by questions not facts
- participants are encouraged to produce their own theories involving mutual respect for the ideas of members
- the focus is on collective goals of understanding rather than individual learning
- participants often work individually but on related projects
- other sources of evidence are pursued such as the range of experiences among members.

The key feature of these communities, for children or adults, is the social emphasis on learning with members of the community *sharing ideas* embodied in phrases such as 'shared decision making; information sharing and communication' (Darling-Hammond 1994), 'shared vision and team learning' (Senge 1990), and 'collective goals of understanding and judgement' (Bereiter and Scardamalia 1993). Yet this feature of *sharing ideas*, central to any notion of community as an educational principle, is not a new concept. One hundred years ago, the importance of sharing ideas in a community to enhance personal learning was a fundamental educational principle in the writings of John Dewey (1859–1952).

The purpose of this chapter is to explain the educational principle of 'community' through the writings of John Dewey and to show how this principle is still applicable in contemporary writings about learning. First, I will outline John Dewey's theory of learning through experience focusing on the role of community as an educational principle which is a key platform in his theory. Second, I will explain a contemporary paradigm for professional development called 'action learning', which is common in the business literature, and show how Dewey's ideas on sharing experiences are relevant to this process. Finally, I will show how the action-learning framework worked in an educational context with teachers in a small high school science faculty who formed a community to sustain their workplace learning for over three years.

THE ROLE OF 'COMMUNITY' IN DEWEY'S THEORY OF LEARNING THROUGH EXPERIENCE

John Dewey wrote over forty books and seven hundred papers in his career, many of which related to his views about education. Over a hundred years ago his theory of learning through experience was clearly laid out in *My Pedagogic Creed* (1897), which established the platform for his educational writings during his career. In an earlier article he defined experience as an interpretation of an event or sensation which has meaning in such a way that

> it is not the sensation itself; it is the interpretation of the sensation. It is the part of meaning. If we take out of an experience all that it *means* as distinguished from what it is – a particular occurrence at a certain time, there is no psychical experience.
>
> (1887: 178)

This is not far removed from a current dictionary definition of experience, 'knowledge or practical wisdom gained from what one has observed, encountered, or undergone' (*The Macquarie Dictionary*, 1990: 322). In both definitions the distinguishing feature of experience is the interpretation or meaning which is gained from participating in some event or occurrence.

Dewey's theory of learning through experience was based on the assumption that learning involves an interaction between psychological and sociological processes. The example he often used in describing this interaction was children learning to talk in the community environment of an educated family:

> I believe that this educational process has two sides – one psychological and one sociological; and that neither can be subordinated to the other or neglected without evil results following. Of these two sides, the psychological is the basis. The child's own instincts and powers furnish the material and give the starting point for all education...I believe that knowledge of social conditions, of the present state of civilization, is necessary in order properly to interpret the child's powers.
>
> (Dewey 1897: 4)

It should also be noted that Dewey did not believe that there was a difference between children's and adult's learning, arguing that the same principles about learning through experience should apply (Dewey 1901).

The psychological process of his theory of experience was the personal experiences that an individual brings to a situation, and 'education, therefore, must begin with a psychological insight into the child's capacities, interests and habits' (Dewey 1897: 6). The sociological process involved interactions with others that consciously and unconsciously influence personal learning, which is embodied in the notion of a community. He believed that organising classroom activities based on the notion of a community generated motivation and a social spirit centred on 'sharing in each other's activities and each other's experiences because they have common ends and purposes' (Dewey 1916: 75). Hence, personal experiences are scaffolded or extended by social interactions with others.

Dewey was a strong critic of traditional education, highlighting that one of the problems is that schools focused on individual learning and were not organised in a way which encouraged students to interact as a community:

> I believe that much of present education fails because it neglects this fundamental principle of the school as a form of community life. It conceives the school as a place where certain information is to be given, where certain lessons are to be learned, or where certain habits are to be formed. The value of these is conceived as lying

largely in the remote future; the child must do these things for the sake of something else he is to do; they are mere preparation. As a result they do not become part of the life experience of the child and so are not truly educative.

(Dewey 1897: 8)

Accordingly, schools which are organised on the basis of a structured curriculum encourage inflexible teaching to individual children instead of a learning environment that fosters flexible teaching based on the sharing of ideas for learning as a group. Accordingly, he proposed that schools should be organised like a community with a curriculum that 'requires a well thought-out philosophy of the social factors that operate in the constitution of individual experience' (Dewey 1938: 21). Hence, education should be an interaction between psychological and sociological processes with 'teaching and learning as a continuous process of reconstruction of experience' (1938: 87).

It is interesting that many of Dewey's ideas written over a hundred years ago are consistent with current educational writings on learning communities. In particular the educative role of a community is to extend personal understanding by sharing ideas with others who may have different experiences and perspectives. This is how Dewey viewed the role of a classroom teacher who should provide subject matter and organise activities to broaden the existing experiences of children:

> I do not know what the greater maturity of the teacher and the teacher's greater knowledge of the world, of subject-matters and of individuals, is for unless the teacher can arrange conditions that are conducive to community activity and to organization which exercises control over individual impulses by the mere fact that all are engaged in communal projects...The planning must be flexible enough to permit free play for individuality of experience and firm enough to give direction towards continuous development of power.

(1938: 58)

In short, it is the social interactions with teachers and others interacting as a community which extend and scaffold an individual's personal experiences. In the next section I will explain how Dewey's educational principle of 'community' plays the same role in a collaborative professional development framework for adults called action learning which is common in the business literature.

'COMMUNITY' AS AN EDUCATIONAL PRINCIPLE UNDERPINNING ACTION LEARNING

Action learning is a collaborative framework to enhance the learning of individuals through experience in order to address personally relevant issues or problems. It is related to Dewey's theory of learning through experience, as action learning begins with an individual posing a problem or issue based on personal experiences and then sharing ideas with colleagues as a community, resulting in an action plan to address that problem. This process has been used extensively in business contexts with small groups of three to seven participants meeting regularly to help each other improve their work practices (Revans 1981, 1982; Pedler 1991; Zuber-Skerritt 1993; McGill and Beaty 1995). This collaborative type of workplace learning has been explored in various business contexts: executives in a textile company (Lewis 1991); supervisors in an electronic firm (Boddy 1991); doctors in a hospital (Winkless 1991); university students in a Masters of Science course (Thorpe and Taylor 1991); and insurance agents attempting to improve the quality of their service (Schlesinger 1991).

There is little reference to action learning in educational literature except in business management courses for higher education. One reason is the confusion that it is the same as action research, which predominates in educational literature (Zuber-Skerritt 1993; Gregory 1996). Action learning is similar to action research as both have cycles of action and reflection, but in action learning the focus is on the social process of learning in a small team, not conducting research by systematically collecting and analysing data. Hence, action learning involves a group of colleagues working together to address the personally relevant problems of individuals and encouraging them to reflect on their practice, share ideas and then put these into action. In effect, participants in an action learning group or 'set' act as consultants for each other to enhance the way that individuals reflect upon, analyse and learn from their experiences (McGill and Beaty 1995).

There are four educational principles which underpin an action-learning framework – *reflection*, *community*, *action* and *feedback* – which interrelate so that each principle enhances learning from the other three. The first educational principle, *reflection*, means individuals analysing their own experiences to identify the reasons for the way they conduct their work practices (Dewey 1938). This is like having second thoughts about your practice and talking to yourself to identify and analyse a particular problem or issue. It is the process of reflection that turns an event into an experience by providing meaning to increase the quality of learning from the experience. For instance, a reflective teacher who has been teaching for ten years will have ten years of different learning experiences, as opposed to a teacher who does not reflect, having ten years of the same yearly experience.

Reflection on an event, however, is bounded by the perimeters of an individual's experiences, and so thinking becomes framed by the limitations of his or her own thoughts. In order to deepen the understanding that a teacher gets from reflecting on a particular problem or experience, a person needs to access the ideas of others and gain different perspectives on the problem he or she is trying to address.

It is the second educational principle, *community*, which provides individuals with different perspectives or ideas about their own experiences. This means participants sharing ideas with a small group of colleagues in regular meetings to discuss personally relevant issues or problems. This is like having a dinner party every month with the same small group of people through which participants develop an understanding of each other's practice. By sharing ideas, participants may compare their interpretations of experiences with others and invite comments which may confirm or challenge their perceptions. Furthermore, interactions with colleagues may extend the way an individual understands their own experiences and possibly reframe how they think about a particular problem. Revans called the community or set the 'cutting edge of every action learning programme' (1982: 14), as this clarifies personal reflections so that action plans crystallise for the individual. Of utmost importance for the educational principle of a community to work is honesty in expressing how we feel and think.

Revans (1982), who pioneered much of the research on action learning, stated that personal honesty resulting in self-disclosure to colleagues was the most important feature of an action-learning set or community. This disclosure establishes a trust that builds up over time between members of a community and enables them to share more personal matters to discuss both their successes *and* failures in attempting to improve their practice.

From this continual sharing of ideas a plan of action evolves to address a particular issue or problem which leads to the third educational principle – *action* – meaning learning by doing, so that participants try ideas that have been generated from personal reflection in the light of group discussions. It is *feedback* received from trying out or testing ideas that provides meaning and becomes the basis for discussions in subsequent meetings. However, the ideas that underpin the action are not based on the sole experiences of an individual; rather they are based on the collective experiences of a small group of colleagues working as a community to address a particular problem or issue. The resulting action confirms or disconfirms the ideas and provides additional experiences to modify action in the light of reflection and discussions with colleagues. In short, there is an interconnection between thinking about a problem and doing something about it so that 'one gets to understand by doing and to do by understanding' (Revans 1982: 49)

The four educational principles, *reflection*, *community*, *action* and *feedback*, which underpin action learning, act like the blades of a propeller to sustain the professional development of a small group over an extended period of time. This is what is different about action learning – the quality of learning through personal experience is enhanced by the combined influence of the four principles. This is because an individual's understanding of a relevant problem is framed by their experiences, and so sharing ideas with others followed by some action provides a wider vision on this understanding. This is similar to Argyris and Schon's (1974) notion of 'double loop learning' to continually build a personal theory of practice, except that action learning is more like 'multiple loop learning', and places more emphasis on the social aspects of learning. This cumulative learning from the four principles has been called 'holistically synergistic' (Cusins 1995: 4) with reflection on personal experiences being enhanced by regularly exchanging ideas with other colleagues and then implementing the most appropriate action. In this way the learning from each principle is enhanced by the other principles, and so the sum of understanding from participating in action learning is greater than the learning from each principle. In addition, the interest in sustained learning is encouraged by having meetings with the group of colleagues every few weeks to further discuss ideas and actions. Figure 1 shows a diagram that represents the recursive nature of the four principles in action learning illustrating the alternating community and action phases.

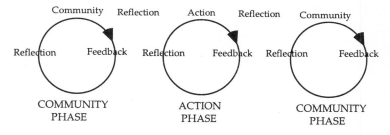

Figure 1 Professional development model showing action learning cycles

ACTION LEARNING IN PRACTICE

This final section describes how a small group of high school science teachers (three teachers in a small rural school in Oberon, Australia) based their professional development on an action-learning framework for over three years. The teachers were encouraged to *reflect* on their practice, share ideas as a *community* on a regular basis, try out ideas as *action* and seek some form of *feedback* from students. To enhance the feedback, teachers were also provided with interview data from students describing their learning experiences at school (Hoban 1996; Hoban *et al.* 1997). These data came from interviews with thirty Year 9 students describing their positive and negative learning experiences across different subjects at high school. These interviews were conducted by the author and data were then analysed and recorded onto sixteen different theme tapes providing eight hours of student data for the teachers to listen to in meetings. These tapes were a catalyst for teacher reflection by providing another perspective on teaching practices which was contextual to their experiences. It took the teachers two years to listen to all the students' tapes in their meetings, which enriched their reflection and discussion. Each of the three teachers has written a personal perspective describing his involvement in the action-learning framework. At the beginning of the study, Craig had been teaching for five years, David for one year and Geoff for fourteen years.

Craig's perspective on his own professional learning

The professional development program that we have been involved in over the last three years is different from any other in which I have participated. This program offered an opportunity to have a great deal of ownership over the process and direction in which it evolved. Power and ownership meant that the process and outcomes were more valued and therefore generated interest to pursue aspects of our own work in greater detail. The initial path of the program relied upon reflecting and listening to student interview data about our own teaching thus making the process potentially confronting. In their comments, students both praised and criticised our teaching. The comments on my teaching practice, however, were the catalyst for thought and enabled me to critically evaluate aspects of my teaching to initiate change. Over time change was further promoted as I reflected on my practice and this was crucial in continually testing ideas.

The collegiate atmosphere that the whole program embodied was also important. The communal sharing provided momentum to change and promoted confidence in experimenting with our teaching. This encouraged all members of the science faculty to exchange ideas on successful and unsuccessful strategies which we tried in an attempt to maximise student learning. However, I don't think that this program would have worked unless all three teachers on the science faculty wanted to be involved. If you look inward and you say 'Right there's a problem, you can do one of two things about it'. You can say, 'Well I'm not going to worry about it' or you can say 'Right I'm going to do something about it.' I think the fact that the three of us were quite happy to listen to the student tapes, take whatever was thrown at us, and then go and try and address any problems was the only reason it probably worked. Even if one of us had said 'Right, I don't want to be involved in the program,' I don't think it would have run very well. It is the sense of community which makes you feel that you belong to a team trying to do something together. So you have to build trust to regularly talk to colleagues about your own teaching because if you sit there in a hole and not talk to anyone, then you will not go anywhere.

This has been a dynamic process with change in my teaching beginning with listening to the student tapes followed by discussions with my colleagues and practically testing my ideas. It's a continually evolving process like a cycle because no group of students is the same and you have to continually reflect and re-evaluate your successes and failures. I don't think you ever get to a final point where you know everything. Just as students change, your ideas will have to change along with them.

David's perspective on his own professional learning

In my experience, traditional one day or after school professional development programs have contributed very little to sustained improvement in the quality of teaching. These types of programs are often good social opportunities and sometimes forums for the interchange of ideas, but on the whole they rarely produce a fundamental change in teaching. For me, the professional development program that I have participated in over the last three years has completely changed the way that I teach. It has helped to make me aware of different student learning styles and the importance of meeting the needs of each and every student in the classroom. A number of critical things have been in place in the program for this to occur:

- Teachers must be *prepared* to change their practice. If this drive or desire is not present then significant improvement in the quality of teaching and learning is prevented from the start.
- Teachers must be aware of a *reason* to change. In the type of action learning that we have been involved, the student tapes provided feedback about our teaching and were the catalyst for the need to change.

- Teachers must be given opportunities to *experiment* and make mistakes just as we as teachers should encourage students in our classes to do the same thing.
- A supportive and encouraging atmosphere among staff must be established and nurtured in order to build the confidence and trust of teachers involved. This *community* also provides a forum for discussion and the exchange of ideas.
- There must be *time* for reflection and discussion of what was tried, what worked and what didn't.

Initially, a professional development program like this is confronting and to a certain extent threatening. Once there develops an open, supportive and encouraging learning community for teachers, change is produced. What is particularly important is the relationship among the teachers so they can share their successes and failures. This sharing would not work as well in a faculty that did not have this collegiality. And through our discussions I think the three of us got on really well and I think that with the relationship between us, we felt safe and secure so that we could try different things and make mistakes and admit it, that type of thing. However, I would be concerned about running a project in a school which didn't have that sense of community. I think that's one of the limitations of the action learning framework.

Students in my class now constructively criticise and praise my teaching on a regular basis. This, I believe, is to be encouraged. The implication is that our teaching is being informed by the learning of our students and to an extent this means that students are in control of their learning. The students now have the confidence to negotiate lessons and ways of learning. This to me is what a classroom learning community is all about.

Geoff's perspective on his own professional learning

After my appointment at Oberon High School as head teacher, development of teaching expertise was to be a priority for me. As a science teacher of 14 years at the time, I had been through the 'mill' of various short term inservice courses that had briefly inspired me to alter my classroom practice to better accommodate the needs of my students as I perceived them, but most of these changes were short lived. This was because ideas were not shared back at school and the hurly burly of a teacher's day leaves little time for reflection.

When first invited to be involved in the professional development program three years ago, I was intrigued – I wanted to hear what students had to say about my teaching and so I readily participated. Listening to the student tapes was an eye opening, or rather a mind opening experience. I was surprised how closely students monitored the practices of their teachers and also their own learning. Some of the things they said reinforced my beliefs about my own teaching, but they also had many pertinent and confronting things to say about teaching and learning in my classes. There is no doubt that the student tapes and the initial set of teacher interviews to discuss, 'Why we teach the way we do?' created an atmosphere for reflection. The student tapes provided the feedback that stimulated discussion and the sharing of experiences which is necessary for real and long term change. However, it was the notion of a shared purpose that had been built up through the collegiality developed within the faculty which carried the process forward – we had formed a community.

For me the cyclic process of action learning shows how it is a self-sustaining professional development experience. The whole thing becomes a cycle of change where you start with the student tapes and you start to reflect on the various aspects of your teaching and then you get change, feedback, more reflection; change, feedback, more reflection; change, feedback – that cycle all the time bringing in ideas from outside, other inputs, your colleagues, and I think if any of these factors had been missing, then it wouldn't have worked. And the important thing about it, and this is where it is different to other forms of professional development and this is why it's caused change, is that it is continually reinforced because it is ongoing and because it has this framework that we keep coming back to. We feel as though we're part of a team and part of a process that's ongoing and not short term. It's not a stick a finger in the dyke here, stick another finger in the dyke there, learn about literacy here, learn about assessment there – it's a whole integrated package.

For the first two years the student tapes gave me fresh impetus to the way I thought about my teaching. I have seen real and long term change in all three of us – changes that make us more responsive to the needs of our students. This is because we heard about their needs directly from them on the student tapes. Because of this we had a better understanding of their perspective and became more in tune with their needs during class time. The student tapes have also demonstrated how difficult good teaching practice is and that there is no holy grail that is excellence in teaching. Rather, it is the process of learning about your own teaching that encourages teachers to respond to students' needs that I find so valuable.

In particular, the sharing of ideas as a community is really important and I think the only way you could do it is if everyone feels as though they're working in a non-threatening environment. It can't be coercive, it's got to be completely voluntary and it's got to be done in the spirit that no one feels threatened and the only way you could do it is to build up a trust relationship. There's no way someone coming into the faculty for the first time could be thrown into this process. I would think I would let them teach for a year in the school, build up a trust, a rapport, you know the going out and having a few social drinks together, all that sort of thing, and see them fall on their face a few times and help them out and realise that you're non-judgemental, all that sort of thing. Once the trust is established, then they may be more willing to share ideas about their teaching and be part of the community.

DISCUSSION

The professional development programme for the three high school science teachers had sufficient momentum to continue for three years because of the synergy produced from the four principles underpinning the action learning framework: *personal reflection, community, feedback* and *action*. In addition, the student interview data on the tapes made the teachers aware of the problematic nature of teaching and provided the catalyst for reflection and discussion as they attempted to improve their practice. Hence, change in teaching practice occurred because the teachers reflected on their practice *and* listened to interviews from their students providing feedback on their teaching *and* shared their ideas as a community *and* were able to experiment with their ideas. So the starting point for professional development was each teacher's reflection on his current practice which was then enhanced by the other principles of the action learning framework on a recurring basis. The result was continuous and cumulative professional development over three years as the teachers gained a deeper understanding of the relationship between *their* teaching and *their* students' learning.

Using student data as feedback to enhance teachers' reflection and discussion was a powerful vehicle for teacher learning because data are contextual to the teachers' beliefs and provided perspectives to extend the way teachers usually frame their experiences. Some of the student data challenged the teachers' beliefs whilst other data confirmed their beliefs about good teaching practice. Furthermore, student data gave the teachers directions for change as data identified effective teaching practice across other subjects within the high school. Also, when the teachers shared ideas as a community it encouraged them to continue in the process because they were committed to developing as a faculty. This willingness to share ideas not only provided a source of new strategies, but provided mutual support that gave momentum to maintain change in their practice. Hence, a sense of community results in teachers being collegial and encourages them to share their experiences. And it is important to give teachers regular time (say once a month) to discuss their own practice in small groups and to encourage collegiality. But often meeting times in secondary schools are designated to tell teachers about school policies or how they should be teaching, not to encourage them to share experiences about what they already do in their classroom.

The notion of 'community' was important for John Dewey's theory of learning through experience as it is for contemporary educational writings. Central to the operation of any learning community is personal reflection on experiences in the light of sharing views with other members. This is consistent with Dewey's views that learning through experience involves both psychological and sociological processes. This process was evident in the action-learning community of science teachers at Oberon High School. Linking personal reflection with discussion and action drives the teachers' action-learning cycles resulting in sustained professional learning for several years. And most importantly, the teachers kept the professional development programme going voluntarily for three years as they were in charge of their own change. Perhaps this is because the teachers were not told how they should be teaching, but instead were provided with a framework to provide the right conditions for effective workplace learning. Central to this framework is valuing the existing classroom experiences of teachers and organising a regular time slot to share ideas and build a sense of community.

Note

I would like to thank the teachers involved in the study, Geoff Hastings, Craig Luccarda and David Lloyd, for their opinions in this chapter; and Chris Tome for his valuable comments on a draft of this chapter.

References

Argyris, C. and Schon, D. (1974) *Theory in Practice: Increasing Professional Effectiveness*, San Francisco: Jossey-Bass.

Bereiter, C. and Scardamalia, M. (1993) *Surpassing Ourselves: An Inquiry into the Nature and Implications of Expertise*, Chicago: Open Court.

Boddy, D. (1991) 'Supervisory development', in M. Pedler (ed.) *Action Learning in Practice*, Aldershot, England: Gower Publishing.

Cusins, P. (1995) 'Action learning revisited', *Industrial and Commercial Training* 27, 3–10.

Darling-Hammond, L. (1994) *Professional Development Schools: Schools for Developing a Profession*, New York: Teachers College Press.

Dewey, J. (1887) 'Knowledge as idealisation', in J. A. Boyston (ed.) (1970) *The Early Works of John Dewey: 1882–1898 Early Essays*, Carbondale: Southern Illinois Press.

Dewey, J. (1897) *My Pedagogic Creed*, New York: E. L. Kellogg.

Dewey, J. (1901) *Psychology and Social Practice*, Chicago: University of Chicago Press.

Dewey, J. (1916) *Democracy and Education*, New York: Macmillan.

Dewey, J. (1938) *Experience and Education*, London: Collier Books.

Gregory, M. (1996) 'Accrediting work-based learning: Action learning – A model for empowerment', *Journal of Management Development* 13 (4), 41–52.

Hoban, G. (1996) 'A professional development model based on interrelated principles of teacher learning', unpublished doctoral dissertation, University of British Columbia, Canada.

Hoban, G., Hastings, G., Luccarda, C. and Lloyd, D. (1997) 'Faculty based professional development as an action learning community', *Australian Science Teachers' Journal* 43 (3), 49–54.

Lewis, A. (1991) 'An in-company program', in M. Pedler (ed.), *Action Learning in Practice*, 111–124, Aldershot, England: Gower Publishing.

Macquarie Library (1990) *The Macquarie Dictionary*, Sydney: Macquarie University.

McGill, I. and Beaty, L. (1995) *Action Learning: A Guide for Professional, Management and Educational Development*, London: Kogan Page.

Pedler, M. (1991) *Action Learning in Practice* (2nd edition), Aldershot, England: Gower Publishing.

Revans, R. W. (1981) 'What is action learning?', *Journal of Management Development* 1 (3), 12–20.

Revans, R. W. (1982) *The ABC of Action Learning*, London: Chartwell-Bratt.

Schlesinger, E. (1991) 'Quality service in New Zealand', in M. Pedler (ed.) *Action Learning in Practice*, Aldershot, England: Gower Publishing.

Senge, P. (1990) *The Fifth Discipline*, Sydney: Random House.

Thorpe, R. and Taylor, M. (1991) 'Action learning in an academic context', in M. Pedler (ed.) *Action Learning in Practice*, Aldershot, England: Gower Publishing.

Winkless, T. (1991) 'Doctors as managers', in M. Pedler (ed.) *Action Learning in Practice*, Aldershot, England: Gower Publishing.

Zuber-Skerritt, O. (1993) 'Improving learning and teaching through action learning and action research', *Higher Education and Development* 12 (1), 45–58.

Part 3

CASE STUDIES OF
LEARNING COMMUNITIES

10

TALKING ABOUT COOMBES

Features of a learning community

Peter Woods

INTRODUCTION

The school provides an exceptional standard of education, which not only pushes the boundaries of imaginative teaching but ensures pupils achieve well in all areas of learning.

Ofsted 1997: 1

This was the verdict of the team conducting a full inspection of Coombes County Infant and Nursery school at Arborfield in Berkshire, England, in December 1997. The judgement is significant, for these inspections are currently framed in a managerialist, technicist discourse, one not ostensibly sympathetic to many of the features of learning communities (Jeffrey and Woods 1998). Interestingly, the only criticisms of the school were of a managerialist nature, but insignificant within the context of the glowing praise for the school's achievements as a learning community. Coombes is a paradigm case of a learning community, as I shall attempt to show in this chapter, and the inspection demonstrates that such schools, against the expectations of many, can survive, and indeed prosper, within a managerialist climate.

Coombes has won international distinction, primarily for its imaginative use of school grounds. In an earlier report (Woods 1995), I described how the school was remarkable for its distinctive ethos which permeated every place and moment of the day, and which marks it out as a notable learning community. Here we find the typical emphasis on common ownership of knowledge, on common engagement with teaching and learning by all participants, on shared and democratic leadership, and on progressive development and continuous renewal, as well as strong links with the environment (Cocklin *et al.* 1996). It was also clear that the teachers favoured social constructivist learning theory, with its emphasis

187

on child- instead of knowledge-centredness, active learning, the importance of context, cooperative learning, caring, and the teacher as facilitator (Sugrue 1997) .

The material in this chapter was acquired during one week spent in the school in February 1996 from open-ended discussions with members of the learning community. These have to be seen within the context of a long association with the school, going back ten years, and containing several other periods of interviews and observation. The main aim of the discussions was to try to articulate the ethos of Coombes and what was so special about it. There are problems here of representation as well as discovery. One attempt at portrayal is contained in a film made in that week (Hill 1996). Here, I complement that presentation by giving voice to members of the community who work and live in the school – parents, teachers, helpers and governors. Four main themes emerged: holism; democratic participation; 'creative learning'; and a charismatic ethos.

HOLISM

All learning

All members of Coombes are learners and they are all teachers. The knowledge contained and skills imparted in this practice are bounded and integrated within lives. There are no limits to what might be learned within this framework.

Rachel Aylmer (teacher and former student) noted: 'It's exciting as a teacher and the teachers are really excited to use the grounds as well and we're constantly learning all the time.' Sue Rowe (deputy head, formerly parent of a child at the school) said:

> My own science teaching is happening at the same time as the children's. I had poor experiences in my own secondary school and always felt I was a duff on science, and it was only since being here and working here that I've started to develop myself personally...Coombes has given me my grounding. It's seeing me grow daily, it's seen my children very nicely, and everyone who walks through the doors here, I believe, is a beneficiary of it...Everyone is a teacher, the children are teachers as well.

There is opportunity for everybody to grow and develop. Sue Rowe claims that Coombes' programme of 'revolving curriculum responsibilities, and curriculum specialisms for all the staff (whereby each of the teachers takes responsibility for a curriculum area for one term), gives us all fresh starts, new approaches. You might be teaching the same subject, but always you'll come at it from a different view-point and the professional stimulation, the personal stimulation that comes from that is enormously gratifying...I want to believe that Coombes will survive into eternity because I believe in it.

Underpinning everything they do at Coombes is, according to Sue Humphries (headteacher)

a sense of worth, about feeling that you have a great deal to con-tribute. It's not about being brilliantly articulate or sparklingly in-tellectual. Those things are lovely if that happens, but it's much deeper than that, and much more long lasting...People come to work for more, a good deal more, than money...It's the old word 'vocation' – that you felt you had some inner light and you want to share that with other people. You actually want to be modified and you want to carry on with your own personal education. You want that very, very badly, and that's why you become a teacher. Lots of people come back into school because their own education never quite satisfied them.

Parents also learn – and teach, like Dee:

At Ella's last school it was something like,'Oh well, you can come in if you want.' Here, it was, 'Well, what can you do? What do you want to come and get involved in?' I come and do a lot of art and painting and model making with the children, and you just notice how receptive they are to everything that you're doing. They're so enthusiastic about what you can put in, and they've got so many ideas to give back to me that I've learned a lot as well.

Learning all

The curriculum provided is an extremely rich one which extends well beyond the expectations of the National Curriculum.
Ofsted 1997: 2

In the prescribed National Curriculum, knowledge is compartmentalised; and the model of the child is one that separates out 'pupil' from child (Woods and Jeffrey 1996). To Coombes' teachers this is anathema. Carole Davies (teacher) described their aim as:

to teach the whole child...It's not just about paper things, it's about a whole person, about their moral development, their social development, their outlook on life, the way they treat other people, and their environment. And also the skills that you need in life, the reading and the writing is just as important but only part of the whole person.

There isn't a 'typical day' at Coombes. It's all about 'enabling children to learn about the broadest possible way of looking at life'.

Carole Cooke (teacher) pointed to research that shows that many young children are bored by maths based on traditional drill exercises. 'But if you can make it dynamic, if you can make it interesting, if you can make it thematic...'. She gave as an example the week's theme of Valentine's and hearts to use a heart symbol – and then she would reinforce the concepts, but with a different symbol:

> perhaps a daffodil, or a leek if we're doing the Eistedfodd, so it makes more fun for them. Because it's cross-curricular, they've been in one room where they've been writing poetry, love poetry this week...comes naturally...instead of using plastic manipulatives to reinforce their number concepts, they're using other cut-out heart symbols.

Navnite (parent) talked of the depth of the children's experiences. All the senses come into play. Judy Allen (teacher) said 'you fill up my senses' summed up the place.

> They don't just show them the movie and read a story to them, they actually all sit around, go in the hall, actually dress up, sing the songs, live them, actually taste the foods they would actually have on those occasions, so it's very positive involvement rather than just on the surface...They feel it, they taste it. This way it stores in their mind somewhere much more...

Ann (parent) confirmed that:

> It gives them a whole appreciation of so many different things. I put a CD on the other day of The Planets, and my daughter knew that piece of music. And the other day we walked through a shopping precinct and she looked in a shop window and said 'Oh look, Mummy, there's a Monet'.

Martin (parent) was amazed at some of the things his daughter knew:

My daughter knows about Chinese New Year, dragons, everything like that, 'beating the bounds' and all these things I'm embarrassed to say that I knew nothing about...If Alexandra is learning that on top of all the other skills then she's got to be best placed for a potentially better academic environment than my wife and I, and we did quite well.

Learning is also continuous. There is a sustained impetus, which continually opens up new horizons for both pupils and teachers. The environment, for example:

> is developed as a living laboratory, right from the early days being used for teaching science but also as a resource for art, language, and all areas of the curriculum. Because it's such a strong base, we've taken the ideas from outside, or used the resources from outside, and we've taken the learning outside. And it's grown beyond anyone's dreams.
>
> (Carol Cooke)

Carol Cooke explains the long-lasting impression made on pupils. She is now teaching second-generation children:

> I taught her daughter, which was about 12, 15 years ago, and she brought in a photograph of herself, the mother, in a dragon dance. It's a personal history. So I think things that happen to the children while they're here they absorb and they internalise...and these things develop inside them and much much later on the children begin to appreciate those sorts of experiences they've had.

DEMOCRATIC PARTICIPATION

> The school's democratic management structure is very effective and assures the school's total commitment towards high achievement in all aspects of pupil development.
>
> Ofsted 1997: 2

Compared with managerial hierarchies (see Jeffrey and Woods 1998), learning communities are based on equal status, and a dovetailing of roles. All are working toward the same endeavour, and combine their skills and interests to maximise the opportunities available.

Common roles

> The school has a highly developed sense of partnership and this per-
> meates the work of the school. Parents and the community are drawn
> into the life of the school by its ethos of valuing all people and this is
> mutually enriching.
>
> Ofsted 1997: 12

Parents as co-educators are more often seen as operating in this role in the
context of their own homes (Macbeth 1994). Within school, such a
partnership might induce feelings of role ambiguity both among them and
among teachers (Thomas 1989). This is not the case at Coombes, where the
very concept of 'role' is not so relevant.

> No one's really ever sure who's the teacher, who's the helping mum,
> who's the teaching assistant, or even who's the Head. We've had
> some funny situations where people have thought that people who
> are on community service [by order of the courts] are actually a
> member of staff.
>
> (Christine – teaching assistant)

> You just wander in and you're met by somebody in wellies who's
> been mucking out sheep, and you don't know who's who. You don't
> know who the Head Teacher is and who the helper is, and it doesn't
> matter because everybody's important at the school...There's no hi-
> erarchy at all, with the children or the teachers. Everybody's got
> something to say and the children are not in the least bit intimi-
> dated by adults. It's not 'Sssh! Be quiet, teacher's talk-
> ing'...Everybody's valued.
>
> (Kim – parent)

Lyn (teaching assistant) thought the teachers 'more like mothers to the
children'. Liz (teaching assistant) found that 'regardless of what job you do
you are treated as an equal'.

The dovetailing of roles applies among the children also.

> If they do have any problems, an older child will look after a
> younger child, a slower child will attach itself to a quicker
> child...That child will spend a certain amount of time to give that
> child enough confidence, and then leave them. They don't go
> around as buddies, they just mix and match, and that gives them
> the confidence to talk to various people of various ages in their
> family groups. They're rubbing shoulders with 5–7 year olds...So
> not only are they getting all the wealth of knowledge from the

teacher, they're getting all the wealth of knowledge from the group that's around them.

Teamwork

Sue Humphries believed:

> There's no greater educator really than the influence of the group...Every group feels its way towards what's right for that group. I think sometimes very strong leadership can stop a group feeling its way outward and onward...For me, the entire movement outwards has got to be wholly felt within the group. It mustn't favour some people and not others, and I think there can be some odd distinctions about who has the best ideas. You don't have the best ideas because you're the Head, or because you've been here longer than anybody else.

Teachers thus work as a team in which they are all leaders. Sue reported:

> Everybody has an inner light, and it's giving space and opportunities for that to be brought out, whether at staff meetings...You can sometimes think 'Oh, that's a whacky idea'. Then when you examine it, you find out that there is something really very trenchant in that way of thinking. It's a matter of accepting the ideas, sometimes sitting for a moment or two in silence...Our staff meetings tend to be rather long drawn out...and rather hesitant sometimes, but that's because everybody's stopping and thinking and looking at what other people have submitted. The ideas, as they are produced, direct everybody's thinking, and the one that does that is naturally the leader for that moment and probably for that activity.

The Coombes staff are a team almost from the point of interview for the job. Carole Davies reported Sue's philosophy as being:

> 'I don't agree with sit-down interviews, you ask me what you want to know.' So I ended up more or less interviewing her...The interviewing process is so often a paper exercise, but she actually gets right down to what people believe education is. The philosophy of Coombes is so important to the way it's run, and that's why it's such a good team, because we all have a similar outlook, and we work well together for the children.

Rachel Aylmer referred to:

the whole team atmosphere, not just between the staff but between the staff and the children and the parents, and everybody that comes in from outside, from the community, visitors from abroad...Everyone's important in making it work.

Even the governors of the school have similar roles. In the legislation of 1988 and afterwards governors were given considerably more power in the new managerial and hierarchical scheme of things. At Coombes, however, they choose to be just as much a part of the community as anybody else. Beryl Ellinor (school governor) explained:

> Our meetings are very informal. They're all involved with activities within the school. Our deputy head is very good on the financial side, and we also have an accountant who's a school governor. We have an ex-teacher who's the vice-chairman, so she adds a little bit of professionalism there. And we all work very well together. There's no question of power where we're concerned. The Head Teacher and her staff are so dedicated to the school that there's no question of the governors wanting to over-rule or exert any power whatsoever. We're behind the staff wholeheartedly.

Teamwork was also encouraged among the children. Gina had a 'very shy child', but every morning they have 'sharing time' where they get a chance to talk about things they've done:

> [At first] she was very reluctant to say anything. Now she can't wait to get to school to share something and even if she hasn't got anything she'll try and make something up...She just loves to share her news, or she wants to bring something in to show...She'll come home and say, 'Have you got something brown or blue or red, or Chinese...' and I think that's very important to bring something from home because they want to share it. It all goes in with being part of the family and sharing with other children.

Jenny Poore (coordinator of PE) thought:

> The philosophy is the fact that everything is shared together, and the sharing is for everybody and everybody's worth. The child, the adult, and the integration of both is so important and underlines everything that's done in the school.

194

Visionary leadership

Notwithstanding the emphasis on democratic management and common roles, at the centre there was visionary leadership – played down by Sue Humphries herself, since she preferred to see it coming through in others, and in the life of the school. Carol Cooke, a long-serving teacher at the school, was captured by Sue's charisma as early as her interview for the post she now holds:

> Sue explained to me that she wanted to put the school back into its rightful setting, because it had a most beautiful backdrop of fields and woods, but had been left by the architects as a barren site. And I thought, 'Oh, this is a woman I could work with!' and it just went from there.

When Sue retires, noted Sue Rowe, 'It will need someone to step into her shoes, with similar visions and a similar inspirational charismatic style'. Leadership may be distributed and shared, but there is still a 'critical agent' (Woods 1995) at the centre of events acting as catalyst. The literature refers to the importance of a school's history (see, for example, Cocklin *et al.* 1996). In the case of Coombes, this is to a large extent Sue's own life history, and her personal long-term vision, which entails what Hameyer (1996) calls a 'long-distance running exercise':

> Twenty-five years ago I had a plan of sorts, a whole lot of things I wanted to realise. One of them was a community school with a team of teachers working in it who very much cared for each other as well as caring for the children. And I had a few ideas about a setting in which I hoped education would take place. But it wasn't a ten-year plan. It was a twenty-five or thirty or forty-year plan. So I'm not going to finish it before it's time for me to retire, because I'm not anywhere close to the realisation that I had or the dream I had at the beginning. So it was bigger than I believed it was.

Openness

> The curriculum is greatly enriched by a wide variety of visitors to school and the extensive and imaginative use of the immediate school environment.
>
> Ofsted 1997: 10

Many schools have a boundary in one form or another between school and the outside world which demarcates different areas of control. There are no such distinctions at Coombes. But there is more than open access. There is involvement. Sue Humphries wanted people to feel that:

> they're always going to be welcome, that they come in and watch us teach or better still, work with us, and that people beyond the community who have talents come in regularly – or even if they don't have any particular talent. It's very much a place where we want the adults to work with the children and to come in and make the atmosphere good for everyone. So it's a sharing place....It's a matter of people seeing a niche for themselves, because there's always room for it here.

Parents attest to the success of the policy. Theresa found:

> The teachers are as fresh at the end of the day as they are at the beginning. They treat every single child as an individual. They get to know them, and they get to know the parents really really well. So that you can go and talk to them about anything at any time.

Martin was impressed with the continuity of learning, stemming from the open policy of the school:

> The school is exceptional in the way they welcome children and parents and anybody that's associated with a particular child into the school, and by making them welcome makes them want to be part of the school, makes them want to learn and take in and share everything they learn here. So they come home and they tell us about it, we talk to them about it, and they come back again the following day and explain again what they have learned. It's just a continuation. They don't actually leave school...We're very pleased with all aspects of work, play, and caring and sharing and being part of an extended family. She doesn't feel as if she is coming to school, she's just coming to another part of her family, and when she comes home to us she comes back to the other part of her family. She's got no problem with crossing the boundary of the school gates.

Cath had recently moved to the area, and came to Coombes to look around, and found:

> they were so very kind when we came in, they welcomed him with open arms. I walked into the wrong classroom, and they said 'Oh Mark, I hope you come into *this* class', and I just thought 'They're so very friendly'...At his previous school he cried for the whole

week! At least when he came here, he cried for one day, and the next day he was quite happy to go to school.

The sense of an 'extended family' here is typical of a learning community (see, for example, Cocklin and Davis 1996). It runs counter to the kind of school some would favour whose function is mainly to separate children from families and to introduce them to wider society (Macbeth 1994). This is the more traditional view of school, with a 'boundary' set up between the school and the outside world, and between teachers and parents. But the Coombes community would not recognise these divisions. They would argue that the interests of society – and of individuals – are better served by combining forces. Martin's child does not 'feel as if she is coming to school', and this allows her to acclimatise more comfortably and to take part more wholeheartedly.

When Theresa phoned up for an appointment she was told 'You don't need an appointment. Turn up whenever you like, go wherever you like.' She found 'you can just wander around, but if you ask if you can help they will find something for you. So you get very involved.' Sidone found the same. She had not enjoyed school herself, and 'always felt on edge walking into a school', but 'when I walked in here they're just so friendly, and I really value the fact that I can walk in at any time, and if I just feel like coming into school and joining in, and that means a lot to me.'

The openness is not restricted to the local world. Kim (parent) told us:

> every culture and race and religion is welcome in this school, and it's accepted that that's the way that country lives, and that's how Chinese or Indian people are....They have a rabbi in to chat to the children, and it's not 'Oh, it's the Jewish religion', it's just a natural process for the school.

CREATIVE LEARNING

'Creative learning' (Woods 1995) involves:

- Acquisition of knowledge that comes to be owned by the child. It is not somebody else's knowledge to be regurgitated in tests, with no internalisation and no change to the child's self. Sue Humphries puts this well:

> You have to work at your own level, and you've got to be constantly open to the children's ideas, because education only becomes genuine when they put in a very strong input. If they don't, it somehow never sits within them as a part of themselves, they have to make

that movement towards it all the time. Otherwise it's being layered on them superficially.

- A learning process that is controlled to some extent by the children. They are not simply being fed knowledge by the teacher through one way transmission, working in a prescribed way and at a prescribed pace.

- Innovation. Learning is a continuous process involving new experiences, new unforeseen developments, new opportunities.

- Relevance to the children's lives, worlds, interests, concerns and background cultures. This includes children recognising learning as relevant. The higher the relevance, the more likelihood there is of the child having control of her own learning processes, which will in turn lead to ownership of the knowledge that results (Woods *et al.* 1998).

These principles feature prominently in the teaching and learning at Coombes as described by the participants, and are met by establishing authenticity, motivating the child, and appropriating the National Curriculum.

Establishing authenticity

> The main strength of the teaching is the use of real world experiences and the quality of resources used to stimulate enthusiasm amongst pupils.
>
> Ofsted 1997: 1

Active learning is the main recipe for establishing authenticity:

> All the experiences are hands-on, real experiences...That's why we keep sheep, and why we use the grounds so that they can actually get out there and do these things, not just look at pictures in a book or read about them or be told about them – they see the sheep being washed and sheared, they see the lambs being born, they go out and do pond-dipping. They don't have to make a day's excursion to the nearest nature reserve to do that, it's part of the ongoing curriculum, and through that the children get a broad outlook on life and they know how to express themselves, and how to communicate with other people and with the environment.
>
> (Carole Davies)

Carole and her children had made a huge dragon for Chinese New Year which housed all the class. Not only was it part of a celebration of an important event, but it served other areas of the curriculum too. The dragon had moved round the grounds with appropriate musical accompaniment before going into the hall for more festivities involving the whole school, and then into their own classroom for a geography lesson.

> Children can go out and plan a route where the dragon might be and then go out and see if they were right, and then come back and plot it on the map of the school. It gives it a reality, instead of just saying 'This is a map, where did we go?' We've actually gone and done it and looked at landmarks and looked at the compass, and discussed whether the compass is agreeing with what we think it should be...Looking at history as well, how they used to say 'Here be dragons' for danger...So it really brings things together which is real life.

Jenny Poore explained how the children practised 'dragon movement' in PE, and how they prepared for the celebration. They spent 'six sessions learning the floor pattern of the movement, practising the different actions, and having ideas about actions, and then putting that all together for the final parades'.

A common strategy is 'transpositioning' – putting the child in the position of others. Rachel Aylmer had been discussing the paintings of Mary Cassatt, which portrayed tender moments between mothers and daughters, with her class, but looking at the paintings was not enough. She arranged for the class to observe a mother bathing her baby, with the children gathered round in a circle.

> We want the children to *feel* that they are writers, we feel that it's really important to give them a really exciting stimulus...so they can actually see a tender moment, they can see the mother looking lovingly at the child, and help wash the child and get involved...then we bring that back to the classroom and talk about how special that moment is....and they can see some more tender moments – a mother brushing her daughter's hair, or washing the child's toes, or the child just sitting with her mother as she's sewing.

The children would then do a 'writers' workshop', some encouraging others, some sitting quietly and reflecting, the teacher also supporting, trying to get them to 'see themselves as writers, believing in themselves and building up their confidence'. Once that has taken hold, you can 'start to correct them' in a constructive way – but not until.

Transpositioning is empowering:

> It's having that curiosity of mind and of spirit, of wanting to know because it's interesting for itself. It's realising that you, too, can do it, you too can be a scientist, a true researcher. Young children can do it as well…For example [in some work on electricity and magnetism] we actually went out and got a plug and a screwdriver, and a piece of three-cord flex for every child, and we've had enormous fun working out why you need three cords, where does the electricity come from when it comes into school, where does it come from before then? So it's starting from simple points, but finding the exciting.
>
> (Sue Rowe)

Children work at their own levels and speeds, after thorough preparation. But they are not left to their own devices, as some critics of child-centred learning claim (Alexander *et al.* 1992). As we have demonstrated elsewhere (Woods *et al.* 1998), growth and development is an important component of the approach. Judith Haynes (parent and teacher) explained how she used the 'Roamer', a mobile robot operated by remote control:

> For several weeks we've been planning out routes, and the children have been devising their own routes, maybe laying down carpet tiles, walking along the routes themselves and turning in right angles, 90-degree turns. This has carried over into PE sessions and music sessions where they've been singing and dancing, doing movements as robots, and actually making these turns…Then we've moved into the IT area, getting children to think about how they planned their route, and programmed themselves, to follow a route and convert that into working with the Roamer, and also on to the computer with a Delta program which is the initial Logo program…They work at their own level and speed. For some children who were perhaps working on the carpet tiles, planning their own routes that way, are ready to work on and move on to something else like Roamer. Those on Roamer are now ready to actually move on to the computer program, and the programs become more sophisticated as you work with them. They start, perhaps, just programming in one route, one thing that they want the Roamer to do, but then which you can work with them to actually build up sequences of movements and routes that you want the IT and the Roamer to do.

Motivating

Pupils have excellent attitudes to learning...Pupils are keen to take ownership of their own learning.

Ofsted 1997: 1

It is of great importance to Coombes teachers how children feel about their learning. Feelings hold the key to cognition. So there is much talk of excitement, joy, fun, happiness, confidence. Sue Rowe recalls her first inspirational memory:

digging a hole, and the children wanting to get in the hole because it was so exciting, to see what was underneath their feet and finding the joy in quite ordinary things, things that you always take for granted, you can never consider. And it was seeing children falling on to the ground with excitement at seeing an earthworm coming out, and it was using that hole so the children were actually collecting clay. And I remember we were making small waterproof bowls from the clay, and giving children some water to carry across the playground. The joy and excitement that something as simple as that generated for me was marvellous – the real stuff of life and of education.

Keith's six-year-old son was sent to the school because 'all the children are happy, and the school develops the child...He has become aware of himself and is a very inquisitive child, as are most of the children.' He contrasts it with his own experiences of school –

I hated it, and they were undoubtedly the worst years of my life...When it came to discussing school for my child, I had to be persuaded to come here, but when I actually came I found it was wonderful. I walked past the windows and saw all these happy faces, and quite frankly I have to eat my words, because he's had a marvellous time here, and it's developed him very well.

Theresa (parent) had benefited from the school's 'open door' policy, going to the school two or three times to have a 'really good look round'. She was impressed with the children's application:

The children were all busy. All the time they were occupied, there was no misbehaving. There seemed to be adults with them on each table...Other schools were sitting one teacher to thirty-plus children. And my child's very active. I just knew that if he went to a school where he had to sit his bottom on that chair and copy what

201

was on the board or wait for the teacher's attention, his mind would
be gone. So he's come here, and he's just flourished.

As Sue Humphries puts it:

> As you grow, you are making up your own story inside yourself and
> that story has to be filled with happiness – it will be filled with un-
> happiness quite naturally – but its construct, together with the in-
> tellectual abilities that are being developed, has to be happy, glad,
> anticipatory, so that you come to school filled with curiosity and a
> sense of 'I want to be here and I want to join in'.

Keith was looking ahead:

> I believe the children should have fun. They should learn to be able
> to develop themselves. When it comes for them to go out in the
> wide world in the 21st century, it's going to be exceedingly diffi-
> cult for them to find jobs and careers, and I think they may well
> have to experience the turmoil of having to re-train two or three
> times within their working lives. The school is preparing them well
> for the ability to adjust and to develop themselves rather than hav-
> ing something thrust at them.

This makes a good basis for learning things like the three Rs. Their success
at that 'comes from the happiness that emanates from the school. All the
children are willing to learn, they're so busy they're happy to learn, they
don't even know they're learning half the time.' Some criticised the school
for not emphasising the three Rs enough; the parents of one boy, who had
difficulty in those respects early on, were assured by staff that if he were
happy, it 'would come'.

> And indeed it has. Two or three years on now, he's Year 2, and his
> reading and writing has absolutely blossomed in the last couple of
> months. Meanwhile he's had this happy experience of school which
> he'll take with him throughout life.

'Fun' and 'happiness' do not mean a free for all. Children's natural and
copious resources have to be channelled to some extent. Theresa, for
example, was concerned to channel her child's confidence

> in the right direction. In some respects, he was 'over-confident' and
> he had found it hard in the nursery school having to 'knuckle under'
> at times. But at the end of his first day in infant school his teacher

202

asked me to come and see her, and the first thing she said was 'This child is so gorgeous I cannot wait to have him in my classroom'.

Theresa 'sort of preened' and thought 'Wonderful! I just hope it lasts for ever!' Martin's daughter had 'been here six months, she's as happy as we could ever have hoped for, and on the back of that she's learning more than we could ever have imagined'. Gina's daughter 'talks about it the whole time. Her love of books is amazing. They nurture a love of books right from the word "go".'

Sue Humphries was sure:

It really has something to do with a confident personality. If the setting is right it's going to help you to fulfil yourself as a person. So that all those qualities that make you fun to be with are burnished, they're going to be brought to the fore and emphasised, because in the end you might be a clever barrister, or a brilliant author or painter or road-sweeper or waitress, but it's going to be the personal qualities that you bring to the job and the way that you relate to other people that's going to mean that you're happy in your life and filled with a sense of achievement and purpose...Education can foster those qualities, and education goes on and on.

Dee's daughter was 'a very bright and receptive child, but she was crippled by her lack of confidence'. She might easily have 'become very intimidated at a very early age' in the current pressurised National Curriculum environment. But at Coombes, 'everything is just fostered and encouraged. Because there is no regimentation, the children find it very easy to find their own level and just pick everything up...Some don't get left miles behind because of an attitude difference.'

This confidence, once established, seemed to stay with them. James felt:

They are confident in the world as they go out today as six or even five year olds. They're holding an adult conversation...and you are happy for them because they're talking sense. You're not embarrassed by your children. If they've been to Coombes, they really are different...[Woman:] They're always constantly surprising you [general agreement]...And you're going 'What?!'

They are also critical. Lynn (parent) felt:

Life is just such an experience to them, they just don't accept anything, they question every single thing. It's like if you tell a child something, they're going to test it out. If they prove it for themselves they learn it.

Appropriation

All teaching within the state sector now has to meet statutory requirements. But Coombes has managed to 'appropriate', rather than, say, 'accommodate' (Woods 1995) these requirements. The National Curriculum has become encapsulated within the Coombes programme, rather than vice versa. The Coombes approach includes a strong emphasis on feelings, and encouraging children – and teachers themselves – to *see and appreciate* the relevance of what they do. This has a circular and cumulative effect, feeding back in to the activity and opening up new opportunities. Sue Humphries explains:

> Everything here underpins the three Rs. You have to have something to write about. You need the means to compose music. If you're going to take art and language and poetry and all the other things, you must have the stimulus for it. And that means lots of personal interaction, it means enjoying a setting where there are things that are beautiful and which bring out the tender side of the human being, and then you move into philosophical and spiritual ideas, and those are what you discover, you write about, you explore, those are what extend you.
>
> The National Curriculum is both a hindrance and a help. It does direct our attention in a very focused way to certain things so that we have always got this eye to good balance. In some regards it's a bit constricting in that it doesn't take the ideas as far as they might be taken. I hope that doesn't obtain here, that we see opportunities, move out towards them and capitalise on them, and that the development is suggested in a way that whenever you leave an idea it's left with masses of possibilities hanging in the air, 'cos you never get to the end of any idea.

Judith Haynes agrees that:

> we incorporate a lot of the experiences into the requirements of the National Curriculum. Certainly the writing and the reading and the maths and the science is very much geared round the topics and the areas we're looking at. For example, with the friendship week we've done this week we've looked at it in terms of maths, writing, science, rather than taking isolated bits of the curriculum...so there's a happy balance between the wonderful experiences they provide for

the children and meeting the requirements of the National Curriculum. The children are getting the best of both worlds.

Jenny Poore explains:

they still do their practice letter writing, but not necessarily on pencil paper, they'll do it in the sand, and through different media of learning to use the motor skills, to help develop writing, maths...every aspect of the school is weights and how big, how small and it's done through hands-on experience of actually seeing the differences.

A governor reported that there were occasional murmurings from some governors in favour of more traditional methods, but: 'everyone accepts that the children that come here reach the same objectives in the end, even though they are taught differently. And in fact they do surpass some children that would not be in such a happy environment.'

Cath (parent) said her son 'is always full of it, something that they've been doing, or eating or making':

The three Rs are catered for excellently here. In my son's previous school he did very badly with his reading and writing. Since he's been here his writing has come on fabulous and his reading is fantastic to what it was. He could hardly read at all when he came here, but his reading has come on in leaps and bounds. My child has a very low concentration level, he wants to be up and jumping around and doing things, being into things and not sitting down all the time – that would be no good for him at all!

A CHARISMATIC ETHOS

The provision for the pupils' spiritual, moral, social and cultural development is outstanding. The school goes across the boundaries of imaginative teaching in enabling pupils to be in touch with their inner selves and that of other people.

Ofsted 1997: 10

There is a captivating, charismatic feel about Coombes which touches nearly everybody who enters, even if only a casual visitor. Judith Haynes remembers the first day she came to collect her child:

He was outside in the playground working with about four others, older than him, measuring sunflowers and counting sunflower leaves, and picking off sunflower seeds, and I just thought 'Wow, this is amazing!' Other children who would have started school that same day were probably sitting writing about their families, about themselves, drawing pictures about themselves...And I just thought 'This is just a wonderful place to be, because they're experiencing things first hand and enjoying it, and getting so much fun from it.'...[As a teacher] it's extremely demanding, hard work, but the rewards you get from it are substantial. It's always exciting, there's always something new going on.

Part of the charisma lies in the fund of rich activities at Coombes. Beryl Ellinor (school governor) reported 'You can walk in and find one group of children with magnets all over the floor, another doing things with keys, others working with stinging nettles, or weaving and harvesting, or counting sunflower seeds.'

Coombes embraces pupils, parents and teachers alike. Jenny Poore has been at the school for twenty-six years: 'I brought my eldest daughter, Jo, as a rising five to the Coombes, and came in as a helping mum, the way we encourage all mums to come in and help, and I've been here ever since.'

Rachel Aylmer was a student at the school. On the first day she thought it was

wonderful. The children just seemed really happy, the staff were really really welcoming, and I could see children using the grounds in such a creative way, I just knew that I wanted to come back, so as soon as there was a place I got back in...I've loved it.

Sue Rowe was similarly captivated: 'I think it was my experience here as a mother, coming in to help, and seeing a style of education that I didn't realise existed anywhere, and becoming increasingly involved.'

Navnite (parent) had found children in other schools withdrawn and reserved, but here:

It was very natural, it had a certain sort of ambience about it...There's nothing fabricated or set up, to me it's just another home away from home because there is so much emphasis on loving, caring and sharing...When the children start, they're always being cuddled by the teachers and introduced to other children, and it's just like a whole big family, it's not like individual children, it's everyone together.

The magnetism of the school also works for the shy child. Dee's daughter was 'painfully shy' and found it 'very difficult to mix with people'. Sue Humphries suggested they spend a day with her prospective class:

I stayed for a bit, then I realised that I could sneak off, she was completely absorbed in what was going on. I came back a little later and she didn't even notice I was there. I decided there and then it was completely what I was looking for...Within a week of her starting here they were making pumpkin soup, then they were burning down houses and eating baked potatoes, then they were moving into the Christmas stuff and I was just like 'Wow! What's this about?!'

There is a kind of infectious, cumulative enthusiasm about the place. Sue Humphries rates this the chief ingredient:

I'd like there to be more people coming in from outside to work and to share their enthusiasms, because it's not always that you need to be talented to come in and work for the children. You really need to be enthusiastic. If you are knife keen on fossil collecting, or you're very switched on to the environment and the leaves and the twigs, and what you can do with it in art work, or whatever it is you've got, it's the enthusiasm which is infectious.

Martin (parent) found:

Every parent I've met and remember, you all seem to be able to re-late to each other. You go somewhere else and you get little cliques over here and over there, but here, I still feel whenever I drop in, like today, I've not met probably 95 per cent of you guys before, but whenever we meet anybody you think, 'Yes, you're saying ex-actly what I want to hear'. And you get so euphoric about it, you're actually excited about it, and this is the buzz, this is this unknown quantity that you just cannot put your finger on...It just exudes from the building walls...There's a magic formula...[Woman: 'Comes from the walls here, definitely.']

Linda (teaching assistant) felt similarly: 'It's a very loving friendly atmosphered school. I love it. As you walk through the front door there's a friendly atmosphere that seems to envelop you. Other schools don't seem to have it.'

When Sue Rowe first visited the school as a prospective parent,

It was the playground developments that immediately arrested the eye, and made one think 'What's happening here?' And that rich quality of environment outside the school made you want to go indoors and see what was happening. That day was actually Hallowe'en, and everyone was dressed up, there were children diving their heads in and apple bobbing, and teachers with green faces and wild hair, and the place was humming, really humming. And it's like that most days...every week there's a dynamic centre to the week.

Audrey (parent) also was 'overwhelmed by what a positive experience it obviously was for all the children'. She thought it was a matter of caring and respect: 'The fundamental thing is that children are taught to care for each other and to share everything, and so they're taught respect for themselves and respect for other people and respect for the environment.'
Carol Cooke (teacher) affirmed, 'There's a very, very strong emphasis on caring.' Beryl Ellinor, reflecting on why Coombes was such a special school, concluded:

There's a lot of love in this school, and I think that's what draws me to it particularly. Because we all need love and this school does generate a great deal...it's the dedication of the Head Teacher and her staff...The parents that are so willing to help, the other members of the community that are willing to help, and the well-being and the love that all that generates is that atmosphere; that, and the way that children learn and the way they're so happy, it's – well – it's magic!

CONCLUSION

We have heard the views of participants in a learning community that has won praise from many quarters. But some words of caution are necessary. In the first place, Coombes is not a 'normal' school (Goffman 1961), and it has taken it many years and much dedication and hard work for it to become 'exceptional'. Many schools find it difficult to break out of normality, especially in current circumstances where the central government has introduced a range of prescriptions and a means of overseeing to determine whether they have been met. Some might claim that the constraints are less on Coombes as a first school than on some others. More importantly, such schools may be only temporary stopping places in a pupil's career, soon to be eclipsed by the demands of the assessment system. What happens to pupils after they leave Coombes is an issue that has not been addressed. Is their flying start maintained, or do they alter course? If the latter, what are the consequences for the child's education? Unfortunately perhaps, Coombes can do nothing about this Balkanised institutionalisation. The focus on 'learning communities' tends to put the centre of gravity within the school. If it were within the community, there might be more similarity and cohesion among the institutions of that community.

There is little mention in the comments in this chapter of political matters, and expressly the need for a political consciousness (Hargreaves 1994). Learning communities do not exist in political vacuums, and where they run against the grain, as in the UK of today, some political planning and strategising is necessary. Coombes teachers have a strong political consciousness, as I discussed in Woods (1995). This enabled them to recognise the political aspects of the government's reforms; to identify more clearly the principles that guided their own teaching; to engage with the National Curriculum in a constructive and productive way; and to establish alliances with governors and local inspectors. They could then cultivate their own brand of ethos which builds up a power of its own. In these ways, Coombes exploits the 'implementation gap' between policy directive and practice (Fitz *et al.* 1994).

Some might be critical of Coombes. There are those who feel there has been 'too much caring and not enough teaching' in primary schools. They would prefer a harder-edged teaching approach of a more traditional kind. The Chief Inspector heads this campaign (Woodhead 1995, 1997). However, as we have seen, Coombes may have won this particular battle with their excellent results on the government's assessment and evaluation measures.

Such points strike a note of caution. Progressive institutions can generate a great deal of euphoria which can come to have a life of its own. Such was the fate of some schools who had adopted a child-centred ideology in the 1970s and 1980s but failed to convert it into effective practice (Alexander 1992). Learning communities are not established in a day. To ensure their success entails vision, a pioneering spirit, conviction and commitment, a great deal of political awareness and groundwork, ambitious but achievable aims, and relentless determination and application. The human investment is total – but so are the rewards.

References

Alexander, R. (1992) *Policy and Practice in Primary Education*, London: Routledge.

Alexander, R., Rose, J. and Woodhead, C. (1992) *Curriculum Organisation and Classroom Practice in Primary Schools: A Discussion Paper*, Department of Education and Science, London: HMSO.

Cocklin B. and Davis K. (1996) 'Creative schools as effective learning communities', paper presented at the British Educational Research Association Conference, Lancaster, 12–15 September.

Cocklin, B., Coombe, K. and Retallick, J. (1996) 'Learning communities in education: directions for professional development', paper presented at the British Educational Research Association Conference, Lancaster, 12–15 September.

Fitz, J., Halpin, D. and Power, S. (1994) 'Implementation research and education policy: Practice and prospects', *British Journal of Education Studies* 42 (1), 53–69.

Goffman, E. (1961) *Encounters*, New York: Bobbs-Merrill.

Hameyer, U. (1996) 'Profiles of productive schools', in R. Chawla-Duggan and C. J. Pole (eds) *Reshaping Education in the 1990s: Perspectives on Primary Schooling*, London: Falmer Press.

Hargreaves, A. (1994) *Changing Teachers, Changing Times: Teacher's Work and Culture in the Postmodern Age*, London: Cassell.

Hill, R. (1996) 'A school for our times?', TV 22, Course E208, *Exploring Educational Issues*, Milton Keynes, England: BBC Productions, Open University Educational Enterprises.

Jeffrey, B. and Woods, P. (1998) *Testing Teachers: The Impact of School Inspections on Primary Teachers*, London: Falmer Press.

Macbeth A. (1994) 'Involving parents', in A. Pollard and J. Bourne (eds) *Teaching and Learning in the Primary School*, London: Routledge.

Ofsted (1997) Inspection Report on Coombes Infant and Nursery School, Reading, Berkshire, 1–4 December.

Sugrue, C. (1997) *Complexities of Teaching: Child-Centred Perspectives*, London: Falmer Press.

Thomas, G. (1989) 'The teacher and others in the classroom', in C. Cullingford (ed.) *The Primary Teacher: The Role of the Educator and the Purpose of Primary Education*, London: Cassell.

Woodhead, C. (1995) *Annual Lecture of HM Chief Inspector of Schools*, London: Ofsted.

Woodhead, C. (1997) Address given to NUT/TES Conference on Progress in Partnership, November, reported in the *Teacher*, November, 10.

Woods, P. (1995) *Creative Teachers in Primary Schools*, Buckingham, England: Open University Press.

Woods, P., Boyle, M. and Hubbard, N. (1998) *Child-Meaningful Learning among Young Bilingual Children*, Clevedon, England: Multilingual Matters.

Woods, P. and Jeffrey, B. (1996) *Teachable Moments: The Art of Teaching in Primary Schools*, Buckingham, England: Open University Press.

11

PARTICIPATIVE LEARNING

The school as a learning community and as a member of a national reform organisation

Susan Groundwater-Smith

INTRODUCTION

It may have become commonplace to say it; but it is worth reiterating. Teachers' work is a complex interplay of emotional, physical and intellectual tasks. Teachers are continually making and enacting decisions about:

- their students' well-being, both emotional and physical
- the ways and means needed to support cognitive and practical learning
- the distribution and quality of 'classroom' interaction, including behaviour management
- assessment and reporting of levels and quality of achievement
- professional relationships with their peers
- their contributions to the corporate life of the school
- the strategies required for enhancing their own professional knowledge.

It is hard and demanding work and has the capacity to be one of the most satisfying of occupations.

Teachers are unlikely to survive the rigours of such a challenging profession if they are not career-long learners. Strategies and techniques continue to change; human knowledge continues to change; students themselves continue to change; and teachers' own biographies change. The teacher who fails to learn from the lived experience of teaching is very likely to be both angry and frustrated. As Hargreaves (1993) has noted, many teachers in mid-to-late career who have become disenchanted with their work no longer hold the good of their students as their highest priority; their work has been stripped of its very purpose.

Much of teachers' career-long learning is grounded in their experience. All the same, experience alone, no matter how satisfying, is not sufficient for sound, advanced, professional learning. It is essential that the experience is reflected upon and interrogated in ways which render it problematic (Tripp 1993). Argyris and Schon (1974) have long advocated the importance of what they call 'double loop learning': that is, where not only the outcomes of teaching are examined, but the intentions, both individual and systemic, are themselves questioned. Sociologists recognise this activity as the distinction between being reflective and being reflexive.

Day (1997) has indicated that for worthwhile professional growth to occur it is important to recognise all of these aforementioned things. He argues that too often provision for teacher professional development has been founded upon the needs of the system, the employing authority, rather than upon the needs of the teachers within it. In this chapter I shall examine the ways in which a process of school renewal became a process of professional, participative learning, through which teachers with many years of experience were challenged and reinvigorated. I shall indicate that what is needed is an understanding that teacher advanced workplace learning is a scholarly and social activity which occurs *in situ*, and that we must cultivate an appreciation of the nexus between the individual teacher and the workplace itself.

As Harris and Volet have observed there is now a significant body of literature which addresses workplace learning and its relationship to organisational change and development (1997: 28). Senge's (1990) book *The Fifth Discipline* gave voice to the concept of the learning organisation as a place where people are encouraged to learn together in ways which are fresh and innovative. While much of the advocacy for organisational learning had its genesis in business and commerce it can certainly be seen to be applicable to educational enterprises.

Sergiovanni (1994) has indicated a preference for the word 'community' to replace 'organisation' in that he sees the former better connotes the relations between the participants. Retallick (1997), on the other hand, has argued that schools after all *are* organisations which are more tightly coupled than a notion of community would suggest. However, in this instance, I shall remain faithful to the idea of a community in that the teachers concerned enjoyed a kind of camaraderie which goes beyond the expectations of an organisation.

To satisfy the goal of placing workplace learning in context this chapter will do three things. It will first of all portray the case, that of the revitalisation of a boys' comprehensive secondary school in an economically disadvantaged community. Second, it will discuss the processes used to reculture the school in terms of participative professional learning; and finally, it will place this learning in the context of a supportive national reform organisation, the National Schools Network, whose singular mission is to support schools as learning communities.

ASHFIELD BOYS' HIGH SCHOOL

The context

Walking from Ashfield railway station to Ashfield Boys' High School tells the story of the many changes which this Sydney suburb has experienced. Old shop walls still bear the faded signs from earlier and quieter days. Others carry names in Greek and Arabic script. But the newer shops are South-East Asian – Vietnamese, Chinese and Korean signs abound. Older, larger houses jostle for space with newer compact units. The local Leagues Club (Rugby League Football) is adjacent to the school, while almost opposite is the Polish Club and around the corner the Ashfield Baptist Church also accommodates a Chinese, Spanish and Ethiopian Church. Italian reception halls and coffee shops vie for space with Lebanese cake shops and restaurants.

Nearly one half of the residents of Ashfield were born overseas in non-English-speaking countries: Indians, Italians, Philippinos, central Europeans, Lebanese, Chinese, Malaysians, to name but a few.

There is little green space in Ashfield; it is one of Sydney's most densely occupied urban environments. It is a regional centre with Department of Community Services Offices, an employment office and a shopping centre which includes a large mall. Many families have been in the area for generations while other families establish themselves here when they arrive from overseas, but once successful they move on.

Only six years ago Ashfield Boys' High School was seen as the place to which students went when there was nowhere else to go. Boys showing academic promise gained entry to a selective high school in a nearby suburb. Others were sent to local Catholic high schools. The 1991 census indicated that more students in the municipality attended non-government secondary schools than did those going to government schools.[1]

Teachers, dispirited by what they saw as low levels of academic performance and aspiration, did not welcome an appointment to the school. Physically run down, graffiti-sprayed, it had all the signifiers of an institution moving into a moribund state. Numbers were falling, students displayed immoderate levels of aggression and absenteeism, literacy levels were low, results in high-stakes assessment such as the Higher School Certificate were poor, and time was wasted.

The current principal, having moved from a high school located in a more privileged area, was distressed to find the school in such a condition. Her first thought was to make the physical state of the school one which was attractive and would enhance the self-esteem not only of the students but also of the staff, including the ancillary staff.

I had this great urge to clean the place up. No school should look like a dump. I wanted it decently painted and carpeted. It was a matter of first things first. You learn better when your surroundings aren't run down and neglected. We had to have the courage to push forward and do things. It's important to see that these things can be quickly fixed so that we can move on to the real educational issues and not be distracted. First and foremost I wanted a 'healthy school'.[2]

Meeting basic needs in terms of the physical environment has paid off. The school is airy and attractive and student work and achievement are displayed in the foyer, the school hall and classrooms. Large tables have been specially manufactured so that students can work comfortably in groups. The exterior walls are remarkably free of graffiti. Students are expected to wear full school uniform and to act with courtesy to others, including visitors to the school. On my own many visits to Ashfield, I was impressed by the manner in which the boys met and directed me when I found myself in unfamiliar surroundings. Often, to cross a secondary school playground is to run the gauntlet; this was decidedly not the case.

Belonging to a community of learners

The core values of the school are embodied in its motto, *Here We Decide*. This signifies the notion of the community of learners in the school being responsible for, and in control of, their own learning. This community includes teachers as well as students. It also reaches out to other educational organisations.

The school acts in collaboration with a Distance Education Support Unit, which works to meet the learning needs of physically disabled students and those who, for emotional and social reasons, do not attend school on a regular basis.

Ashfield Boys' High School was for many years a designated disadvantaged school. It takes part in the Staying On Program, which seeks to enhance student retention rates in less affluent communities, and it is linked to a local university, not only for purposes of the practicum, but to take part in programmes of research and development.

Approximately four hundred boys attend the school, a very large proportion of these coming from language backgrounds other than English. Their needs are met by a teaching staff of forty, half of whom have been in the school for over six years, i.e. prior to the changes which the reculturing brought to the school.

It is important to note that Ashfield Boys' High School is characterised by multiple innovations, each of which interacts with the other. Student welfare and literacy are paramount in planning and change, all of which have

214

as a focus the notion of understanding and promoting learning in a secure and accepting environment. It is expected that teachers will be sensitive to different learning styles and develop pedagogies collaboratively to accommodate these. The leadership of the school encourages all members of the staff to see themselves as active and informed agents of change. Decisions are negotiated and policies developed collaboratively.

The innovation with which this case study is concerned is that part of the school's activity which focuses upon Years 7 and 8. By restructuring the ways in which the teachers work it has been possible to divide each year into four groups. Each group is the responsibility of a team of four teachers, most of whom teach more than one key learning area. Teams take the students from Year 7 into Year 8. Each team meets weekly for the equivalent of two periods to discuss student learning, in terms of both achievement and needs. The day itself is organised into double, even triple, periods thus cutting down on movement between classes. From time to time teams work together on integrated themes which run over several weeks with a culminating day.

The emphasis upon the junior years is significant in that, as one teacher observed, 'if you can catch people in Year 7 then part of the battle is won'. The home/school link is considered to be of great importance. Teams do not hesitate to contact students' homes to discuss with parents any difficulties which the student may be experiencing, or to advise home of particular achievements which home and school can mutually celebrate. Regular bulletins are published. These give information about school events and individual student achievement. They also address particular educational issues in a reader-friendly fashion.

Central to the innovation is the enhancement of teacher professional knowledge. While less explicit in planning documents it is clear that there is a planned process which ensures that teachers have access to innovative thinking from both within Australia and overseas. International associates from organisations such as the US Coalition of Essential Schools, for example Professor Ted Sizer, visit the school and contribute to its continuing professional conversation. When Professor Jennifer Nias, from the United Kingdom, visited the school she was impressed by the ongoing professional exchange which she witnessed and she commented to me:

> Of course teachers are going to talk about private and domestic things with each other. But, in my experience, it is unusual to find teachers, in the staffrooms, on the stairs, in the corridors, talking so much about their pupils and their needs. It is really a form of professional development and a very powerful one at that.

Another feature of the innovation is the acceptance of a flatter management structure. Although, and very clearly, the principal plays a key role in inspiring and motivating her staff, she is also very active in mentoring staff and encouraging them to take leadership responsibilities in planning and implementation. During my association with the school (over two years) several new leaders have emerged and have been supported in developing and articulating policies in the school. Key players have moved on to support the innovation in a larger context. For example, a maths teacher has moved on to become a consultant in his discipline and to draw attention particularly to multiple learning styles and processes of group work and problem-solving in the junior secondary years. A senior science teacher has become the state coordinator for the National Schools Network, a reform organisation whose work will be discussed later in this chapter. As a result of her work at Ashfield, she has been able to draw upon her practical experience of change to encourage others to engage in the risky business of rethinking teachers' work practices.

In summary, the innovation is one which emphasises teaching and learning for all. The report of the quality assurance review in Term 2, 1995, put it thus:

> In the focus area of 'teaching and learning' the school has been commendably successful over recent years in creating and achieving an agenda for change in learning and teaching practices to improve student learning outcomes. The school is essentially characterised by proactive risk taking and informed intellectual discourse about contemporary best practice. Educational leadership is shared and enhanced at all levels by a variety of collaborative decision making structures. Students are able to articulate high level understandings about learning and increasingly demonstrate improved learning outcomes. The school has an atmosphere of purposeful, cooperative learning which is strongly supported by quality relationships among students and staff...

While there can be little question that the generally held view is that the innovations at Ashfield Boys' High School have taken hold, it is important that a portrayal of the kind attempted here should look more intently at the work of the school through the eyes of the teachers and learners themselves. The two sections which follow, 'Teachers' voices' and 'Students' voices', will examine the ways in which teachers and learners talk about learning, pedagogy and the curriculum in the context of the middle years of schooling, organised as they are in the aforementioned team framework.

Teachers' voices

In order to capture teachers' insights and understandings of the middle years at Ashfield Boys' High School I became an observer at a series of team

216

meetings for one Year 7 and one Year 8 group. I also requested annotated samples of work from these two groups and recorded teachers' commentaries on learning as exemplified in this work. I attended staff meetings, particularly one with an overseas visitor focusing upon authentic assessment. Finally, individual teachers were also interviewed.

Team meetings followed an agenda which was developed collaboratively. The meetings were chaired on a rotational basis. Action statements were recorded as a means of following through decisions. These statements are themselves reviewed from time to time to ensure that such follow-through has occurred.

Below are notes from one such meeting. They are reported here in detail as they exemplify the kind, and level, of discussion which teachers conducted.

> The first item discussed was the newsletter. It was noted that there had been an attempt to carry more of the students' work and to acknowledge them individually. Strategies were suggested for ensuring that the bulletins went home. It was proposed that code numbers be assigned and that those which were returned would be entered into a book club prize.
>
> The meeting then turned to individual cases. Two major offenders in terms of persistent lateness were discussed. It was indicated that phone contact had been made with home and that positive improvement had been noted. The achievement of the two students, across the key learning areas, was of concern, and it was clear that the discussion was well informed. Two larger issues arose from these individual cases and were in turn analysed. One of these was the extent to which the team worked together to facilitate a balance in homework tasks; the other was a management question in relation to handling mixed ability groups in such a way as to maximise the learning for all. Of particular concern was the attainment level of the more able students in mathematics. The team exchanged strategies which had worked for them with this particular group of students.
>
> A third student, D., was then cited. His nervous demeanour and isolated behaviour appeared to manifest itself in all of the classes. It was seen that the school counsellor should be consulted: 'to me it's getting bigger than us, we need the counsellor's help if we are to best help D.' The specific case again led to a more general discussion of the value of the Classroom Management Plan which was routinely used for students at risk. In this plan the problem was cited, the action taken was recorded and the action requested was noted. It was seen that because D. was a new boy it would be important to arrange for his parents to meet the team. While D. was

negatively constructed as argumentative, having poor study habits and a difficult prior history; the team made an effort to ensure that his positive assets were also outlined. It was seen that he was particularly strong at analysing his own performance and that this skill should be built upon: 'It's important that we build on even the slightest glimmerings...'

Again a general issue arose; this was in relation to students meeting with the team when there was concern about academic and social progress. It was also seen that teachers who were not members of the team, but who also taught the class, needed greater access to the team's deliberations. For example the teacher of Japanese was experiencing some difficulties and might be able to better manage if she could be party to the team's intense knowledge of the boys. A number of strategies for the teacher of Japanese were proposed, for example reordering the seating, and a member of the team delegated to discuss them with her.

The team then turned to their stated aim which was to inculcate independent learning habits among the students: 'If the whole aim of our work is for the kids to become independent learners they still have a long, long way to go!' The team recognised that there was a fine line between nurturing the boys and disengaging from them, so that they took greater responsibility. The item was nominated for further discussion. The minutes and actions were then quickly reviewed.

It is clear, from the team meetings, that students in Years 7 and 8 cannot render themselves invisible as they so often do when they move from primary to secondary schools. Where teachers' work is structured so that they see hundreds of students weekly, often for very short periods of time, and where they are isolated from other teachers, it is very difficult for them to come to know the students as intimately as they do at Ashfield. The teachers are focused and purposeful in their discussion of students; their aim is to enhance learning and they believe they do this best by knowing the students, and the conditions under which they learn, well.

It is also clear that strategies for teaching are regularly discussed. Motivation, classroom management, application and assessment procedures all have their airing. The teachers are by no means satisfied by what they do. They believe that now the school is more settled they need to find ways of boosting performance, particularly among students with significant academic potential, not only so that these students can gain personally, but also so that they might be mentors for their peers.

Staff focus group discussions were held with the same teams as those observed. Teachers were asked to recollect a critical learning moment in the classroom and to reflect upon it. They were also asked to provide evidence of learning and to comment upon it.

One example of a critical learning moment (for teacher as well as student) was of a student taking a maths test which was a form of group-based practical problem solving:

> He came up to me afterwards and said 'I really liked that test, why can't we do more like it?' Well it wasn't a common test and it was more fun because it was testing their learning in context. [This led to a more general discussion of the conduct of testing and its purposes.]

> Partly it's for placement in Year 9. You have to decide, when it comes to the crunch, who is going to a level and it's difficult to decide, for one person, so we need plenty of information. I suppose the mark is a bit of a crutch for us, not that we depend on it entirely. There is a lot of discussion with the teachers about how they [the students] work et cetera, et cetera. We keep all the marks, it's not just the one common test, there are four of them, and the class tests.

> We also need to think about who it's for. We tend to think it's only for us, but if a parent asks they're entitled to know, but at the moment we think about it as being information for us.

> [In response to the question 'Well, how do the lower-achieving students feel about the common tests, you are describing them just as a tool, do they see them that way?']

> They (the lower achieving students) get very demoralised. But it's one of the benefits of an ungraded class that the students do know their own scope. When they are streamed they can have great fun, but they have no idea of what they can't do...it's a dilemma, because in a streamed, low ability class you can do a lot, they just do their class tests at their own level and they feel competent, there is the other side, they're in the bottom class and they know they are in the bottom class; but they find the common test a terrible letdown. It's very difficult to teach ungraded classes in maths, very difficult...we can't let them fall behind in Years 7 and 8 because they will be disadvantaged when they start to work in Year 9. See some of them are already thinking about the TER [Tertiary Entrance Rank for university admission] and we are not going to decide for them 'You're not university material so it doesn't matter'. I worry about the top students because I think they may be held back and I worry about the bottom students, the ones in the middle are OK...

> This particular test [the group test which set this discussion running] was a real challenge for B. because he doesn't like working

in groups. He just went off and did his own thing, so he didn't do very well, and he's used to getting top marks. He's very bright, but he's not very good at working with other people...It would be good to introduce a practical part to the common test, but it's not going to be easy.

By way of contrast, in physical education it was seen that assessment could be far less exact. Students were closely observed in performance tasks, but there was no task analysis; instead the judgement was a subjective one: 'It's just a report on how they try...whether they want to improve or not.' While there is no specific programme, as such, students are encouraged to observe each other's skills and provide each other with feedback. They also demonstrate skills: 'that gives them a real kick and the others think "well if he can do it, maybe I can do it"'.

This one critical learning moment led to a protracted discussion regarding assessment practices generally and the ways in which they needed to be consistent with the philosophy of learning held by the school. Currently the junior school is reconsidering its reporting practices and is asking each faculty for advice regarding terminology and layout. Again the matter of high-stakes assessment in the form of the Higher School Certificate (HSC) meant that teachers felt themselves pulled two ways at once. They had a commitment to the school's policies, but were concerned about meeting their responsibilities to their students as they moved into the senior years. On reflection, though, the teachers believed that they were continuing to move on this issue, in spite of the many difficulties:

Sometimes I forget how far we've come in this school. Of course you can get demoralised. I think 'oh golly there's so much still to do'; but this school is so aware of its different students, it's so aware of students' learning. Sure you can look at things like essays, but we try to look at the ways they work together, the ways they do their work.

While it is not possible here to reproduce the many pieces of work which the teachers submitted as evidence of learning, it is interesting to note that the demonstration of learning can take many forms including artefacts, performance, planning and preparation. As one teacher commented:

I believe that there are many different learning styles and that people have different aptitudes for different things. As a result of this belief the format of the attached assignment is one that I often use. It covers three sections: written, oral, auditory or visual, so that each student has a chance to perform well in the area they feel more comfortable in.

Working in teams, being investigative, communicating findings, these are commonplace in the primary school context, but they are activities which often fade away in the secondary school. Ashfield Boys' High School, by working in these ways in the junior years, is facilitating the transition from primary to secondary school. While not perceived as one of its major aims, it is clearly a significant outcome.

While teachers, in their discussions and actions, are working hard to change pedagogy at the school, they also are open about their concerns; these revolve mainly around questions of assessment and reporting. During the conduct of the case study it was possible to be witness to a morning's conversation with a visiting teacher from an innovative high school in the Bronx. Dinah asked the participants to note what was good about working at Ashfield, what excited teachers and what 'bugged' them. Below is a digest of the teachers' responses:

The good – relationships, openness, the kids, being a teacher–learner, teams, mutually supportive (teachers help teachers, kids help kids, teachers help kids, kids help teachers!), meaningful work, at home and welcomed, enthusiasm of students, professional development, growth and development of the school as a whole.

The exciting – teams, challenges, ownership, real outcomes, assessment no longer a punishment to be feared but an opportunity for a different relationship with students and their parents, being able to demonstrate to parents what has been achieved, learners being proud of their work, learners knowing where they are going and why, possibilities for alternative forms of assessment, opportunities for students to make decisions about what constitutes good work and why.

Bugs – rate of change in official thinking, enormity of the task of assessment, system constraints, unrealistic expectations, time, intensification of work (not really a bug), but the difficulty of negotiating when you *really* want to improve things and it's not just on the surface, continuing curriculum change, isolation, Departmental thinking (DSE), lack of public understanding of what is being achieved, dominance of HSC.

Clearly the rapidity of change beyond the scope and control of the school was a matter of concern to the teachers, but equally clearly they perceived that they were in a context where significant features of change were in their hands and that these features produced satisfying professional rewards.

Student opinions are important in the context of the work of Ashfield Boys' High School. How do students see their learning and the ways in which their teachers support them? This portrayal now turns to the students' voices.

Students' voices

Students were asked to examine a series of eight pictures of adults: some young, some old, male and female, Anglo Australian, Ethnic Australian. They were asked to choose an image of a 'helpful teacher' and explain their selection. They then answered the following questions: What do teachers do to help you learn? How do you know when you have learned something? How does your teacher know when you have learned something? and What other things would you like your teachers to do to help you learn?

The images enabled students to discuss the attributes of teachers whom they liked and respected. Being humorous, considerate, knowledgeable and kind were the most often cited teacher behaviours which were seen as helpful.

Students from Year 7 saw the following strategies as ones which helped them to learn: being clear and specific; explaining well; repeating instructions and explanations in more than one way; listening, being patient, encouraging; pointing things out; giving many examples; working in groups; giving 'hands on' activities; allowing students to ask questions; conducting class meetings; and talking with parents. The list from Year 8 was similar but with a greater emphasis on class management: 'they need to be strict but fair', 'ensure that everyone is attending'. One student summed up the helpful teacher in this way:

> They shouldn't rush us. They should give you a chance at trying and be positive.

The majority of students in Year 7 believed that they had learned something when they could answer questions. They also significantly cited merit awards, marks, results and reports. They believed that when their teachers recognised them by congratulating them they were also learning. Fewer relied on their own assessment of competence; an exception to this was the following response:

> When it sticks in my head and it seems easier to talk to friends and explain to them.

Year 8 students had far more diverse responses. Merit awards, tests, and positive reinforcement from teachers were mentioned several times, but in the main the focus was on the students' internalisation of success:

When I can get started easily.
When I can do the revision.
When I remember and can explain it to someone else.
When I can do it for homework and not worry.
You just get this feeling that tells you it's easy.
When you can tackle something new.

And how do their teachers know that they have learned something? Answering questions again rated the most common response among Year 7 students. Marks, homework, correcting work, observation and noticeable improvement were all suggested. Year 8 students had similar indicators and included slightly more sophisticated responses, such as:

When I can communicate freely with them.
To be honest they don't really show it so I have no idea.

Finally, in considering other ways in which their teachers might be of assistance, Year 7 emphasised active learning, fun, games, excursions and camps. They also looked for more homework (although one student suggested less homework) and more discussion time. Only two students had negative observations related to less shouting. More analysis when things go wrong was also seen as helpful:

Explain when I get something wrong, explain step by step – go slowly.

Year 8 students were also keen to see learning made more fun and based on concrete experiences. Games, excursions and camps were popular. Shouting was a problem for one student. Others suggested more personal help, for example 'Single out all the things I'm not good at and help me with them'. Following up homework was also seen as important. One student thought that his teachers should encourage him to try things, even if he might not be successful straight away. Two students turned directly to content:

Cover fewer topics well.
Teach more in the time available.

In the discussions which were conducted following the personal responses students were most forthcoming. They did not add new ideas but they felt comfortable and confident, in front of their teachers, to discuss these issues. They also appeared to be anxious to assist each other in clarifying their responses, especially where a student was struggling with the vocabulary.

Ashfield Boys' High School is a school on the move. There is a sense that teachers and students are justly proud of the school's achievements. Years 7 and 8 are critical ones for establishing student self-esteem and establishing study habits and attitudes for later years. But the participants are not easily satisfied; they can see where there is room for further growth and continue to work towards it. Assessment and reporting are clearly areas of concern to the teachers. Increased active learning is of interest to the students. Continuing professional growth is important to the principal.

It could be said that the school is an authentic learning community where learning with others, learning through others and learning about learning itself is valued. As a researcher I have seen the experience of constructing the case study as a form of learning – learning that secondary school teachers, given the opportunity and challenge, can come to know their students with the kind of intimacy not normally considered possible in that context; learning that students can and will discuss their own learning with insight and clarity; learning that educational leadership is as much to do with letting go of authority as with exercising it.

PARTICIPATIVE PROFESSIONAL LEARNING AND THE ROLE OF THE NATIONAL SCHOOLS NETWORK

So how did the school manage the change which resulted in teachers perceiving themselves as engaged in their own ongoing professional learning? It has already been indicated that a critical factor was the role played by the educational leaders in the school; not only the principal, but a number of key teachers, not all of whom were necessarily in executive positions such as head of department.

In addition, importantly, the school was a foundation member of the National Schools Network (NSN).The Network recognises that schools are complex communities which breed complex problems. The NSN does not have technical solutions which are to be applied to those problems; rather it creates the conditions for schools to enquire into their own problems, identify the challenges and generate their own resolutions. Throughout the process of change the school was supported by the NSN. It is to the work of the Network that this chapter now turns, for it is becoming clear that schools are not learning communities within a professional vacuum; they operate as members of larger learning organisations, in this case the NSN.

The National Schools Network as a reform organisation

As a reform movement the NSN has some unique characteristics. It was born of a national project which was established to examine the quality of teaching and learning in Australia (National Project on the Quality of Teaching and Learning, NPQTL 1994). From its inception it has been founded on a partnership between employing authorities (both government and non-government) and teachers' unions in each Australian state and territory. Ordinarily these relations can be said to be somewhat uneasy and at times difficult and competitive. States and territories guard their education portfolios carefully and are suspicious of federalism. Similarly, relations between employing authorities and unions are often problematic. So the partnership is unusual in a number of respects.[3]

It is not surprising that it was the Work Organisation and Related Pedagogical Issues working party of the NPQTL which gave rise to the National Schools Network. It became clear to the working party that the ways in which teachers' work was organised and regulated had impact upon pedagogy. The key reform questions which were to be addressed by the NSN were:

1   What is it about the way teachers work, in particular the way they teach and organise their work, that gets in the way of student learning?
2   How can educators support each other to make the changes that are good for both learners and teachers?

Clearly the agreements which were developed between employing authorities and teachers' unions were critical in enabling teachers to conduct workplace reform and reculturing in ways which stepped outside regulatory frameworks, on the understanding that practices were judged to be safe and socially equitable.

Member schools, such as Ashfield Boys' High School, agreed to the following nationally negotiated set of principles:

- to be responsible for improving learning outcomes for all students
- to encourage greater student participation in the learning process
- to establish equality of access, opportunity and outcomes for all students
- to examine current work organisation to identify good practices and impediments to effective teaching and learning
- to develop a model of participative workplace procedures and decision making that includes the whole staff

- to understand and accept the industrial rights and responsibilities of all parties
- to encourage whole community involvement in decision-making about the reform process.

(NSN Website 1998)

Schools within the ambit of the NSN began to experiment with innovative forms of team-teaching, cooperative learning, timetable restructuring, assessment and reporting practices, parental and community involvement and sub-school development (Groundwater-Smith 1996a).

The Network, in association with the Australian Teaching Council, developed a series of residential professional development schools where successful practices could be more widely disseminated. Partnership links were established with individual teacher education academics who themselves became co-learners with classroom practitioners. The NSN simultaneously hosted a series of seminars with university-based teacher educators where issues of workplace culture and adult workplace learning were debated (see for example Retallick and Groundwater-Smith 1996). The seminars brought together teacher educators, school principals, classroom practitioners and training and development officers of state departments of education. A keynote speaker on one occasion was the principal of Ashfield Boys' High School. At the centre of her paper was her own workplace learning as an educational leader in a reforming school.

At the same time as it worked to directly support schools as learning communities the Network was establishing a research register of academic practitioners willing to commit themselves to the NSN principles, while at the same time maintaining a critical voice. Partnership research practices, which developed notions of participative practitioner research, were employed and not only resulted in a number of publications but also provided a form of professional development for teachers (Groundwater-Smith 1996b; Sachs and Groundwater-Smith 1996).

The NSN focus for action is best summed up in the concluding comments (NPQTL 1994: 35) of the review of the National Schools Program from which it arose. Such areas of action could include:

- collaborative working relationships among and between teachers, non-teaching staff and students
- changes to school culture and climate to make schools a better workplace for teaching and learning
- structural/organisational change (such as changes to timetabling etc.); this includes cooperative arrangements with external bodies able to contribute to the work of the school.
- applications of technologies to increase the effectiveness and efficiency of teaching, learning, assessment, etc.

Clearly, it is under the aegis of these areas of action that Ashfield's work progressed and the learning community was built.

Finally, in this brief discussion of the work of the National Schools Network it is important to recognise that it sees for itself a responsibility to systematically enquire into the reforms themselves. The Network has a research office whose task it is to 'build a culture of research in member schools as an integral part of their rethinking processes' (Harradine 1996: 1). To foster the development of such a research culture the Network has established a Faculty of Educational Researchers in the field of school reform. As well as supporting research at the local level the office commissions cross-site enquiries focused upon issues of strategic significance as they are identified by the NSN's Steering Committee. It is expected that such enquiries will be participative and liberatory.

Indeed, it is the result of such a research project that this chapter came into being (Groundwater-Smith and Currie 1998). As an accredited researcher, one is afforded by the NSN an opportunity to work with schools in ways which change the social relations between the outside and inside voices. This chapter has undergone several revisions as a result of negotiations between the NSN, myself and Ashfield Boys' High School staff. For example, it was the school's decision to name itself, rather than be given anonymity as is normally the case. In addition, and more importantly, the school saw the discussion of the chapter as another opportunity for professional development and workplace learning.

CONCLUSION

Clearly the work described in this chapter is scholarly in nature. It recognises teaching, not only as a learning profession but as a learned profession. Consider this entry on Bertrand Russell, the philosopher:

> His aim was always to find reasons for accepted beliefs, whether in the field of mathematics, natural science, or common sense. He was a consistent Sceptic, not in the sense that he denied our claims to knowledge, but that he questioned them.
>
> (Urmson and Ree 1989: 285)

Teachers at Ashfield engaged in continuous questioning regarding the nature of their work. They were participative learners who took responsibility not only for their own learning but also for that of their peers and colleagues. They were in the richest sense of the phrase a learning community. I suggested at the beginning of the chapter that teachers' work is hard and demanding. It is also courageous work when it is undertaken in the transformative ways described in the case study outlined in this chapter.

Notes

This chapter draws upon a study undertaken for the National Schools Network (Groundwater-Smith and Currie 1998). It also has some of its origin in a key-note address delivered to the biennial conference of the Queensland Agriculture Teachers Association (Groundwater-Smith 1998).

1   State-wide figures for New South Wales reveal that 70 per cent of students attend government schools.
2   This paragraph has been constructed from several conversations with the school principal.
3   It should be noted that the NPQTL itself grew from a reform climate based upon an evolving accord between employers and unions more generally. With a change in federal government this accord is no longer operative. Nonetheless, the NSN has survived with the support of state systems of education, teacher unions, a coalition of member universities (14) and their host, the University of Western Sydney (MacArthur), and individual membership. A recent senate enquiry into the status of teaching in Australia has strongly recommended that the NSN be revivified and supported by the Commonwealth.

References

Argyris, C. and Schon, D. (1974) *Theory in Practice: Increasing Professional Effectiveness*, New York: Jossey-Bass.

Day, C. (1997) 'In-service teacher education in Europe: Conditions and themes for development in the 21st century', *British Journal of In-Service Education* 23 (1), 39–54.

Groundwater-Smith, S. (1996a) 'Putting teacher professional judgement to work', paper presented to the Practitioner Research and Academic Practices Conference, Cambridge Institute of Education, 4–6 July.

Groundwater-Smith, S. (1996b) *Let's Not Live Yesterday Tomorrow: A Study of Curriculum and Assessment Reform in the Context of Schools' Reculturing*, Ryde, Australia: National Schools Network.

Groundwater-Smith, S. (1998) 'The scholarship of teaching: Professional workplace learning', keynote address to the Queensland Agricultural Teachers' Association Tenth Biennial Conference, 14–17 January, Coolum, Queensland.

Groundwater-Smith, S. and Currie, J. (1998) *Learning is When...*, Ryde, Australia: National Schools Network.

Hargreaves, A. (1993) 'Dissonant voices, dissipated lives: Teachers and the multiple realities of restructuring', paper presented to the Fifth Annual Conference of the International Study Association on Teacher Thinking, Gothenburg, Sweden, 12–17 August.

Harradine, J. (1996) *The Role of Research in the Work of the National Schools Network*, Ryde, Australia: National Schools Network.

Harris, L. and Volet, S. (1997) *Developing a Learning Culture in the Workplace*, Perth, Australia: Murdoch University.

NPQTL (1994) 'Report of the National Project on the Quality of Teaching and Learning', 1991–1993, Canberra: NPQTL.

NSN Website (1998) http://www.schnet.edu.au/nsn

Retallick, J. (1997) 'Workplace learning and the school as a learning organisation', in Faculty of Education (eds) *Exploring Professional Development in Education*, Sydney: Social Science Press.

Retallick, J. and Groundwater-Smith, S. (1996) *The Advancement of Teacher Workplace Learning*, Wagga Wagga, Australia: Centre for Professional Development, Charles Sturt University.

Sachs, J. and Groundwater-Smith, S. (1996) 'Celebrating teacher professional knowledge: School reform and teacher professional judgement', paper presented to the Re-engineering Education for Change Conference, UNESCO and Asia Pacific Centre of Educational Innovation and Development, Bangkok.

Senge, P. (1990) *The Fifth Discipline: The Art and Practice of the Learning Organisation*, New York: Doubleday.

Sergiovanni, T. (1994) *Building Community in Schools*, San Francisco: Jossey-Bass.

Tripp, D. (1993) *Critical Incidents in Teaching*, London: Routledge.

Urmson, J. and Ree, J. (eds) (1989) *The Concise Encyclopedia of Western Philosophy and Philosophers*, London: Unwin Hyman.

12

BUILDING A LEARNING COMMUNITY IN A DOCTORAL PROGRAMME IN PROFESSIONAL DEVELOPMENT

Jim Henkelman-Bahn and Neil Davidson

INTRODUCTION

A doctoral programme in professional development was initiated in the 1980s at the University of Maryland College Park with the express intent of building learning communities as the basis of the programme. This chapter will describe the programme and some of the lessons that have been learned about the issues that arise in the building and sustaining of learning communities.

DESCRIPTION OF THE PROGRAMME

This experientially based Doctor of Education programme was conceived by a small faculty consisting of a group of five people associated with the Department of Curriculum and Instruction in the College of Education; this included our colleagues Larry Nash, Richard Arends and Charles Brand. It began in 1985 with a cohort of twenty-five graduate students who were seeking new ways to have impact as professionals. Most persons participating in the programme did not want to be administrators or managers. They were preparing themselves to become effective change agents in educational systems, government service agencies and private enterprises. They were interested in improving the effectiveness of people and organisations through the use of the applied behavioural sciences in professional development, staff development, organisation development, human resource development or training and development. They were generally full-time

230

mid-career employees in a variety of settings who attended classes on a part-time basis.

The commitment of the faculty who designed the doctoral programme for professional development was to use the concept of the learning community as the basis for an experiential programme to develop self-reflective practitioners in human resource development and staff development. During the past decade, the faculty and students in the three cohorts that have participated in this programme have together learned valuable lessons about the nature of community and its relationship to the development of self-reflective learners.

Goals of the programme

The goals of the programme are simple. Professionals are being prepared to become effective change agents for individuals and organisations through training and consulting interventions. Professionals are also being prepared to add to the knowledge and practice of the field through a variety of research methodologies.

The programme

The applied behavioural science skills, competencies and knowledge included in this programme can be conceptualised as in Table 2. This matrix defines twelve specific areas by combining three arenas (one-to-one, small group, organisation) in which the skills are demonstrated, and four roles (member, leader, trainer, consultant) for each of these arenas. The skills, competencies and knowledge in each area are important for an effective practitioner in this field. In order to develop the skills for Area 12, it is necessary to develop the skills in the preceding areas.

Table 2 Matrix of skills, competencies and knowledge required for the doctoral programme in professional development

Roles	Arenas One-to-one	Small group	Organisation
Member	1	2	3
Leader	4	5	6
Trainer	7	8	9
Consultant	10	11	12

Source: Adapted from Leadership Institute of Seattle (LIOS) model

In order to illustrate the skills/competencies/knowledge that are associated with each area in the matrix, consider the small group column (Areas 2,

5, 8 and 11). In the member role in a small group (Area 2), a person completing the doctoral programme would understand group development theories and be able to use these theories as a diagnostic tool or lens through which to understand the dynamics of the group and function effectively as a group member. In the leader role in a small group (Area 5), a person would know leadership theories and be able to assess his or her own leadership style in a small group in order to lead more effectively. In the trainer role in a small group (Area 8), a person would understand how adults learn and be able to design an appropriate experiential education event in a small group. And finally, as a consultant with a small group (Area 11), a participant in the programme would learn different processing tools and be able to help a group to reflect on its effectiveness after a working session.

The doctoral programme is designed to meet the many objectives, like the ones illustrated above, that follow from the matrix as well as curriculum/instruction and research objectives. Course work and traditional requirements in doctoral programmes are moulded to attain these objectives through an experiential community-based approach.

Course work

The course work which most of the cohort took together differed slightly from one cohort to another. Below is a listing of the courses that are involved for the most recent cohort. This course work was offered over a period of three and a half years with one or two courses each semester or summer term. Dissertation work then followed.

- Pro Seminar in Professional Development
- Communication Issues in Human Resource Development
- Group Dynamics and Leadership
- Consulting and Training Skills
- Organisation Development and Change Processes
- Theories of Conflict Resolution in Human Development
- Three Internships in Varied Settings
- The Adult Learner
- Computers in Instructional Settings
- Introduction to Instructional Design/Development
- Introduction to Research
- Research on Teaching
- Quantitative Research Methods I and II
- Intermediate Statistics in Education
- Introduction to Evaluation Models
- Introduction to Field Methods of Research
- Doctoral Seminar

In addition to the course work, there were regular community meetings, residential experiential learning laboratories, and support group meetings.

A METAPHOR

The second cohort group began with an experiential outdoor education weekend designed to begin the process of community building. This event became a metaphor for the development of the learning community as well as an experience of community building. A brief telling of this story indicates some of the flavour of the programme and also raises some important community issues. After this story has been told, each of the major components of the programme will be explored for insights into learning communities.

The event was planned by the students themselves with minimal input from the faculty. The students had to perform this task while the group was still in the formation stage. On the whole, they managed to pull it off successfully and most participants were pleased with the event. However, problems occurred which illustrated some of the issues in building a community.

It was the end of the second day of the initial retreat for the beginning of the doctoral programme in professional development. A group of tired students and faculty members climbed into the school bus for the trip back to the retreat centre after an all-day canoe adventure on the Shenandoah River. Most of the students seemed satisfied, but there was some uneasiness. One of the guides had stayed behind to wait for two students who had not yet landed their canoes at the final destination and for two other students who had paddled back upstream to find the missing canoe. In this stranded canoe were two students who simply could not manage the canoe as it turned in circles in an eddy in the river. When they finally got free and ended the trip, they couldn't believe that they had been left behind.

This canoe trip was a metaphor for the way in which students struggled with the nature of community and their responsibility to each other while at the same time expressing their individuality in the doctoral programme. While planning the canoe trip on the previous day, the group of twenty-five students, who were mostly strangers to each other, had made a commitment to stay together and support each other. Some of the students had never participated in this kind of event, and a few were very definitely frightened of the water. During the morning on the river, the group did seem to stay close together — checking with each other and encouraging those having troubles. There were a few mishaps; for example, one student fell into the mud while disembarking on an island for lunch.

However, in the afternoon some of the pairs of students decided to take their canoes on individual explorations. The group became more and more spread out. Finally, when all but the last canoe had arrived at the final destination, it was decided that the bus would head back to the retreat centre and return later to pick up the remaining students.

During the processing of the day's events that evening, some very significant questions were raised. Amidst tears of anger, one of the stranded canoe occupants asked, 'How can I trust you to support me in the doctoral programme, or how can I trust you to help me write a dissertation when you don't even keep your word about my safety?' She felt a deep sense of abandonment when she and her partner were left stranded in their canoe on the river. After all, the group had made a decision to stay together for support. Indeed what would be the nature of community in this doctoral programme? Could people trust each other?

The planning for the canoe trip had also been difficult. Getting twenty-five students, most of whom did not know each other, to agree on what to eat for lunch, whether to buy or make the lunch, and who was to handle which chores, was not easy without input or help from any of the faculty. Was this an example of what the relationship would be between the faculty and the students in this doctoral programme? Who would be responsible for decisions or for the learning?

COMPONENTS OF THE PROGRAMME: LEARNING COMMUNITY ILLUSTRATED

Three cohort groups of approximately twenty-five students each have experienced this programme. Each of the cohorts developed distinct personalities and demonstrated different lessons concerning community. Examples are drawn below from each of the three cohorts to illustrate aspects of the learning community. The faculty and students together made the concept of learning community come to life and evolve over the years of the three cohorts. The components of the programme that are examined are: cohort, mutual learning community, internships, varied experiential learning processes, residential learning events, accommodating the needs of participants, continuous improvement, research as a foundation, emphasis on writing as a medium of thinking, becoming reflective practitioners, and a support system for dissertation completion.

Cohort

In each of the three cohort groups of the doctoral programme in professional development, the students were admitted to the programme at the same time. Most of the course work for three years was completed by the students in courses that were designed specifically for the doctoral programme. As the students took these courses together, the cohort provided emotional, intellectual and professional support for the individuals.

During the ethnography research course in the first cohort, a team of six students and three faculty members, including the ethnographer who was the instructor for the course, conducted a study of the culture of the cohort (Henkelman 1989). Students were invited to describe the programme and some of the different ways in which it affected their lives. The students and the ethnographer on this research team reached consensus on the emergence of the following key themes that uniquely described the culture of the organisation and shaped the development of the individuals in that culture: 1) community, 2) group evolution, 3) experiential learning, 4) individual growth. It is important to note that these themes emerged from the transcripts of the interviews. Questions were not asked about community or other possible components of the programme. The questions were open ended. One student expressed it as follows:

> I can't overestimate the value of having an intact group with each other over periods of time. We celebrate at weddings and good things that happen, and we mourn at losses, deaths, and illnesses within the group. We rally around and give each other support.

The major conclusions around the community theme in this research were:

1 The community of learners supported each other through camaraderie and caring.
2 The participants learned about working effectively as a group.
3 The group was strengthened by its diversity (to be described later).
4 The participants created a professional state-wide network.
5 An atmosphere of risk-taking and challenge encouraged members to experiment with new behaviours and to trust themselves and the group.
6 There was a sense of family that will last a lifetime.
7 People grew in ways they had never before experienced.

Mutual learning community

The concept of a mutual learning community was an ideal that was sought from the beginning of the programme. Obviously, a cohort does not automatically become either a community of learners or a full-blown learning community, in which the community itself becomes a deliberate vehicle for learning. When each cohort first met, most participants did not have any relationship with the others in the group. They were a disparate group of students in the same programme cohort. Intentional interventions helped move the disparate group into a community of learners and finally into a mutual learning community involving both faculty and students.

The mutual learning community was developed not only by each cohort attending classes together but also through intentionally setting aside time for community meetings that were not specifically course related. Generally at least one half day per month was set aside for a community meeting. Sometimes these community meetings were on the same day as a class, and sometimes the community meetings were part of a weekend retreat. The purpose of the community meeting was to provide an opportunity for the entire community of students and faculty to experience decision-making, support and learning in a group of twenty to thirty people. Basically, the life of the cohort was determined by decisions made in the community meetings.

During the community meetings, individual students took the roles of facilitating, recording and processing the meetings. Ways of organising groups for decision-making were explored. Different models of processing were used to enhance the learning. For example, a reflection process known as EIAG (Experiencing, Identifying, Analysing, Generalising) was often employed. What was done was typically intentional and examined for learning.

In the mutual learning community that evolved, participants and staff took responsibility for their own and for each other's learning. The learning community extended beyond the community meetings. Classes and related group projects and internships contributed to the mutual learning community. A couple of examples will illustrate some aspects of this.

During the professional seminar course at the beginning of the second and third cohort programmes, the decision was made to utilise more fully the background of individuals in the programme. Several students who had extensive professional experience were invited to become a part of the team responsible for the course. In addition, two of the faculty members participated as students in the introduction to research course in the first cohort programme. Hence, students became faculty members, and some faculty members became students at times. And everyone shared responsibility for helping each other learn.

During the second cohort, the instructor of the evaluation research course, who was highly competent in his subject area and weak on his pedagogy (he hadn't heard of andragogy), was perceived as a challenge by the cohort. They decided to offer him ideas and methods for greater participation and involvement of the students in the class so that the learning would be enhanced and the classes would be more vital. After some negotiation between the instructor and the class, a group of students met with the instructor and helped him plan a more participative classroom process. The instructor probably learned as much about teaching and learning as the students did about evaluation research.

Internships

Each year of the course work in the programme, students were expected to complete an internship. These internships were supported in the community by meetings to plan, report on progress, and evaluate. Students were expected to have internships in different sectors of the society – education, government and business. In many graduate programmes, internships are arranged by the faculty in order to provide experiences in new areas. In this doctoral programme, the students used their evolving consultation skills to arrange their own internships. In addition, the students formed coaching pairs to work together as they developed, analysed and assessed their internships These coaching pairs were one form of community support.

During the ethnographic research project in the first cohort, the internships were identified as a key part of the experiential learning theme. One student expressed it as follows:

> The internship actually allowed us to try out our skills and truly, I think, master those skills. For me, the internship has meant, not only growing professionally, but has led me to a new job.

The change of job through the internship and other aspects of the programme was common. After two years of the programme for the first cohort, all of the participants had changed jobs.

The community was fully utilised in arranging and supporting the learning in these internships. One example of this occurred during the second cohort. One of the students was an experienced internal organisation development (OD) consultant in a large corporation. Since she was already conducting OD interventions as a part of her daily professional life, it made no sense for her to carry out another OD intervention as an internship. So she proposed that she put together a team of graduate students from the cohort to conduct a major OD project in her corporation. She had never organised a team of external OD consultants, and the members of the team had never conducted a major OD project. The mutual learning was substantial for all concerned parties.

Varied experiential learning processes

Every opportunity was taken to provide a variety of experiential learning processes to expand opportunities for learning in the cognitive, affective and behavioural domains. Classes, community meetings and internships were opportunities for each person in the community to engage in new experiences. For example, in classes, a range of cooperative learning techniques, simulations, and role-plays were introduced. Students began to develop skill in employing these techniques in their class presentations, internships and community meetings. The programme became the vehicle for learning skills and processes rather than just a collection of courses and examinations.

Perhaps this can be illustrated by the way in which two courses in the second cohort programme were adapted to provide a variety of experiential learning processes in all domains. It was important for all those who completed the programme to be competent in the use of computers for learning purposes and instructional design. A timeframe of one year was established for the completion of the combined courses. The decision was made to break down the usual course boundary barriers and to establish a team to organise a series of experiences for the students. The team of one instructor and several students was given a budget for hiring the expertise needed. An instructional design instructor headed the team and specified that each student would develop an experiential learning package using all the steps of instructional design and development, incorporating the use of computers in the product. Students were at a variety of levels in computer competence, with experience with different software. A series of workshops was established at different levels involving varied software. Some of these workshops were taught by students in the course, expanding their skills and self-confidence. Others were taught by experts hired from the funds available. All students did not participate in all activities. Each student, working with others in the community, determined what resources were necessary for completion of the tasks. Initial fears of computers on the part of some students were overcome and outstanding products were developed.

Residential learning events

One of the key experiential learning processes was undertaken through applied behavioural science laboratories offered in collaboration with the Mid-Atlantic Association for Training and Consulting (MATC). Each cohort participated in three five-day residential training events:

1 Human Interaction Laboratory: a basic T-Group (the experiential interactive group model used by MATC) experience for intrapersonal and interpersonal skill development
2 Group Development Laboratory: focus on group processes and group development
3 Experiential Education Design Skills Laboratory: focus on development of the skills for designing and delivering experiential learning events for adult learners.

Making these residential training laboratories a part of the programme provided the opportunity for in-depth experiential learning. In the ethnographic research project, one participant described her T-Group experience like this:

> Talk about significant. T-Group was really significant for me. I really, really grew and learned a lot from that experience. Painful, but growth producing. I had no idea what my effect [was] on others.

In addition to the residential training events, several weekend retreats were set aside for the doctoral programme. These weekend retreats were planned and designed by the faculty and the students and provided the opportunity for community meetings; mini-workshops on specific topics; ongoing class meetings; internship planning, reporting and evaluating; and informal time together.

These residential events played a key role in the development and sustainability of the community. It was interesting to note that although many of the students, and the faculty members, found the residential events demanding in terms of time commitment, they were judged by nearly all to be key to the positive life of the community.

Accommodating the needs of participants

The faculty intentionally worked to accommodate many of the needs of the participants. At first the faculty attempted to determine the needs and adapt the programme. However, during the first year of the first cohort programme, it became clear that students wanted a larger share of the decision-making regarding the programme. A steering committee was established which met regularly to make decisions for the community as a whole. The steering committee consisted of one or two of the faculty and a half-dozen students whose membership rotated each semester by different schemes. The agenda and leadership for the community meetings were determined by the steering committee. Important decisions were taken to the community meetings. The steering committee and the community meetings provided excellent opportunities for negotiation between faculty and students. As each cohort evolved, the students took on more and more of the responsibility for the total community life.

Many decisions were made to provide the best possible learning opportunities for the students (and the faculty). Students often find the rigid schedule of courses with meeting times fixed on a predetermined basis a block to their best learning; in the doctoral programme times and dates for the classes were negotiated between students and faculty. This often led to some highly innovative arrangements. For example, consider the typical bare and uninviting university classroom with rows of chairs which seem unproductive to learning, especially group activities. Compare this with the doctoral programme wherein the places for meetings were negotiated, and spaces were found with carpets on the floor, tables to sit around, places for resources to be shared, and space for refreshments to be available. The environment for the community was clearly an important factor in building and sustaining the community.

Continuous improvement

The concepts of total quality management and continuous improvement became increasingly important as the cohorts evolved. By the time of the third cohort, the programme was addressing these important concepts in professional development and organisation development by fully modelling the concepts in the programme. Class teaching was based on the concepts rather than simply being about the concepts. In addition to espousing and living total quality management, a number of very specific techniques were developed to implement the idea.

One simple technique was the use of pads of self-stick notes at the tables where the students were sitting in a class. As the class progressed, students were encouraged to write comments or ask questions that they wanted to express while not wanting to interrupt the presentation or the discussion at that time. Students placed the notes on an easel in front of the room and the instructor would regularly check to see what the students needed and accommodate them when possible. This might range from answering a specific content question to turning down the heat in the room. Students were seen as the customers of an instructor at that point in time.

Research as a foundation

As in any doctoral programme, research is fundamental. In addition to the usual quantitative and, not quite as usual, qualitative research courses, the community-based programme provided an excellent opportunity to involve students in creative research. Every student was expected to conduct an ethnographic study, an evaluation study, a quantitative study and an action research organisational diagnosis study as part of the course work prior to dissertation research. Often these studies were conducted in teams. Naturally, the dissertation research varied from experimental design to case studies, to ethnographies, to action science studies, to phenomenologies.

One example of the way in which the nature of the supportive community was exploited is provided by the team of eight students who joined with one faculty member to carry out a massive study of the effects of different aspects of a teacher education programme in the classrooms of the teachers during their first years of teaching. The entire team participated in the literature search and accumulated several file drawers full of pertinent research literature. Then the team conceptualised the overall project and developed instrumentation to address the individual issues that each student was studying in depth. Interviewing teachers and observations in the classrooms led to the collection of data which were shared by all of the students as they analysed their research questions. By jointly carrying out this research study a much larger scope of investigation was possible. The study required the collaboration of the entire team in the overall planning and coordinated gathering of data. Individuals wrote their own dissertations on different topics based on the common data pool. One of the major pay-offs for the students was the completion of eight doctoral dissertations and a 100 per cent completion rate within the expected time.

Emphasis on writing as a medium of thinking

As in all graduate programmes, writing as a medium of thinking is an important competency. In the doctoral programme in professional development this was addressed in many ways including journal writing, scholarly papers, internship reports, and dissertations. The usual model for writing in graduate school is for individuals to write papers and for professors to evaluate those papers and return them to the students for their learning. A much more productive model for handling all written assignments grew out of this doctoral programme. Before any paper would be read by a faculty member, it had to be first read by a peer. The peer read the paper for content, clarity of expression and editorial soundness. After revision as needed, the peer reader then signed off that the paper was ready for the faculty or dissertation research committee to review. The quality of the writing of the graduate students improved dramatically upon the initiation of this peer-review process which mirrored the peer-review process that is expected in scholarly journals. In addition, important editing skills were learned. Even very good writers believed that their skills improved through peer editing.

Becoming reflective practitioners

Each component of the doctoral programme was designed to develop self-reflective practitioners. The journal writing, the processing of community meetings, all of the experiential elements including the human interaction laboratories, and the continuous improvement efforts contributed to each doctoral student becoming a reflective practitioner. The ability to be reflective on an individual as well as a group level is essential to the development of true community where the individual gifts are enhanced through a supportive community.

As several graduates of the doctoral programme have moved into positions as faculty members in graduate programmes, they have established programmes based on a learning community which are developing self-aware reflective practitioners.

Support system for dissertation completion

At the end of the three years of course work in the first cohort, the community as an organised entity disbanded in order for the individuals to work on their dissertations. Although many of the students continued to support each other as they worked toward completion, it was clear that withdrawing the formal community structure meant that doctoral students did not find the support they needed for completion. Although the completion rate to date for the first cohort was over 50 per cent (compared to our college completion rate of under 25 per cent), we wanted to improve that completion rate.

Beginning with the second cohort, a systematic support system was built in to take advantage of the community in reaching a higher degree of completion. In addition to several examples of groups of students working together on a larger research problem with one or more faculty members, regular meetings (monthly or bimonthly) were established where faculty members and students share their progress on the dissertation research and where joint problem-solving takes place. In addition, by the third cohort, students presented their research proposals to the community before they were presented to the individual faculty dissertation committees. The completion rate for the second cohort is currently 88 per cent with a 92 per cent completion rate projected, based on one student currently finishing her dissertation. It is expected that the third cohort will be at about the same level of completion as the second cohort.

Utilisation of the community support system has had an enormous pay-off in the success of students in completing their doctorate. One of the doctoral students conducted an in-depth qualitative study to examine in detail the factors that led to these results (Rode 1998).

BUILDING COMMUNITY

There are a number of lessons learned about the issues involved in building and sustaining learning communities. A number of examples have been included in the above discussion of the components of the programme. However, there are several issues which deserve some additional attention.

Collaborative attitude

It would be impossible to design and develop a community-based doctoral programme without the commitment of the faculty and the students to working together in a spirit of collaboration. For the faculty, this meant challenging some of the traditional roles and attitudes of the academic world. Universities are commonly organised around highly competitive, individual achievement. The cooperation necessary to build a learning community in a university setting must be held as an important value by those who want to reap the benefits of community.

Cooperation and collaboration were fostered through deliberate use of cooperative learning techniques and multiple approaches to collaborative group work and team work. Cooperation and collaboration do not mean a lowering of standards on the part of the faculty, although this is the fear of some in the academic world. In fact, our experience has been that what makes the learning community a vital enterprise is just the opposite. Setting high expectations results in everyone collaborating to reach those high expectations. The integrity involved in striving toward the full development of each of the members of the community is critical. The pressures of group thinking can work in either direction. The persons in the group can be reduced to the lowest common denominator, or each individual in the group can be challenged to reach his or her highest potential. As long as there are members of the learning community who continually challenge the others to grow, the spiral of high performance will be upward. The commitment of the faculty to provide both support and challenge is essential.

Setting the climate

Establishing a learning community is best accomplished when intentional efforts are made throughout the programme. As an example, when the third cohort was convened, the first thing that was said by the faculty to the students was quite different from what is often said in some law schools, i.e. 'Look at the person sitting to your right; look at the person sitting to your left; only one of the three of you will be here on graduation day.' Instead, in this doctoral programme the following was said: 'Look at the person sitting to your right; look at the person sitting to your left; our collective responsibility is to support every one of you to complete this programme successfully.'

The seeds to build each cohort into a community were sown even before the first meeting of the students. Recruitment for the programme was undertaken by advertising and extending invitations to selected individuals. These individuals were identified by persons in the region who were professionals in staff development or human resource development. A representative number of these professionals served on an advisory committee for the doctoral programme. The invitations recognised the accomplishments of the potential students and made them feel affirmed before they even applied for the programme.

At the time of selection of students for the programme, a day was set aside for presentations by and interviews with prospective students. The presentations of the potential students were made in small groups with the faculty members, current students, and potential students as the audience.

Interviews for the newcomers were also conducted with faculty members and current students present. The entire day was designed to begin the process of building the community of learners.

Another way in which the climate of the community was established can be illustrated by the metaphor cited earlier in this chapter. The strong emotions expressed by the student who felt abandoned by the community in this first reflective processing of the second cohort set the tone for the full acceptance of the individual in the community – emotional aspects as well as intellectual. The faculty modelled this acceptance of all aspects of the life of the student.

Conscious use of a diverse community for learning

The learning community in the doctoral programme was intentionally used as more than a support system for a community of diverse learners. Reflection was structured into the community meetings and other gatherings of the learning community so that community became a major vehicle for learning. When one of the students facilitated a community meeting, she or he received feedback about their effectiveness as a facilitator. When the community was in conflict, everyone learned a little more about organisational conflict from the experience and the intentional reflection on the experience. The opportunities for learning from experience were endless.

In order to enhance the learning community, efforts were made to recruit a cohort of students who would represent a wide diversity of individuals. The first cohort was composed predominantly of white females from the field of education. The third cohort represented more people of colour, a few more males, and a variety of work sectors of the society. For example, the first cohort included only 12 per cent people of colour; the third cohort included 33 per cent people of colour. The second cohort was between these figures. The word had spread that this doctoral programme was perceived as a safe environment for people of colour. The commitment of the faculty to create an inclusive community enabled the issues of diversity to be addressed in the community. Racial and gender issues that were raised in the learning community also became opportunities for learning.

Barriers to community development

Scott Peck (1987) lists the following as characteristics of true community: (1) inclusivity, (2) commitment, (3) consensus, (4) realism, (5) contemplation, (6) safe place, (7) lab for personal disarmament, (8) a group that can fight gracefully, (9) a group of leaders, (10) a spirit. The learning community in the doctoral programme satisfied most of these characteristics, in fact seven out of ten.

Three characteristics of community were not fully reflected in the doctoral programme. Full realism was one of them. Peck defines realism as dealing with everything that is happening in the group – the unpleasant as well as the pleasant. This includes what is normally not talked about in public. Although many hard issues were raised in the doctoral programme learning community, there were a few issues which were not openly discussed. These were interpersonal issues which were simply too difficult for the community to tackle. Hence the full reality of the situation was not confronted. This also meant that the group not only did not fight gracefully on these issues, but avoided the issues altogether.

Another characteristic of a true community that was not fully attained was that of all members as leaders. All members of the group did take on leadership roles, and some of the faculty took on student roles. However, the reality of faculty giving grades and supervising dissertations kept the roles of faculty and students basically distinct. As long as evaluation, as opposed to simply challenge and confrontation, is a function of the faculty in a learning experience, there seems to be no way for the central leadership role of the faculty member to fade and all members of the group to be fully leaders. However, students definitely shifted from a status of dependence to interdependence in the learning community of the doctoral programme, even though some aspects of true community were not fully realised.

Balance of individual and community

One fundamental philosophical issue is always present: the polarity of the individual and the community. This is not a problem to be solved; it is a basic polarity. Choosing to put the emphasis on the individual, as is most common in institutions of higher education, leads to a competitive atmosphere that creates many losers along with a few winners. Putting the emphasis on the community at the expense of the individual would be counterproductive. Using the community as the way to maximise the full empowerment of the individual seems sensible.

This struggle between the individual and the group was reflected in the attempt by the second cohort to reach consensus on a mission statement. There was basic agreement, but the wording could not be resolved. There were individuals who were afraid that their individuality would be sacrificed if they were to be held responsible for the successful completion of all participants in the programme. On the other hand there were individuals who were concerned whether they would get the support needed for completion of the programme if others were not willing to commit themselves to supporting them. The cohort was never able to reach consensus on this issue. This was probably a healthy result since the tension between the individual and the community was fastidiously preserved.

CONCLUSION

We believe that the creation of a learning community for a doctoral programme is not only feasible, but critical. Our data show that retention has been high, and completion rates have far exceeded those of other programmes. We have also observed that student and faculty learning has been extensive and the empowerment of those who participated has been impressive. The professional and personal outcomes of the programme have been documented by a doctoral student in a dissertation research study (Thompson 1998). A tribute to the success of our community-based experiential doctoral programme is the extensive use by our graduates of experiential learning and learning communities in public education, university, non-profit and corporate settings, where they are teaching and showing leadership in varied roles. As one graduate of the programme recently wrote, 'Again, thanks for a wonderful educational experience that equipped me well. Of course I'm still learning – and that's the fun of it.'

References

Henkelman, J. (1989) 'The power of community in HRD programs: An ethnographic study of the culture of a graduate HRD program', 1989 HRD Professor's Network Conference Proceedings, Boston: ASTD.

Peck, M. S. (1987) *The Different Drum: Community Making and Peace*, New York: Simon and Schuster.

Rode, W. (1998) 'Role of a learning community-based program in doctoral dissertations: A case study of program factors related to dissertation completion in a professional development program with an emphasis in staff development', unpublished doctoral dissertation, University of Maryland.

Thompson, S. (1998) 'A multiple case study of professional and personal outcomes of a professional development doctoral program with a learning community base', unpublished doctoral dissertation, University of Maryland.

PRIMARY SCHOOLS AND CLASSROOMS IN IRELAND

What kinds of learning communities?

Ciaran Sugrue

INTRODUCTION

This chapter seeks to document the dominant characteristics of Irish primary classrooms and schools primarily through critical analysis of sixteen in-depth interviews with teachers where they describe in detail their interpretations of official policy (which advocates a child-centred approach to schooling), and how they intend to reconstruct their interpretations in and through their pedagogical routines. The purpose of this analysis is to gain insights into the nature of Irish primary schools as learning communities for teachers as well as pupils from the perspective of practitioners. The chapter begins with a brief account of traditions of schooling in the setting and indicates the system's dominant characteristics, to provide a backdrop for analysis and to enable that analysis to identify continuities and changes over time.

This introductory section includes a brief historical perspective, current realities of primary schooling in Ireland, and identification of key aspects of official policy that bear heavily on subsequent analysis. This is followed by a selective review of current literature on schools as learning communities to describe their dominant characteristics. These characteristics become part of the interpretive framework of the chapter's analysis of dominant aspects of primary school cultures in contemporary Irish classrooms. Analysis of empirical data is presented under four separate subheadings: images of teaching, planning intentions, pedagogical intentions and collegiality–collaboration. While each is treated separately, collectively they are intended to provide a comprehensive pastiche of dominant characteristics of these teachers' routines of teaching and patterns of behaviour in schools. A concluding section provides a summary of the evidence presented and makes some suggestions about possible reforms if Irish primary schools as places of learning for teachers as well as pupils are to be integral to rather than incidental to the system.

Background perspectives

When I was a primary school pupil in rural Ireland in the 1950s and early 1960s, my maternal grandfather came to stay with our family during summer vacations. A memorable if amusing element of this annual ritual was to be asked by him: 'What book are you in now?' His question reflected his own rather brief encounter with formal schooling during the final decade of the nineteenth century. There were apparently four books in total, and most 'scholars' ceased to attend school long before they reached the heady heights of the fourth book – the boys to assist on the family farm or to sell their labour to neighbouring farmers or further afield, and the girls to go into domestic service. My grandfather's question was a source of amusement as my experience of schooling was to advance annually from one class (or grade) to the next while there were those unfortunate contemporaries who suffered the indignity of 'being kept back', thus spending more than one school year at the same level.

Though the industrial revolution scarcely penetrated peasant and rural Ireland until the last quarter of the present century, the factory model of organising primary (elementary) school pupils into age cohorts espoused by Joseph Lancaster and Andrew Bell was deeply embedded in the national educational system (Holmes 1911). Consequently, advancement (rather than progress) through the system was determined primarily by chronology, so that 'moving classes' was an annual ritual for the vast majority. Knowledge, instead of being packaged neatly between the covers of four texts, was divided into smaller morsels that teachers dispensed through a 'transmission mode' of teaching or 'teaching as telling', and frequently coerced pupils into consuming by means of corporal punishment, without time or opportunity for cognitive mastication (Samuelowitcz and Bain 1992; Sugrue 1997, 1998).

After independence in 1922, the curriculum for primary schools, frequently still referred to as national schools, was harnessed for the purpose of revitalising a national identity characterised predominantly as being Gaelic, Catholic and Republican. Consequently, much emphasis was placed on the introduction of the Irish language as a compulsory subject from the beginning of schooling (Coolahan 1981). As much as 50 per cent of the school day was spent teaching Irish, and as part of the last remnants of the payments-by-results system of the last century, primary teachers' salaries continued to be influenced by the general rating awarded them by the inspectorate for the quality of their teaching. It is generally accepted that these ratings were influenced primarily by standards achieved in the Irish language. For a time, the youngest pupils (4–6 years) were taught entirely through the medium of the language; there was a general narrowing of curriculum content, resulting in an almost exclusive 3Rs' diet of Irish, English and mathematics rather than the more usual 'reading, writing, 'rithmetic'. Standards and the curriculum's narrow focus were reinforced further by a national system of examinations; the Primary Certificate (abolished in 1967 when universal secondary education was introduced); and a national system of school transport. For virtually the first seventy years of this century the system of primary schooling in Ireland can be characterised as conservative, narrow and restricting, while providing an important backdrop to more recent educational reforms.

This brief historical sketch has importance for situating analysis of more recent educational changes and practices for, as Goodson suggests, 'The traditions through which particular practices are transmitted and reshaped never exist in isolation from larger social traditions' (1992: 242). While attempting to establish the nature of contemporary Irish classrooms as learning communities, this larger socio-historical canvas is vital, for 'to ignore or disregard our past is to remain in corrosive collusion with it' (Kearney 1985: 37).

Reform of this traditional primary curriculum arrived late by international comparison, and was characterised by a 'radical shift' in primary schooling in 1971 with the introduction of a policy of child-centredness (Coolahan 1981; Sugrue 1997). More than a quarter of a century later, remarkably little research has been conducted in the setting to establish the extent to which this policy has become embedded in teachers' classroom rituals and routines. The general evidence suggests that the rhetoric of child-centredness was adopted by practitioners, while there are many continuities with traditional forms of schooling that remain as dominant features of the educational landscape (Sugrue 1990).

Contemporary Irish primary schools and classrooms

There are more than 3,200 primary schools in the Irish Republic, and despite rapid urbanisation in recent years more than four-fifths have eight teachers or fewer, while there are 650 schools with just two teachers (Sugrue 1997). Though the legal requirement is for children to begin formal schooling at the age of 6, many begin after their fourth birthday, and virtually all 5-year-olds attend school. There are eight years of primary schooling: junior and senior infants followed by grades 1 to 6 so that children typically transfer to secondary schools at age 12. Since the introduction of child-centred teaching in 1971 there has been no major review of primary teaching, while, at the time of writing, a revised curriculum is to be introduced into primary schools during the school year 1998–99.

249

The Irish system is at once highly centralised and decentralised. While the government Department of Education has responsibility for determining curricula, each school is responsible for the hiring and firing of teachers through individual boards of management. Schools, though state funded, are denominational and owned by the Churches, with the vast majority being Catholic. In response to a more pluralist and diverse society, fifteen multi-denominational schools have been established in recent years, and there has been a proliferation of Irish-medium primary schools, now more than 115 in total.

There are no regional educational structures, and because teachers are employed by individual schools, mobility is severely constrained in a system that is relatively small and limited in career opportunities. Since 1994, thirty-five million punts have been made available for the professional development of teachers through European Structural Funds. With this funding there has been a significant increase in the availability of in-service courses for primary teachers, but there are many practitioners who remain untouched by these activities. Teacher–pupil ratios have also improved significantly during the past twenty years, from being the highest in Europe with an average of 36.5 pupils per class to 23.5 at present, yet there continue to be many classes with more than thirty pupils.

Official policy

As previously indicated, a policy of child-centred teaching was officially introduced into Irish primary schools in 1971. Retrospectively, it has been suggested (Department of Education 1990) that this policy is underpinned by five principles:

- full and harmonious development of the child
- recognition of and attention to individual difference
- teaching/learning to be characterised by activity and discovery
- curriculum content to be integrated
- teaching and learning to be environmentally based.

Available evidence suggests that Irish primary teachers readily embraced the rhetoric of child-centredness while practice, in many instances, continues to be dominated by class teaching and didacticism (OECD 1991; Sugrue 1997). Despite the fact that policy-makers have been criticised for not clearly articulating this policy perspective and that these principles have not been debated publicly (Coolahan 1981), they became the basis for substantial curriculum reform introduced into schools during 1998–99.

With this historical and policy scene-setting for Irish education, it is necessary now to identify briefly from current literature, some of the more salient features of learning communities.

CHARACTERISTICS OF LEARNING COMMUNITIES

Roland Barth asserts that:

> Just as potters cannot teach others to craft in clay without setting their own hands to work at the wheel, so teachers cannot fully teach others the excitement, the difficulty, the patience, and the satisfaction that accompany learning without themselves engaging in the messy, frustrating, and rewarding 'clay' of learning.
>
> (1990: 49)

This assertion runs counter to traditional schooling, where the primary function of teachers was to transmit the received cultural wisdom of previous generations to the minds of learners; a neat if unsophisticated division of labour where teachers taught and pupils learned (Cuban 1993). The essence of this process is captured in the immortal lines of Oliver Goldsmith's poem 'The Deserted Village', where it says of the 'village rustics' who sat in the 'master's' classroom:

> and still they gazed and still the wonder grew,
> that one small head could carry all he knew

In a postmodern world, however, characterised increasingly by loss of certainty and consequent instability, by the simultaneous presence of potency and precariousness, Hargreaves suggests, 'doubt is pervasive, tradition is in retreat, and moral and scientific certainty have lost their credibility' (1994: 57). He identifies the immediate consequences of the postmodern condition for teachers and learners in the following terms:

> as scientific knowledge becomes more and more provisional, the validity of a curriculum based on given knowledge and incontrovertible fact becomes less and less credible. Processes of inquiry, analysis, information gathering and other aspects of learning-how-to-learn in an engaged and critical way become more important goals and methods for teachers and schools.
>
> (1994: 57)

Such scenarios have led policy-makers, internationally, to devolve responsibility and decision-making to the individual school as a paradoxical response to the globalisation of educational reform rhetorics (Department of Education 1992, 1995; Ball 1994). In a society where all knowledge is tentative and provisional, and the pace of change continues to quicken perceptibly, teachers too must become lifelong learners, and, the argument

251

goes, schools must become places of learning for teachers as well as for pupils. It is necessary in such conditions that a school 'make strides toward becoming a community of learners' (Barth 1990: 62).

As Abbott indicates: 'Time was, not so long ago, when young people learned about work by working, and about the community by direct participation within it' (1995: 6). As a consequence of a combination of industrialisation, urbanisation and mechanisation, learning has been increasingly sanitised, homogenised, and virtualised within the artificiality of schools and classrooms divorced and disconnected from first-hand experience. Consequently, many have lost sight of the fact that learning is essentially a social activity (apprenticeship) and that it relies much more on knowledge construction than on transfer. Traditional forms of schooling have tended to focus on the individual as the 'unit' of learning and to emphasise memorisation and abstraction rather than meaning making and connectedness. Dewey indicates his awareness of this false dichotomising when he states that 'the learning in school should be continuous with that out of school. There should be free interplay between the two' (1916: 358). However, the learning should not be confined to pupils only. Klein-Kracht summarises this perspective in the following terms:

> Conceiving of schools as communities of learners demands a new understanding of teaching and the re-definition of the roles played by school members. In a community of learners, everyone involved is a learner, including teachers and administrators.
>
> (1993: 393)

This stance recommends a fundamental shift in thinking in the minds of many teachers from transmitters of information to co-inquirers along with colleagues and their pupils so that schools become 'communities of inquiry' (Klein-Kracht 1993; Abbott 1995), 'learning organisations' (Senge 1990; O'Neil 1995) or 'learning communities'. A learning community or organisation is described by Senge as one that:

> is continually expanding its capacity to create its future. It is not enough merely to survive. 'Survival learning' or what is more often termed adaptive learning is important – indeed it is necessary. But for a learning organisation, 'adaptive learning' must be joined by 'generative learning', learning that enhances our capacity to create.
>
> (1990: 14)

He acknowledges that, so far, there are very few serious attempts to build such organisations. Schools, being primarily in the public domain, are much more likely to lag behind than organisations in the private sector, driven, as the latter are, by the bottom line to stay ahead of the competition.

Nevertheless, 'teacher collaboration' has become an important 'generative principle' in literature on school reform and restructuring in tandem with concepts such as 'instructional leadership' (Fullan 1993; Hargreaves 1994; Sarason 1996). Sarason makes the critically important point, however, that 'until we have more comprehensive and dispassionate descriptions of the process of change in the school culture any effort to introduce change maximises the role of ignorance with its all too familiar consequences' (1996: 37). It must be recognised also that despite decades of attempted school reforms, a 'culture of individualism' continues to be pervasive in schools (Hargreaves 1994). Visiting experts from the Organisation for Economic Cooperation and Development (OECD) in the early 1990s commented on the 'legendary autonomy' of Irish teachers while nationally teachers have been characterised as displaying a 'dependency culture' (Coolahan 1994). Recent policy perspectives have advocated a 'whole school' approach to planning in an attempt to build more collaborative cultures in Irish schools (Department of Education 1995).

THE STUDY

The data that provide empirical evidence in this chapter were generated as part of a much larger investigation into Irish primary teachers' intentions and classroom actions (see Sugrue 1997). Three levels of data were generated: interviews with sixteen teachers to establish their interpretations of a national policy of child-centred teaching; mini-case studies in six of these teachers' classrooms to identify common patterns in their teaching constructions; and a major case study in one of these classrooms where an in-depth investigation of emergent themes was documented and critically analysed. However, this chapter focuses on interview data only, while the two other data sets become part of the framework of analysis of teachers' interpretations and intentions of policy.

Collaborative teaching strategies which reflect the principles of child-centredness outlined above seem to be the only way forward towards the development of learning communities in high schools. Even these are dependent upon the teachers' own images of teaching.

Images of teaching

A central feature of interviewees' images of teaching includes rapport and relationships with pupils. Helen, working in a school officially designated as disadvantaged, characterised the importance of relationships in the following terms:

I don't want the children in my class to fear me, they respect me, and they know, they understand the rules, they know exactly what the border-line is. Like I am firm with them but fair, and I think there's a happy atmosphere in the class. The sense of humour, I enjoy them...the repartee there with them. And they're not afraid to be wrong, they're not afraid to comment on something, they're not afraid to ask questions.

(transcript 8)

This is in sharp contrast to traditional classroom relations that were frequently characterised by fear, intimidation and silence (Sugrue 1998).

Another teacher in a similar social context contrasts the classroom of his own childhood with his present struggles to cultivate qualitatively different relationships and a positive classroom atmosphere. Since the abolition of corporal punishment (in the early 1980s) he has had to work hard at leaving the past behind.

I think you have to devise ways and means, you've got to have better relationships with them, because I mean before that you could just 'sling two' and that was the end of it, but I can tell you, you've to work a lot harder, and you've to spend a lot more time talking to them as individuals now...I've certainly spent far more time since [the abolition of corporal punishment], and I think it's made better teachers out of a lot of people, that they had to draw on some other side of themselves to discipline, [and] if you can achieve [it], it's far nicer discipline than the stick, but there again, I often wished to God I had it back you-know, for...certain individuals.

(transcript 2)

These comments are illustrative of teachers' perceptions of how classroom relationships have changed and their importance for creating a positive classroom climate. However, they do not signal that this is a collaborative effort clearly articulated as a whole-school approach. Rather, it is something that they have had to work out for themselves in response to legislative change and changing social mores and expectations. Despite a concerted effort on their part to cultivate rapport, there is recognition also of the need for professional distance. There are inevitable tensions between intimacy and distance so that teachers are not compromised by getting too close to pupils' problems (Hargreaves and Tucker 1991). The following is illustrative:

I want them to be as happy as possible. If you get very emotionally involved with all their problems you won't be effective as a teacher either. So there's a very thin line there between being so worried and concerned about them that you say, Ah well, just don't make any demands of them. So you have to be very careful.

(transcript 8)

It is generally accepted in Irish society that primary schools are much happier places today than they were some decades previously, and it is reasonable to suggest that this is in large measure due to much warmer and informal classroom relationships. While this is a very positive development, when it comes to putting aspects of school planning and teaching intentions under the microscope, the extent to which teachers continue to function in isolation becomes more apparent.

Planning intentions

Whole-school planning has been official policy since the advent of child-centredness in 1971. However, it is not a policy that has been promoted with great rigour until more recent years. An education bill currently before Parliament (1998) will oblige schools to provide such plans annually to their respective boards of management. Whole-school planning is intended to provide for continuity throughout the primary school, to deploy teacher expertise in the most effective way possible, and this necessitates breaking down the walls of privatism by promoting teacher collaboration (Fullan 1991; Hargreaves 1992). By carefully scrutinising teachers' intentions in this regard, further insights are gained into Irish primary schools and classrooms as learning communities.

According to the *Rules for National Schools* (Department of Education 1965) teachers are obliged to provide short- and long-term preparation and monthly progress records. These requirements speak to a system where there was a highly centralised and prescribed curriculum and teachers did their own preparation without reference to colleagues. Despite advocacy of a more collaborative approach, these rules still apply. For many teachers, therefore, whole-school planning is perceived as an additional bureaucratic requirement imposed by policy-makers.

When asked about the extent to which they adopted a whole-school approach when planning their work, interviewees indicated that to a significant extent their planning was private and individual without reference to colleagues. One of the idiosyncratic aspects of this whole process is the manner in which teachers almost invariably refer to the school plan as the *plean scoile*, which is the Irish version of the English term, thus suggesting that this is an official term and an imposed requirement by the Department of Education and its inspectorate.

Frank is rather unclear as to what a plan actually is; guidelines for its completion have been scant and rather vague (INTO 1990), so that teachers react to the requirement with varying degrees of scepticism. An uneasy

255

alliance between older rules about planning and a more recent requirement to provide a whole-school approach is evident in his comment that 'there is a kind of a plean scoile there. I wouldn't call it a plean scoile but it's a certain scheme of work that goes right through the school' (transcript 6).

Jane's comments suggest that attempts to develop a collaborative approach to planning have been sporadic, lacking in commitment and thus of limited value. She says: 'We had half a plean scoile but it never got finished. I think it died through lack of interest' (transcript 10). However, she indicates that in another school she did benefit from the presence of a plan:

I found it [the school plan] a good jumping off point for my work. I would have been very confused starting off with second class, 'cause I like kids a bit older than that. It gave me good ideas as to how to begin with them until I got to know them and what they were like.

(transcript 10)

While her comments indicate the presence of a school plan, there is nothing that suggests that it promoted any teacher collaboration; she continued to work in the isolation of her own classroom.

When Kate began teaching she got a scheme from a teacher who'd been teaching first class the previous year, and as she laughs heartily at the manner in which she procured this manuscript, she states: 'Well I had to get one some place [laugh] and it had been given to the school' (transcript 11), thus suggesting that far from the scheme being a collaborative endeavour within the school, it was the borrowed efforts of another individual teaching in another context. This suggests that the overriding concern is to have something down on paper, something that meets a bureaucratic requirement that may also be of assistance in the teaching/learning process. Kate concludes that a school plan is 'handy to have' but it is not something to which there is a great deal of commitment.

There are tensions also between the teachers' perceptions of the potential of a school plan for cohesion and continuity and perceived risks to their autonomy. Frank states: 'I don't think it's right to limit teachers to what's in the plan' (transcript 6), and Emer expresses the view that this does not occur anyway, because in her experience 'Teachers have gone on doing what they were doing anyway, regardless of the plan' (transcript 5).

Despite the intentions of whole-school planning to promote greater collegiality and collaboration among school staffs, these interviewees' comments suggest a very strong, and deeply embedded, 'culture of individualism' in their schools (Hargreaves 1994). This perception is reinforced by Noel's comments when he states: 'there is no plean scoile, so my planning would be individual to myself without much recourse to other teachers' (transcript 14). Mark also indicates this pervasiveness in his school context: 'we don't have much of a plean scoile; it's all very much up to ourselves' (transcript 13).

Paula too, though she is highly committed to planning and, unlike many of the other informants, does much of her planning quite independently of textbooks, does so without reference to colleagues. She too is concerned that planning should not set boundaries to pupils' learning:

> I don't use my planning though as...having a kind of imprisoning effect on the children. Anything that comes up from the children or enters the subject spontaneously, I then develop that. If I could develop it within the bounds of the classroom I would, or if I couldn't, I would bring it with me and I would try to develop it for the following day or whatever. So I don't allow that [to] restrict me or make my teaching rigid in any way.
>
> (transcript 15)

While Paula's commitment to detailed planning and responsiveness to children's interests and expressed desires are laudable, they testify to a rugged individualism rather than anything that resembles planning as a collaborative endeavour.

Orla, however, paints a significantly different picture. Music is a subject to which she has strong commitment and expertise. It is not without significance therefore that this subject has been chosen for collaborative planning throughout the school in which she is principal. Being principal makes it easier to promote such planning and what is not evident is the extent to which the plan is hers rather than being the product of collective and collaborative endeavour. She declares commitment to a collaborative approach. Since a whole-school approach has been promoted more vigorously by the inspectorate in recent years, she says:

> we have tried to stay with that, and not just give it lip service. We are trying to do it [school plan] subject by subject. Music is one area that comes to mind but we decided to work on a scheme and see if it satisfied what we saw as our aim in teaching music. Now we are trying to keep with that and to review it.
>
> (transcript 7)

It appears, therefore, that in the lives and work of participants in this particular study, there is very little evidence of a collaborative approach being espoused by them in relation to their approach to planning. In these circumstances, it is reasonable to anticipate that pedagogical intentions will be equally individualistic.

Pedagogical intentions

The *Teacher's Handbooks*, the Government's articulation of espoused policy, anticipate that a child-centred curriculum would confer greater 'freedom' on 'the individual teacher', which would 'bring added responsibility' (Department of Education 1971: 21). The practitioner would have responsibility for 'over-all planning of work', which includes making 'adequate provision for each stage of learning'. The *Handbooks* suggest that teachers would need to be aware of 'the varied needs and interests of...pupils', and in constructing appropriate curricula it would be necessary to appraise 'the environment for the opportunities it provides' (1971: 22). These proposed changes in the role of the individual practitioner anticipate greater collegiality to 'ensure continuity and avoid unnecessary duplication' (1971: 21).

The more recently published report on the Irish education system by the Organisation for Economic Cooperation and Development concludes that 'despite the vision and thoroughness' which had been envisaged in the rhetoric just quoted above, 'the evidence suggests that emphasis is still largely on a didactic approach and often in the later primary years in a relatively narrow range of subject matter' (OECD 1991: 59). The report further suggests that a satisfactory curriculum balance has not been struck in the primary (or indeed the secondary) school. However, the visiting committee does not indicate what a 'balanced' curriculum would actually look like in practice, and their comments were made without the benefit of any observational or interpretive research conducted in the setting.

This present focus provides a significant opportunity to peer behind the pedagogical facade at the intentions of practitioners as they anticipate and reflect on their teaching routines. Analysis is confined to comments on the extent to which their pedagogical repertoires include collaboration with colleagues; and the extent to which pedagogical expertise is shared to enhance pupils' learning or to further teachers' professional skills and understandings.

Collegiality–collaboration

There was general agreement among the interviewees that 'the secret to running a good school', as Barry expresses it, 'is leadership' (transcript 2). Paula added the caveat that it needed to be 'leadership as a member of a team' and not 'leadership from up there' (transcript 16). However, when the teachers were asked about the extent to which they were part of a team or isolated in their classrooms, a more complex pattern began to emerge.

Emer has worked in a number of schools during the past five years and this has enabled her to make perceptive observations regarding the prevalence of 'collegiality' in schools (Nias 1989; Fullan 1993).

> I think a lot depends on the principal and on the kind of teachers in the school. And I think it also depends on the history, 'cause as a teacher coming into a school you don't know what's been going on before; I've been very lucky in one particular school, the staff were just together, like you're always going to have tensions.
>
> (transcript 5)

These comments acknowledge that leadership at the level of the school is critical for creating a climate conducive to collaboration, while they recognise also that a system's history and dominant aspects of school culture cast long shadows on present patterns of practice (Sarason 1990; Nias *et al.* 1992; Smyth 1994).

Kate had some experience of teaching abroad before returning home to a permanent post. Her first job gave her the enthusiasm to establish 'a very high standard' and she found the level of cooperation from colleagues to be 'brilliant...so professional'. Her colleagues were 'very helpful' because of the climate created in the school: 'it's the principal, he's like that too' (transcript 14). However, there is no indication that this cooperation violates the traditional autonomy of the class teacher.

Helen and Gemma argue that cooperation is dependent on the teachers who have responsibility for the same age group and the extent to which, as individuals, they get on together, thus suggesting a type of 'balkanisation' (Hargreaves 1994). Consequently, the degree of cooperation varies from one year to the next. Helen expressed this succinctly when she said: 'it depends really, but on the whole...you would feel quite isolated'. Nevertheless, she identifies what may be termed a chain of command which 'sets the whole atmosphere for the school...if you have strong leadership you will have a very happy staff...happy teachers and happy children (transcript 8).

In a forthright manner, Frank indicates that there is a tension between the 'legendary autonomy' of the class teacher, and a more collegial climate, suggesting that what has emerged in his context is a more cooperative spirit which does not encroach on the sanctity of the classroom citadel. The following comments are illustrative:

> Well once I'm inside my own classroom like on my own, there's nothing I can do about it. It's as simple as that. But we do work as a team in the school. And we often teach the same ways, and we teach the same things...We often swap round as well; I've often found that...I like doing the P.E....I'm not mad about music, so I often find maybe a teacher will do my music for me and I do her P.E.
>
> (transcript 6)

Traditional recruitment into primary teaching insisted that female entrants be able to sing while this compulsion did not extend to male applicants. As a consequence of this policy many schools were dependent on female staff to 'do the music'. This practice may also have helped to perpetuate the myth that music was feminine and not sufficiently macho for boys to take seriously. The 'master' by way of reciprocation would take the boys for (Gaelic) football. There is a sense therefore that Frank and his female colleague are perpetuating this tradition. It seems the shadows cast by dominant aspects of school cultures in the past continue to shape present routines, so that the walls of privatism continue to be buttressed by levels of professional cooperation that do not intrude and archetypal notions of teaching are perpetuated and reinvented (Sugrue 1997, 1998).

In contrast to this cooperative climate, Mark declares that relatively small initiatives have failed in his school, owing to lack of agreement among staff. He says:

> I'm not part of a team, it's fairly much autonomous [within] my own four walls. We'd tried, we thought about grouping at some stage in maths – that we'd group all the 5ths according to ability. This was to improve the maths teaching, supposedly to improve it, but we couldn't get agreement among all the teachers.
>
> (transcript 13)

This attempt to stream pupils across a particular age range was attempting to enhance learning for pupils, while teachers would continue to work in isolation.

Similarly, David indicated that he was 'reluctantly...the boss' in his own classroom, and the tensions manifest in Frank's comments above are expressed more acutely in his case when he says, in relation to the school plan, that: 'without telling anybody, I can just calmly abandon it and do my own thing in my own class' (transcript 4). He also indicates that there was unlikely to be any change in this situation without a shift on the part of principals from administrative duties to assuming a leadership role. Paula likewise feels that her work is 'very much in isolation', but she also spoke with obvious nostalgia for a school she had worked in previously in which 'everybody seemed to have...a kind of passion' and commitment to the collegial enterprise (transcript 16).

Except for the nostalgic comments above, the general pattern is one which places emphasis on teachers working in isolation rather than something more genuinely collaborative. The concept of good teaching within the tradition of primary schooling in Ireland is prefaced on the strong personality of the individual teacher, central control of syllabuses, and standards being policed by an influential inspectorate. In these circumstances, emphasis is on individual salvation rather than collective action. Even younger interviewees suggest that individual practitioners should be free to do their own thing.

However, it seems to me that with appropriate leadership and cooperation a school programme which is carefully planned and structured would provide a much larger stage for a practitioner with particular expertise and the yen to display and develop it beyond the confines of an individual classroom. The interviewees' comments suggest that a significant change of emphasis from the strength of the individual teacher to team strength is not part of their experience, though this may be a function of selecting 'good' practitioners as collaborators in the inquiry. If this is the case, then it provides further evidence that 'good teaching' continues to be defined on traditional criteria rather than the principles of child-centredness (Sugrue 1998). Without a collegial approach, the challenge of providing a more balanced curriculum is a severe test of the knowledge and skills of the individual practitioner working in isolation, and postpones the prospect of schools as places of learning for teachers as well as pupils. Despite the espousal of schools as more collaborative institutions, this collaboration has been promoted primarily to enhance teaching and learning for pupils, while the need for ongoing professional development of teachers has not been part of the equation. In fact, provision for, and government support, of lifelong learning for teachers has been entirely inadequate (OECD 1991). Provision has improved significantly since £35 million of European Community money was made available for this purpose (1994–99), yet research indicates that professional development initiatives are largely individual rather than a collaborative enterprise entered into by entire school communities. The culture of individualism and its attendant characteristics that are frequently regarded as antithetical to collaboration continue to be prominent features of Irish primary schools.

CONCLUSION

The evidence presented above suggests a very definite shift in practitioners' intentions in Irish primary classrooms from the classrooms of my childhood where didacticism reigned in a frequently hostile environment, where sarcasm, ridicule, humiliation and physical abuse were commonplace and what learning did take place was accomplished from fear of the consequences. By contrast, today's classrooms are characterised by good rapport and relationships between teachers and pupils, and a heavy-handed approach, be it verbal or physical, is no longer acceptable. Smaller classes and more resources enable teachers to construct learning encounters that leave room for pupil initiative and interest. While there is general evidence that class teaching continues to be the dominant mode of teaching, it is generally characterised by greater levels of interaction between pupils and teachers, and these exchanges, for the most part, are distinguished by warmth and a focus on the positive with greater respect for individual difference in evidence. Primary classrooms can generally be regarded as more conducive to learning in all its complexity for pupils than heretofore, but this is no more than might be expected.

There are, however, significant continuities with traditions of teaching in the setting, as the legendary autonomy of teachers, reinforced (in the past) by an oppressive system of school inspection, pervades schools through a culture of individualism. Despite policies that espouse a whole-school approach to school planning that is intended to encourage collaboration, the sharing of expertise, and the deployment of teachers' talents for the benefit of entire school communities, teachers in general continue to operate in the privacy of their classrooms or sustain a balkanised approach through cooperation (rather than collaboration) with teachers who teach classes of the same grade or are located immediately adjacent to them.

More recent policy perspectives, which resonate with international trends, and seek to promote schools as the locus of reform and lifelong learning for teachers, appear to be problematic from a number of perspectives. Exhortation alone will do little to alter a pervasive culture of individualism. Existing structures of the school day militate against teacher collaboration as timetabling does not provide for release from teaching responsibilities, and long-established practice decrees that teachers finish work at the end of the school day, at the same time as pupils. An influential primary teachers' union has so far resisted any attempts to renegotiate teachers' conditions of employment to lengthen the school day thus providing space and time for more collegial and collaborative approaches. Where collaboration does exist, in a minority of schools and classrooms, its primary focus is on benefiting pupils rather than teachers' professional development, and this tends to be reinforced by the existing (inadequate) provision of in-service courses (Sugrue 1998).

It is reasonable to conclude therefore that contemporary Irish primary schools are more conducive to pupil learning than in the past, but there is very little evidence that they have become, or are in the process of becoming, places of professional growth and renewal for teachers, except in an incidental, unplanned and unsystematic manner. Consequently, the system is poorly equipped to deal with the accelerating pace of change, and with the increasing need for teachers to acquire new understandings and skills to enhance their pedagogical repertoires and to restructure teaching and learning in ways that anticipate and provide for emergent social, economic and educational needs. In these circumstances, there is a strong temptation on the part of policy-makers to advocate collaboration as an unqualified good, and to exhort teachers to take up this challenge.

However, the very notion of collaboration itself must be understood as being problematic in the setting. Until policy is directed towards overcoming the existing constraints and structures which impede collaborative endeavours, it is unjust, as well as impractical, to expect teachers to embrace the principles of learning communities. If teachers are to take primary responsibility for their ongoing professional development, they require policy-makers to restructure the system in ways that make this possible and worthwhile.

References

Abbott, J. (1995) 'Children need communities', *Educational Leadership* 53 (8) (May), 6–10.

Ball, S. (1994) *Education Reform: A Critical and Post-Structural Approach*, Buckingham, England: Open University Press.

Barth, R. (1990) *Improving Schools from Within: Teachers, Parents, and Principals Can Make a Difference*, San Francisco: Jossey-Bass.

Coolahan, J. (1981) *Irish Education: History and Structure*, Dublin: Dublin Institute of Public Administration.

Cuban, L. (1993) *How Teachers Taught: Constancy and Change in American Classrooms 1890–1990*, London: Teachers College Press.

Department of Education (1965) *Rules for National Schools*, Dublin: Stationery Office.

Department of Education (1971) *Teacher's Handbooks, Part One and Part Two*, Dublin: Stationery Office.

Department of Education (1990) *Report of the Review Body on the Primary Curriculum*, Dublin: Government Publications.

Department of Education (1992) *Education for a Changing World*, Green Paper on Education, Dublin: Government Publications.

Department of Education (1995) *Charting Our Education Future*, White Paper on Education, Dublin: Government Publications.

Dewey, J. (1916) *Democracy and Education*, London: Collier Macmillan.

Fullan, M. (1991) *The New Meaning of Educational Change*, London: Cassell.

Fullan, M. (1993) *Change Forces*, London: Falmer Press.

Goodson, I. (1992) *Studying Teachers' Lives*, London: Routledge and Kegan Paul.

Hargreaves, A. (1992) 'Cultures of teaching: A focus for change', in A. Hargreaves and M. Fullan (eds) *Understanding Teacher Development*, London: Cassell.

Hargreaves, A. (1994) *Changing Teachers, Changing Times*, London: Cassell.

Hargreaves, A. and Tucker, E. (1991) 'Teachers and guilt: exploring the feelings of teaching', *Teaching and Teacher Education* 7, 5–6, 491–505.

Holmes, E. (1911) *General and Primary Education in Particular*, London: Constable and Company.

Irish National Teachers Organisation (INTO) (1990) *School Plan: A Report by the Education Committee*, Dublin: INTO.

Kearney, R. (1985) *The Irish Mind: Exploring Intellectual Traditions*, Dublin: Wolfhound Press.

Kleine-Kracht, P. (1993) 'The principal in a community of learning', *Journal of School Leadership* 3, 391–9.

Nias, J. (1989) *Primary Teachers Talking: A Study of Teaching as Work*, London: Routledge and Kegan Paul.

Nias, J., Southworth, G. and Campbell, P. (1992) *Whole School Curriculum Development in the Primary School*, London: Falmer Press.

Nias, J., Southworth, G. and Yeomans, R. (1989) *Staff Relationships in the Primary School*, London: Cassell.

O'Neil, J. (1995) 'Schools as learning organisations: A conversation with Peter Senge', *Educational Leadership* 52 (7) (April), 2–23.

Organisation for Economic Cooperation and Development (OECD) (1991) *Reviews of National Policies for Education: Ireland*, Paris: OECD.

Samuelowitcz, K. and Bain, J. (1992) 'Conceptions of teaching held by academic teachers', *Higher Education* 24 (1), 93–111.

Sarason, S. (1990) *The Predictable Failure of Educational Reform*, Oxford: Jossey-Bass.

Sarason, S. (1996) *Revisiting 'The Culture of the School and the Problem of Change'* London: Teachers College Press.

Senge, P. (1990) *The Fifth Discipline: The Art and Practice of the Learning Organisation*, London: Random House.

Smyth, J. (ed.) (1994) *Critical Perspectives on Educational Leadership*, London: Falmer Press.

Sugrue, C. (1990) 'Child-centred teaching in Ireland since 1971: An assessment', *Oideas* 35 (Spring), 5–21.

Sugrue, C. (1992) 'Teachers' constructions of child-centred teaching', unpublished Ph.D. dissertation, University of Toronto/OISE.

Sugrue, C. (1997) *Complexities of Teaching: Child-Centred Perspectives*, London: Falmer Press.

Sugrue, C. (1998) 'Student teachers' lay theories and culturally embedded archetypes of teaching: Implications for professional development', in C. Sugrue (ed.) *Teaching Curriculum and Educational Research*, Dublin: Grenham.

14

GUMLY GUMLY PUBLIC SCHOOL AS A LEARNING COMMUNITY

Sifting the rhetoric to locate the reality

Barry Cocklin

INTRODUCTION

In the 1960s Bob Dylan sang 'The Times, They Are A-Changing', an anthem then, but perhaps a lament of the present where an ever-increasing complexity of technology, demographic change, environmental crises, increasing urbanisation, changes to our economic base, moral uncertainty, and crises of national identity, confront us in a rapidly changing world. Yet, we can also identify strong values-conformity in some aspects of postmodern life. This 'McDonaldization' (Ritzer 1996) of society is characterised by a uniformity of product, architecture, technology and work practices. Accordingly, we have the paradox between the flexibility and differentiation that supposedly characterises the postmodern world, and a rigidity, inflexibility and rationality that owe more to the modernist era (see Craft 1996).

Education also experiences these processes and contradictions, at an ever-increasing rate, with the development of new agendas and terminology, and with the political control and uniformity associated with a marketplace rhetoric where managerialism and economic rationalism dominate (see Bates 1993; Marginson 1993). Teachers are expected to do more, faster, and better than previously (Apple 1986; Hargreaves 1995; Woods 1995). There has been an increase in bureaucratisation, externally derived policy and curricula, often associated with calls for a return to the so-called traditional ways of teaching and Fordist approach. Despite the realities of knowledge expansion, there are increasing indications of a return to notions that knowledge is objective, linear, sequential, rational, quantifiable in the one-right-answer sense, to be delivered to the 'group' in a uniform format (see Drake 1996).

These managerialist agendas and political constraints do little to provide either teachers or pupils with the necessary skills and knowledge to make sense of and survive in a rapidly changing future, where teaching requires flexibility (Woods and Jeffrey 1996). However, it is evident (see Ball and Bowe 1992; Fitz *et al.* 1994; Woods 1995; Woods *et al.* 1997) that some teachers are adopting a discourse and pedagogy directed towards the best interests of the pupils and which seek to manage the influences of change. We note such occasions when, as a visitor, one enters a school and there is a certain, very subjective, feeling that things are working. The pupils and teachers appear comfortable with their situation; there is a sense of enjoyment, and a feeling that learning is taking place. Furthermore, there is a strong sense of community and interaction, and often support derives from the wider community context.

I first visited Gumly Gumly Public School in September 1995, having been allocated supervision of two practicum students (see Cocklin 1997, 1998). My first impressions, confirmed over subsequent visits, were of the community participation, the mutual ownership of teaching and learning by all, of shared leadership, child-centred practice (see Sugrue 1997), active learning, with the teacher as a facilitator, and strategies towards emancipation and empowerment for all members. In short, the context indicated that there was a particular social emphasis on learning with members of the community sharing ideas (see Hoban, this volume).

On my first visit to the Upper Division room (Years 3–6) to see the practicum student, Ken Davis (principal) said 'Don't just stand there, do something', and immediately involved me in working with pupils, a policy and practice which apply to all visitors who can contribute. During the rest of the year, I spent as much time as possible at the school, establishing an ongoing contact with staff, pupils and the local community, particularly parents (see Cocklin 1998). While the initial subjective feelings were confirmed, Ken and I determined to seek to find the factors which contributed to the perception that the school worked, that it was successful and provided an environment in which effective learning – by students, staff, and community – occurred, and which led to their description of the school as a 'learning community'.

SITE AND RESEARCH

The research commenced in January 1996 and continued over the following eight months, although an ongoing contact and involvement continues to the present. Derived from the contacts the previous year, the research question was broadly stated as:

What is it that makes the school what it is, and how can this under-standing be better used and translated into more effective learning for the school and its community?

The focus was upon participant accounts of their lived reality as they acted to develop the experiences of schooling (see Smyth 1995). We determined to start with a description of the culture of the school; then, through an action orientation, use these findings to examine and reflect upon the situation, effecting strategies and processes of development as a result (Cocklin and Davis 1996). The conduct of the research was one of involved participation, where at various times I took the roles of 'teacher', 'friend', 'critical advocate', in a context where I sought to have a shared experience of the school in action. The research involved interviews of staff, pupils and some of the parents, as well as extensive observations by myself, while Ken used oral history interviews to focus upon:

What has happened in the past that has bonded the community and the school so closely together and how does this affiliation work to make the school the learning community it seems to be?

Data collection and analysis (see Cocklin 1998) within a broadly based interactionist paradigm derived categories which were then related to the overall notions of creative teachers (Woods 1995) and learning communi-ties (Johnson 1995). As other chapters in the present text indicate, the term 'learning community' is subject to differing, and at times contested, interpretations, while also used as a generic descriptor of schools. The adoption of the term in itself has the potential to become another paradox, when, as argued elsewhere (see Cocklin *et al.* 1996), it is taken as synonymous and used interchangeably with 'learning organisation' (Senge 1990), derived from the business and managerial contexts. Accordingly, I have taken the term 'learning community' as an educational concept (see Wagner 1993), but within a framework which allows for the interchange of ideas between both perspectives, 'community' and 'organisation'.

The notion of community adopted here is one of working together, wherein difference and even contestation are valued, and which places particular emphasis upon the everyday lived reality of the school context. This notion of community 'puts the emphasis on process, and involves intuition, spontaneity, "tacit knowledge", enthusiasm and fun' (Woods and Jeffrey 1996: 34). The basic premise of a learning community, then, is one of participation by all:

Our traditional concept that teachers teach, pupils learn, and ad-ministrators manage is completely altered. In a community of learners, everyone is about the business of learning, questioning, in-vestigating, and seeking solutions. The basis for human interaction is no longer a hierarchy of who knows more than someone else, but rather the need for everyone to contribute to the process of asking questions and investigating solutions.

(Kleine-Kracht 1993: 392)

Overall, this study sought to celebrate the Gumly Gumly perception that learning is the primary focus of education, their emphasis upon collegiality, involvement in curricular, pedagogical and professional development, a democratic school culture involving pupils, parents and community, a secure and stable school, maximum and effective use of learning time, and continuing resource allocation, especially that of time. In this chapter, then, I have allowed the participant voice to describe the features of the lived reality of their school.

GUMLY GUMLY PUBLIC SCHOOL

In 1996, Ken Davis taught Upper Division, and Bev Osborne, on a one-year casual contract, taught Lower Division, while there was also a part-time release teacher/librarian, school secretary and school handy-person. There were thirty-eight pupils at the start of the research: eighteen (9 girls, 9 boys) in Upper Division, twenty (9 girls, 11 boys) in Lower Division. Although the majority of pupils came from the school district, reflecting both parental and pupil choice others travelled past their local school to attend Gumly Gumly Public, representing a growing awareness within the wider community that the school has something to offer.

As Ken was already aware, and my initial involvement in the school indicated, certain elements derived from the context and the history of the local district had a marked influence upon the school and its relationships, both interpersonal and with the community.

The context

Although only a few kilometres outside a major rural centre, the school and community are very much isolated and independent of their larger neighbour, reflecting both history and geography where the district is on the banks of a large river subject to occasional flooding precluding denser settlement and preserving the rural nature. The initial forty-one settler families, balloted for the blocks in the 1930s, arrived in an area covered with weeds, no houses or roads and no boundaries to the farms. With the Great Depression in full swing, some were among the unemployed, and all were pioneers with little more than the basic tools and a willingness to turn their block into a home to sustain them. Separated from the town by poor roads and a lack of transport, they came to rely on each other, and from early accounts they rapidly developed a strong sense of community. Most occupied their land living in tents or shacks for the first few years while they built a permanent home. They walked to town for food, drew water from the river, and worked together to get their land prepared. As the Depression eased, some of the men obtained work in town, leaving further development of the farm to their family, and to evening work. Indeed, accounts describe fencing activities undertaken at night where lanterns were placed on posts to align them, and 'all the community turned out to help'.

In 1935 Gumly Gumly Public School was opened, in response to considerable lobbying from the local community, who then provided additional facilities such as fencing, trees, and general work around the school grounds, further reinforcing a strong community – school linkage which continues to the present. For most of its history, it has been a two-teacher school. These antecedent factors of history and size have contributed to a pattern of constructive community involvement and interaction within the school. In the present, the independence from the larger centre, and the sense of sharing and working together continue, reinforced by the number of descendants from the original settlers who remain. This has directly influenced feelings of ownership by all stakeholders, represented in a particular allegiance to the school and the learning that occurs within.

History, ownership and involvement

There was certainly a perception within the school that history and tradition exerted an ongoing influence on the present, which, as Ken suggested, should serve to remind us that:

> The school has 'reaped the rewards' from the historical develop-
> ment of the community and will continue to do so as long as it
> remembers its origins and 'feeds' the needs of the community to
> be involved.

Rather than seeking the continuous improvement derived from the corporate sphere (see Senge 1990), which underpins much of the change rhetoric at present, within educational contexts there are elements of the school characterised by heritage, tradition, continuity and a consolidation of processes, practice and content which we may wish, upon critical reflection, to preserve (Hargreaves 1995). For schools, then, change for change's sake alone should not be the goal, nor should we allow the learning community notion to be appropriated within the managerialist discourse.

From the oral history interviews, certain characteristics of the school, and school-community relationships, emerged. One of the dominant themes was that of 'pride', as Liza, a past pupil from 1938, recounted:

> It went from one generation to the other and that went down through the school. All grew up like one big family – real close ties – all the generations of children [from the original settlers] went to Gumly Gumly School. You took a pride in your school...because we were all so close...so much so that even when we grew up, the ones that didn't shift away from Gumly Gumly still continued that same effort that your parents had.

There was an ongoing contact with the school reflecting both an allegiance and ownership, demonstrated at various school functions where members of the local community and past pupils were regularly in attendance. For instance, at the end-of-year concert in 1995, there were over a hundred and fifty people present, from a school with a population (parents and pupils) of approximately eighty. The ongoing contact with the school also includes past pupils who, when they had a day off secondary school, came and sat in on classes, took part in lessons, and offered assistance to the teachers and pupils. This ownership and relationship with the school continues, as Casey (parent) commented about her older children who had left the district:

> Even with the bigger girls now, they pretty much think of Gumly Gumly as 'their' school. I've got to tell them about it because they want to know what's going on – anything that's got to do with Gumly Gumly they just help.

Across-generational ties also continue, with a parent of two current children noting that not only were she and her mother past pupils, but it was her grandmother who 'got the school going'. There remains a continuity of involvement with the school, certainly amongst a core who have returned as parents in the Parents and Citizens committee (P&C) but also in general among the local community who, as one noted, 'look on the school like it's our school'. Indeed, even once their own children have left the school, parents continue to be involved, as Ken recounted:

> Their girls have been gone now for three years, but she keeps coming back and says 'what's the P&C running now that I can help with' – that sort of thing. Normally, when people finish with a school, that's it – you're finished with the school, the kids go elsewhere, you go elsewhere. That doesn't happen at Gumly – you finish with the school, you keep coming back.

There has, then, been a sense of pride, involvement, allegiance to and ownership of the school from the early days, all of which continue to be demonstrated in the current context. From the time of initial settlement, and continuing to the present, the strong sense of community and working together for the benefit of all underpins the ongoing perception that 'what we do is for the kids'.

Overall there has been a degree of continuity of relationships between the local community and 'their' school, an involvement from the outset. The 'degree' signifies that there have been occasions when relationships have not been so harmonious, and indeed the sense of community has been lost primarily through the actions of the principal of the time in excluding parents, two instances of which will be noted. Accordingly, it may be suggested that it is the overall culture of the school, including aspects of history, which is the factor influencing the development of this sense of community, one which develops over time and through particular relationships and strategies involving all concerned. In other words, a learning community must be developed; it is not something to be imposed nor one that can be achieved without a number of contributory factors.

OUR GREAT SCHOOL: PUPIL OWNERSHIP AND EMPOWERMENT

The strong sense of pride in 'their' school was emphasised by the current pupils, reflected in Kat's remark, 'I don't really want to change the school'. The sense of ownership also came through strongly, expressed in terms of 'our' school and their loyalty to it, as Mark indicated when asked to sell his school to me:

> To make you come here I'd tell you how great we are.... Well, I've been to two other schools. The first one was really good, the second was a bit down in the dumps, and this one is great.

For those parents from outside the district, it was evident that they had selected the school after either experiences with, or considerations of, alternatives, as Danielle commented:

> Mainly because it was a small environment. Because everywhere we went it wasn't much different than what you would get around Sydney – they were concrete jungles....How big was the school – that was the first question – how many kids. Then, the teacher/child ratio, and resources....And how Ken was over the phone. When I rang [their closest school] the principal up there – at the time – didn't sound very good. Then we rang Ken and you

271

just had that good feeling – just the way he sounded and the way he talked to you.

The bases of such selections, as Beth (parent) commented, reflected a variety of factors, including:

Being a split [multiple grades] class situation, it allows them to expand, and progress and grow, as they feel comfortable, and I guess a lot of that stems back to the ability of the teachers....He has come home and said 'I've got Year 6 homework'. He complained a bit and I told him he should be proud of himself because it was a great effort. Now if he was in a structured school he wouldn't have that flexibility and that's where I believe that our kids are fortunate...

Throughout all parent comments, there was an emphasis upon the context, the relationships, the one-on-one teaching assisted by strong parental involvement, and the approach and approachability of the teachers, which many had discovered from comparisons with other schools.

Perhaps indicating the attitude towards school, particularly by the pupils, were remarks Bev Osborne made during Term 1 upon the unusual situation at Gumly Gumly, where 'you have to kick the kids, and some of their parents, out at the end of the day'. Here Bev was commenting on the fact that at the end of each day there were always some pupils still in the classroom playing on the computers, talking with each other, or with the teachers, or playing around the grounds. Often, too, the parents stayed after school, talking with each other or with the teachers. As Bev noted, in all her prior experiences, pupils were always in a rush to leave the school, and few if any parents entered the school grounds other than on formal visits, a difference Ken also focused upon:

They notice their parents there – and they notice their parents are helping – and they do appreciate the fact that they've got the opportunity there for their parents to be involved in the classroom, be involved around the school.

I don't know whether that's something the school does differently – from other, larger schools? I think there is a difference. Not so much the fact that the parents work in the school, and they help with the school, but the fact that their parents can come to the school – even if they're not working. They put their head in and say, 'How're you going, dropped off such and such's lunch'. They feel free just to come into the school. They park themselves under the trees in the afternoon – where they're happy to talk. And the other thing is that it actually occurs within the school – most other schools the parents who are there to meet their kids – it's outside the school grounds. It's not a lot of places that they will come into the playground and classroom.

The enthusiasm for school by pupils was noted by parents as well, as Beth remarked:

> The best thing my children have learnt is the fact that they like school and it's not a common thing for children to like school....It's rare that we have had to drag them out of bed. Most mornings Mark's up and dressed by 7.15, ready to go. He would walk out the door there and then.

Certain features emerge from such comments, in particular the notions of size and relationships, including those involving teachers.

'Togetherness': a sense of family and community

The perception throughout the community, pupils, and parents, of the nature of the context was summarised by Ken as:

> I tend to refer to it not as a 'school' but as an extended family. Alluding to the fact that you're not only teaching kids skills, and things like that, you're also teaching them living skills, social skills.

One important feature of the school was the 'togetherness' within the school environment, including benefits such as space provided by the large area and small number of pupils, relationships in terms of making friends, and the teaching/learning situation, as Nicole comments:

> There's not much people – so there's not much bullying. We all get to learn a lot more because there's not many of us and the teacher has more time to teach us. Most of us get along very well. And so you could have more chance of getting friends in other classes. You just get to know other people in higher grades who know more.

Throughout all the pupil comment, there was a strong emphasis upon the notion of learning together, and all as equals in the process, including the teachers and parents. During the research, for instance, a focus was being placed on computer technology. The teachers said to the pupils, 'you make the mistakes, you teach me', in a process of collaborative learning and teaching, which the pupils were encouraged to share with parents and visitors. This also included pupils taking responsibility for constructing their own web page, emailing local and international schools, and publishing stories and projects.

The sense of working together in a collaborative environment was also noted by Casey (parent):

> I took them up to [nearby school] for a week and the kids nearly died. They didn't like it. It was too big, too much of a shock for them. They were used to having, not only me, but other parents. They were really used to having that 'closeness' with everybody else. Then I brought them down here and that was the end of it.

The people at Gumly Gumly generally considered the small size to be a definite factor in the formation of a particular set of relationships – between pupils, with teachers, and with the wider community. The central factor, however, is the pupil–teacher ratio, which needs to be given consideration in larger schools, as well as relationships and community involvement. Again these are things which all must work towards, which can be neither implanted nor created over a short period of time. Given the current political agenda, where efficiency is often equated with a 'big is better' view, and issues of class size are being overlooked, we can take encouragement from the fact that teachers, pupils and parents realise the considerable advantages in the small school (or class) environment (Cocklin 1997). Again, size alone will not create the community without the approach to learning and teaching, the collaboration and the leadership within the school which allow these issues to emerge. As teachers and parents recounted, there were other small schools which they did not consider as learning communities, and some larger ones which were.

The interpersonal relationships, both in and out of the classroom, were supportive and seen by pupils such as Taylor as a central benefit arising from the Gumly Gumly context:

> *Taylor:*   It's got good kids. Some (bad) behaviour – well, some of them – but there are no bullies. Because everyone cooperates. Yeah, like a family thing. Some fight but not as much. We sort it out.
>
> *I:*   Who 'sorts it out' – teachers or pupils?
>
> *Taylor:*   Both.

This concept of 'family' was noted as a defining characteristic of Gumly Gumly, by parents, pupils and teachers, with even disagreements and fights being akin to a form of 'sibling rivalry'. However, it was the strong group loyalty which Taylor, for instance, emphasised, noting that they 'stuck up for each other', and 'against everyone – in the school and out of the school'. An incident at an inter-school athletics carnival illustrated this when, as one of the senior girls competed in the 800 metres race, a parent gathered both adults and pupils into a cheer squad, and, when by the final lap the girl could only walk, many of her peers went out and accompanied her to the finish. This involvement and support are evident not only amongst the pupils, but in the community as a whole supporting all Gumly Gumly children. They are also clearly evident in the general relationships at school where, for instance, if one is hurt or upset others rally around and offer help, and all take pride in the achievement of others:

> They support each other – no matter what it is. On Wednesday when we came back – when Colin and Ben had been to the Rugby League trials – all the kids asked them 'how did it go?' – it was really good. The fact that Taylor and Kat who have that natural ability to perform really well at sport – there's no feeling 'how come it's you all the time?' The other kids take the pride in the fact that it's a Gumly kid who is achieving.
>
> (Ken)

Overall, the general point was made by parents that:

> Gumly Gumly seems to bring out that protective attitude. It's taught them a lot about relationships. Because they've got all the kids, they've got the teachers, then they've got the parents, then the community – everybody is so involved, and there are so many different personalities involved – it gives them a good grounding. It is like a family.
>
> (Casey)

This sense of 'supportive community', contributed to by the historical context, was not a given; rather, it required conscious effort and leadership, initially when Ken was appointed as principal:

> Second objective, I suppose, was to build up the community support again, because it had suffered a little because of a previous principal. He 'locked' himself in the office and wouldn't talk to anybody. Another objective was to get out and make the school a community school again, and reinforce some of the things that people had been saying that they wanted done.

This approach and philosophy have resulted in a continuation of parent involvement in a variety of in-school and out-of-school activities. It was also very evident that parents felt comfortable about coming to the school, even just for a look during the day, with the commonly held view being expressed by Emma (parent) in these terms:

To everybody it is their school. They'll donate their time, they'll donate their energy, they'll donate their money. Everybody looks out for everybody else, too, other people's kids.

While the historical context of involvement in the school, the ongoing sense of community and ownership, contributed, it was the size of the school and the actions and leadership of staff which were seen as central, as Joel (parent) stated:

Because it's a small school – you can really have a say – make a contribution. The guy we've got there promotes that type of thing. You get to see how the school runs, you get involved in policy sort of issues, discipline codes, this sort of thing. So, you really get an idea of how the school runs...

The school, then, has an open-door policy, involving a process of negotiation with parents, and reflecting Ken's view that:

the parents know that they're welcome, that it is 'your school' and 'they are your kids, you've got just as much right to have a say in what happens'. You know, 'you don't have a right to tell me what happens, but you have a right to have a say'. In the final analysis, it's my decision as to what actually happens. But most of them take that fairly well.

As Ken notes, collaboration is encouraged where the approach is one of partnership.

A 'partnership'

The parents also gave particular emphasis to this partnership with the school, as Casey (parent) commented:

It's good. I mean, if you're having problems with the kids – or the kids are having problems – I have always felt perfectly comfortable with coming in. The teachers will help you. It's a two-way street...working with the parent....And the parents coming in and actually helping with the kids. So, if those [teacher and parent] combine and it's sort of like a run-on from home to school – and they've got a good working partnership. I mean, they won't always have a 'good' partnership – they will disagree – but, if they feel comfortable to disagree – they'll work it out like that. I think that's the most effective way. Not only that, but parents are very interested in education and the educational processes. I think it's got to be a partnership to work.

At Gumly Gumly, parents are encouraged to come in and assist in the teaching and learning activities, as reading tutors, helping with craft, and any other area where they feel able to contribute. In turn, this further enhances the notions of learning community, but also particularly those of involvement, ownership, and centrally the contribution to the self of the adult, as Beth (parent) notes:

> As much as having my children at school I probably even get more pleasure out of helping out there;...when I help kids like Duane that is probably a really great thing and that's when I grow. When I see a child like Duane or one of the others suddenly take off I really think I had a bit to do with it.

The pupils appreciated this school/community linkage, and the 'extended family' situation which existed both outside and inside the school; as Mark (pupil) indicated, these were very important:

> The community, how it is involved in the school. We just have days when the community comes in and walks through – they always know something about Gumly Gumly School. It helps a lot with the pupils as well. The parents know the teachers, and they work in the school with reading and things like that.

However, there was also that extent to which they were emphatic that it was 'their' school and, while help was appreciated, parents needed to acknowledge that ownership was the responsibility and perhaps right of the current pupils:

> *I:*   So, you think there is a need for people to listen to the kids more?
>
> *Colin:*   Yes! Not parents being able to rule the school!

The pupils also contrasted the responsibility teachers gave them at school with joint school-community events where parents needed to do the same, as Kat remarked 'Some parents are pains – you know the fair we had – well, they wouldn't let us do anything'.

Enhancing children's learning

As well as the emphasis placed upon the notion of community and involvement, there was a strong sense in which the approach to leadership and teaching was a crucial component in maintaining the learning community in action. Staff, parents and pupils all noted a contrast with previous experiences. For example, Casey (parent) remarked that:

> To start off with, the parents were perfectly willing to be friendly, welcoming, helpful. But it was made quite clear to them from the start that they weren't welcome at the school. In fact, the further away they stayed the better. The kids were basically told right from the start that they knew nothing. The kids weren't academically brilliant, but they loved going to school. But, they were turned off. There was no homework done, they had totally no interest in school. They weren't interested in anything – they were becoming disruptive. It took all their self-confidence away.

Given this situation, some parents seriously considered withdrawing their children from the school. For all participants, this provided a point of contrast with the current context, and a basis for their elaboration of the central contribution of leadership and teaching to establishing and maintaining the sharing of ideas and processes central to having a learning community. It was also used to illustrate the importance of school–community relationships, particularly in situations where the community has a sense of ownership and involvement in the school.

The pupils often used this situation to contrast their perceptions of 'effective' teachers with those held in less regard. Here, they noted that 'good teachers spend more time with you' (Bruce), 'they help you, they tell you how to do things, you seem to work together better' (Petra), or there was just a general perception across both content and relationships that 'they understand everything – they understand stuff' (Kylie). Throughout, the teachers sought to extend knowledge, and encourage the pupils to seek out understandings across a variety of topics and resources (see Woods, this volume). Pupils also noted the emotional/self-security support such teachers provided, an attribute Ken himself emphasised:

> That's the beauty of the school, too, the fact that they do feel happy that they can divulge their deep, intimate, dark, life secrets. And they're quite happy to share them with you, without somebody ridiculing them – saying 'that's stupid'. The thing is that they do support each other – as often as possible.

Overall, pupil perceptions were markedly similar to those documented in the literature on creative teachers (see Woods 1995). The pupils also reported their ability to differentiate 'We can tell a good teacher and a bad teacher in about five minutes' (Mark), and the influence upon learning: 'Because if you don't like the teacher you won't find yourself learning very much' (Nicole).

The job is to teach children

At Gumly Gumly, also central to the relationships, then, was the approach to teaching where there was a focus on catering for the individual child, and teacher and pupil were involved in a collaborative learning experience (see Sugrue 1997). As Woods notes, this learning is where 'pupils have control over their own learning processes, and ownership of the knowledge produced, which is relevant to their concerns' (1995: 3). As Ken expressed it:

> The 'job' is to teach kids not get 'bogged down' in management – and not a 'fixed structure' – need to be adaptable and open to change – change to make learning for staff and kids more effective. And 'push the Department line' – that's what we've got to say [laugh] – the 'systemic' – we realise we're a political body, we have to do what we're told – in some aspects, you just can't get away from it, but there are other parts that you work within. Translating what the system wants us to do, but putting it in to the kids' and community needs. You're looking at utilising those things, but around the kids' needs. But, there are things that kids need to be taught that they don't want to learn. It's their development – and sometimes their development has to be structured – it can't be free rein all the time. It's a combination of a number of factors.

While there is no such thing as a 'typical day' at Gumly Gumly, indeed the variety of teaching and learning is a defining characteristic, over time the teachers could be observed working with individual pupils, groups, or the class on the floor, sitting at the pupil desks, learning together on the computer, and in front of the class, in either classroom, with children outside, in the library, throughout delivering content, skills, and facilitating individualised learning processes. Both teachers also noted their strong sense of enjoyment derived from the school context (see Woods *et al.* 1997). The context was dynamic, where the teaching could be best described as both 'teacher-centred' and 'child-centred' (Woods and Jeffrey 1996; Sugrue 1997). Children moved around the room and school, helping others, seeking information, discussing issues, debating with the teachers, often with a level of working noise, and equally the teachers were open about their learning from the pupils. In the classroom there was very much an ethos of working with pupils in a collaborative learning style. The pedagogy was constantly varied and flexible, reflecting teacher philosophy, morals, values and beliefs, influenced by children's needs and the requirements of curriculum, a focus on children learning, rather than merely encountering content (see Woods and Jeffrey 1996). Underpinning this was constant reflection, a willingness to 'take risks', to experiment, where the teacher is, even if not formally, undertaking reflection-in-action (Schon 1983), where 'You have to develop them [ideas/strategies, etc.] – and you have to keep developing them. Trying them out, chucking them out – trying something different' (Bev).

The overall approach was directed towards an emancipatory praxis, one where staff sought forms of critical, self-reflective and collaborative work to create conditions where they themselves, the pupils and the parents came to develop a greater sense of control and ownership of knowledge and practice (see Grundy 1993). In describing the 'school', Ken suggested that in the context:

> Everyone is given the opportunity, and everyone has to participate – we just don't have the numbers, so everyone is given the opportunity to do something. It gives them a sense of achievement all the time.

The emphasis was on the individual child, and on their achievements, a sense of empowerment and control, a sense of collaboration, working together, where 'It's the way Ken runs it, everybody gets a go – encouraged to participate rather than competing' (Danielle, parent).

This was evident throughout the research, where both teachers noted the need to be 'adaptable', to be 'flexible', to focus on the children learning, to work with all members of the school community, but within the reality where, as Ken noted:

> you can't do everything to please everyone. Somewhere along the line you have to make a decision – 'the people I should be pleasing, should be looking after the most, are the kids' – the focus is on what they should be doing, not a minority or a particular group want to do.

With this approach such teachers engage with pupils, with colleagues, and with others including those within the community, and are more than willing to welcome the contribution visitors can make to the teaching and learning. Thus, Ken and Bev sought to engage the children in an active process of contributing to both practice and content within the classroom environment, as part of a strategy of providing the pupils with a sense of belonging and empowerment.

Both teachers, then, sought to provide an individualised content, a focus on learning skills and processes, based within but not dominated by content, one where the learner was in control and exerted ownership leading towards empowerment. As a Casey (parent) summed up, such teachers have:

> Attitude. I think most parents – they don't see the need for their child to be 'the top' but they do want their child to feel comfortable and intelligent – and they want their child to be working to the best of their ability. Some teachers haven't got that attitude – they are there to 'teach at' the kids – they are not there to work with the kids....[the 'good ones' have] put a lot of enjoyment, a lot of thought, into what they do for the kids – the kids are actually learning because they are enjoying it and they're interested in what they're learning. And nobody is left out. They've got a little bit more time, a little bit more thought, about ways in which to approach that child to get them to want to learn....Instead of seeing the classroom as 20 or 30 kids that you've got to teach this thing, they see it more as an individual thing. It's 20 individuals, rather than '20 kids' or 'a class'.

Both teachers demonstrated in a variety of ways that they were learning leaders for the children, and potentially for the community, and also leading learners as they found themselves learning with and from the children and community. In other words, they have become facilitators, seeking to allow children to develop an emancipatory perspective, where process rather than content is a focus; they support the development of the self of both themselves and pupils, engage in a positive interaction with pupils, are knowledgeable, are 'in control' but through processes of management, have a sense of humour and humanity, and work with all in a sense of collaboration and participation.

Overall, the teacher/pupil relationships at Gumly Gumly were very 'close'. Partly, this can be attributed to the size factor, as both teachers said: 'In a small school you're never off duty'; but it seems to have more to do with an attitude of involvement, as Mark commented: 'It's them [teachers] being with the children all the time. I think it's great'. At both recess and lunch, the teachers are out in the playground, often joining in games and participating in activities, and always available, for support, for learning, for interaction. In such situations, the teachers and pupils have opportunities for engaging in interpersonal interactions separate from the classroom context, allowing both groups to 'understand' and 'know' each other in a deeper and more personal sense, and also provide a strong context for learning by both teachers and pupils. Similarly, visitors to the school are also expected to participate – both in class and outside, which certainly blurs any distinctions between teacher, parent or visitor, and leaves the pupils only distinguishable on the basis of age.

This is not to suggest that an idyllic setting existed; there were occasions when disciplinary actions were required, where parents were upset with situations, staff were under stress, and where either individuals or groups of children were reminded of their obligations. However, the children reported that they expected to be told off for some of their behaviour, but saw this as entirely legitimate under the circumstances, and in no way as a threat to the relationships. The context, even when Ken resorted to his 'principal's voice', was one of classroom or individual management – a situation of negotiation, maintaining individual and mutual respect and self-image (see Woods 1995; Woods and Jeffrey 1996).

Creating responsibility and self-confidence

Another significant issue involved the sense of responsibility the pupils were given by the teachers, in terms of both the content and issues of relationships:

> Mr Davis has said heaps of things we should do – and we've been doing wrong – we've fixed all of these things – and it's become fairer now. He says 'this is what we should do' and 'this is what we shouldn't do' – every couple of days we write down what we're going to do and what we're going to change of each other. It's like – well, when we write down those things it's like a commitment. Yeah – it's a pretty good idea. It gives you some responsibility.
>
> (Petra)

This responsibility included a variety of aspects, one of which Ken noted:

> Another comment I got from one of the parents, a couple of weeks ago, was the fact that they liked the idea of the fact that the kids are given the opportunity to actually get up and accept, say, the Swimming Shield on behalf of the school – next time it's someone else, next time someone else has to get up and say 'thank you'. That's something Sandy [parent] really appreciates – and a lot of the other parents do too. The fact that the kids are given the responsibility.

This also extended to the teaching and learning aspects. One important factor was the multi-aged context, allowing for teaching to stages rather than the age-grading approach; this had important consequences for both relationships and for teaching/learning, and all pupils saw it as beneficial:

Instead of working on your own, if you've got a problem you've got another person next to you to ask to help you out with it. It's just like one big class instead of just 1, 2, 3...It's better to be all together.

(Colin)

This extended to the general school context, particularly in that there was an overarching philosophy of 'working together', including pupil-as-teacher and teacher-as-pupil. In other words, there was an interactive partnership of learning characterising the context, where both teacher and pupil took responsibility for their own learning. Such a peer-support approach provided a teaching context wherein pupils had access across levels of ability; they were encouraged to work for themselves and their learning style, at their ability, but also challenged, encouraged and supported to extend themselves. Equally, teachers actively engaged in their own learning with and from the children, along with an ongoing commitment to continuous professional development and knowledge extension. Both teachers noted that 'You never stop learning in this job'.

Each child was seen as an individual, and an emphasis was put on a caring and sharing relationship. The children were allowed to make mistakes, and encouraged to take responsibility for their own learning and development. Both teachers were constantly alert for all the nuances of the experiences of the children, and were not averse to providing emotional support. The emphasis at Gumly Gumly was upon an individualised approach to learning, varied and interactive, collaborative, and contributing to creative learning (see Woods 1995).

That approach also appeared to contribute to a view that 'learning' was something that would continue throughout their lives; as Mark commented, he would always 'be learning', no 'end'. Perhaps, then, an outcome of such relationships and teaching approaches is the development of that elusive notion of lifelong learning. Certainly, it does indicate that where experiences and perceptions are positive, where interest is engaged, and the self is developed, an allegiance to learning is encouraged, but this requires a multifaceted set of contents and relationships, particularly in the nature of the teaching approach (see Woods 1995; Woods and Jeffrey 1996). That they were successful in this was shown by a student teacher's comments during the research:

The kids had a lot more personality, and were a lot more outspoken than in other schools that I've been in and also I think they feel more comfortable in their setting. They're prepared to let you know those things. I reckon they're encouraged, too. Like, with Ken and them – he 'trains' them to just be themselves, and not just 'do this', 'do that'. To stand up for themselves.

EDUCATIONAL 'LEADERSHIP', NOT 'MANAGEMENT'

As Ken has already stated, he saw his primary role as one of teaching the children, who were central to all aspects, with the consequence that:

> The administrative role within the school sort of takes a bit of a nosedive – when I've got so many other things. There's mail sitting on my desk that's been there for about a month – that I haven't been through yet. It just had to be left behind. There are policies, there's structure of the school, there are school plans, there are all sorts of things that get done so quickly, you know, it's the bandaid to what you really want to do if you had the time to sit down and work through. In a big school, you'd negotiate for somebody else to do it, whereas in a small school, you've got it all on top of you. But your first priority comes back to the kids in the classroom. If they're not working, if they're not organised and functioning properly, then nothing else will get done anyway. The administrative side, I just tend to fax off and say, 'Sorry, I forgot, it didn't get done'.

This was reflected in Ken's approach to aspects of the principal's job:

> We'd sit down at the beginning of the year and have a look at the sorts of things that they [other teachers] wanted to do, the sorts of things they wanted to do in the class, and then we'd look at the possible avenues. But, there's no real structure – as to a line between who's principal and who does this, and who does that. Everyone's got duties and has responsibilities, and they're always delineated at the beginning of the year, but there's no structure as to, 'This is the way we're going to behave, this is the way I want you to work'. I think I give them the freedom to create their own classroom, create their own atmosphere, without trying to force them. Realising that there is a certain set of standards that the kids are going to have to follow.

Certainly, both teachers took leadership roles and responsibilities, they worked together during the school day, and equally, parents and pupils were encouraged to have input. In this sense, the notion of 'roles' becomes considerably blurred, as all are collaborating towards maximising the benefits for all in the community (see Woods, this volume).

The situation at Gumly Gumly derived partly from the historical context, but more specifically from the teaching and leadership, and consequent relationships and interactions with and between staff, pupils, parents and the wider community: in short, through the culture (see Cocklin 1997, 1998).

CONCLUSION

In presenting this account of Gumly Gumly I have focused upon a celebration of 'what works and why'. I have sought to provide the participant description, noting that there is a wider support for the perception, of a learning community that is highly regarded by those who are involved. The intention has not been to present some idyllic notion of a school, but to recount a lived reality where, overall, but not without the normal cycle of ups and downs, a sharing of ideas is found in action. The outcome is, as the participants noted, not a 'typical school', but a community where all experience ownership, a right and indeed obligation to participate in the school and educative processes and contexts. They also placed particular emphasis upon the ongoing nature of such a community: it was dynamic, not static, and needed to be subject to continuing reflection, analysis and development. As such, it is an outcome of culture, but more particularly an approach to leadership and teaching, collaboration and negotiation, involving all members of the learning community in taking action, involvement, and responsibility (see Smyth *et al.* 1996). The result is an educative context for all, but one which does involve contestation with the political and economic agenda (see Woods, this volume). If the notion of the learning community is to continue, we need not only to recognise this contestation, but to seek means of ensuring that it is not overwhelmed, or worse appropriated, by the managerialist discourse. As the people at Gumly indicate, the reward is worthy of the effort.

References

Apple, M. W. (1986) *Teachers and Texts: A Political Economy of Class and Gender Relations in Education*, New York: Routledge and Kegan Paul.

Ball, S. J. and Bowe, R. (1992) 'Subject departments and the "implementation" of National Curriculum policy: An overview of the issues', *Journal of Curriculum Studies* 24 (2), 97–115.

Bates, R. (1993) 'Educational reform: Its role in the economic destruction of society', *Australian Administrator* 14 (2/3), 1–12.

Cocklin, B. (1997) 'Towards a "learning community": The case of Rana Primary School', *Education in Rural Australia* 7 (2), 1–11.

Cocklin, B. (1998) 'Towards a creative school: A case study from rural New South Wales', in G. Walford and A. Massey (eds) *Children Learning: Ethnographic Explorations*, London: JAI Press.

Cocklin, B., and Davis, K. (1996) 'Creative teachers and creative schools: Towards a learning community', paper presented at the Annual Ethnography and Education Conference, Oxford, 9–10 September.

Cocklin, B., Coombe, K. and Retallick, J. (1966) 'Learning communities in education: Directions for professional development', paper presented at the British Educational Research Association Conference, Lancaster, 12–15 September.

Craft, A. (1996) 'Nourishing educator creativity: An holistic approach to continuing professional development', *British Journal of In-service Education* 22 (3), 309–23.

Drake, S. M. (1996) 'Towards a new story in education', *Orbit* 27 (1), 1–3.

Fitz, J., Halpin, D. and Power, S. (1994) 'Implementation research and education policy: Practice and prospects', *British Journal of Education Studies* 42 (1), 53–69.

Grundy, S. (1993) 'Educational leadership as emancipatory praxis', in J. Blackmore and J. Kenway (eds) *Gender Matters in Educational Administration and Policy*, London: Falmer Press.

Hargreaves, A. (1995) 'Changing teachers, changing times: Strategies for leadership in an age of paradox', Australian Council on Educational Administration Workshop, Melbourne.

Johnson, N. (1995) 'Schools as learning communities: Curriculum implications', paper presented at the Australian Curriculum Studies Association Biennial Conference, University of Melbourne.

Kleine-Kracht, P. A. (1993) 'The principal in a learning community', *Journal of School Leadership* 3 (4), 391–9.

Marginson, S. (1993) *Education and Public Policy in Australia*, Melbourne: Cambridge University Press.

Ritzer, G. (1996) 'The McDonaldization thesis: Is expansion inevitable?', *International Sociology* 11 (3), 291–308.

Schon, D. (1983) *The Reflective Practitioner*, New York: Basic Books.

Senge, P. (1990) *The Fifth Discipline: The Art and Practice of the Learning Organization*, New York: Doubleday.

Smyth, J. (1995) 'Teacher's work and the labor process of teaching: Central problematics in professional development', in T. R. Guskey and M. Huberman (eds) *Professional Development in Education: New Paradigms and Practices*, New York: Teachers College Press.

Smyth, J., Hattam, R., McInerney, P. and Lawson, M. (1996) 'Finding the "enunciative space" for teacher leadership and teacher learning in schools', paper presented to the Australian Association for Research in Education, Brisbane, November.

Sugrue, C. (1997) *Complexities of Teaching: Child-Centred Perspectives*, London: Falmer Press.

Wagner, T. (1993) 'Improving high schools: The case for new goals and strategies', *Phi Delta Kappan* 74 (9), 695–701.

Woods, P. (1995) *Creative Teachers in Primary Schools*, Buckingham, England: Open University Press.

Woods, P. and Jeffrey, B. (1996) *Teachable Moments: The Art of Teaching in Primary Schools*, Buckingham, England: Open University Press.

Woods, P., Jeffrey, B., Troman, G. and Boyle, M. (1997) *Restructuring Schools, Reconstructing Teachers*, Buckingham, England: Open University Press.

NAME INDEX

SUBJECT INDEX